Disaffection from School?
The Early Years

Edited by

Gill Barrett

The Falmer Press
(A member of the Taylor & Francis Group)
London • New York • Philadelphia

UK   The Falmer Press, Falmer House, Barcombe, Lewes, East Sussex, BN8 5DL

USA   The Falmer Press, Taylor & Francis Inc., 1900 Frost Road, Suite 101, Bristol, PA 19007

© Selection and editorial material copyright G. Barrett 1989

First published 1989

British Library Cataloguing in Publication Data

Barrett, Gill
   Disaffection from school? The early years
   1. Great Britain. Primary schools. Students.
   Disaffection
   I. Title
   372.18′1

   ISBN 1-85000-440-4
   ISBN 1-85000-441-2 pbk

Library of Congress Cataloging in Publication Data is available on request

Jacket design by Caroline Archer

Typeset in 10/12 Garamond by
Chapterhouse, The Cloisters, Formby L37 3PX

Printed in Great Britain by BPCC Wheatons Ltd, Exeter

Contents

Part IV: Learning and Knowing: Policy and Practice

Acknowledgements

As contributor of Chapter Three I would like to acknowledge the work and commitment of the teachers who worked on the project on which this chapter is based. In essence it is their experience, reflection, questions and understanding that makes the chapter feasible. I hope I have represented them adequately.

As editor I would like to thank Neville Jones for inviting me to compile this book, those people who contributed, and those who guided, encouraged, and supported me on the way to completion. In particular, my thanks are due to John Isaac, who from conception of the idea has been instrumental in the formulation, criticism and production of the text.

I would also like to join with the Series Editor to record our thanks and appreciation to Christine Cox at Falmer Press, for her cooperation and encouragement at the planning stage and for providing support and guidance with a never failing equanimity, to bring this book into existence.

Preface

The books in this series are published as part of the work being carried out on the Disaffected Pupil Programme in Oxfordshire (DPP). The Programme is essentially about learning and personal development in primary and secondary schools, and the social context within which teachers and pupils are engaged in the process of education. Given that schools are the context in which disaffection finds expression and where solutions to pupil alienation have to be found, the focus of the Programme and these books is on effective school management, skilled and imaginative teaching, and appropriate curriculum for all pupils.

The approach to pupil disaffection being taken is that schools do matter and do make a difference in the way pupils grow and develop during early childhood and adolescence. This is a positive philosophy that has to be developed by all teachers in all our schools, taking account of what early learning experiences all children bring to their learning in school. Essential to the task of preventing educational disaffection is that every pupil should feel, and is engaged upon, purposeful learning and be seen positively as a potential learner. The Programme, therefore, aims to look at what can be achieved in ordinary schools by virtue of good practice.

The books in this series examine both the factors that prevent positive learning taking place and the good practice that enhances a pupil's experience of schooling irrespective of previous background experience and learning. This volume is concerned with pupils at a particular stage in their education. It is one in the series that ranges from when pupils are prepared for schooling in playgroups, day centres and nurseries, through primary and secondary schooling, to further and adult education. Each volume attempts to identify those factors which encourage disaffection at a particular stage in education. The series has been planned in recognition that there are strands of disaffection — attitudinal, management, teaching and curriculum — that thread themselves throughout the education service. These affect pupils in a variety of ways, depending both on individual susceptibility and the characteristic features of school organisation and management. Disaffection is, therefore, a multi-dimensional phenomenon.

The continuities that thread their way through the different phases of education include attitudes towards ability and achievement, gender, disability and race together with those attitudes which tend to determine how we structure our education system, establish its aims and goals, and determine its casualties. So at each stage in the education process there are characteristic features of school management, teaching techniques, and curriculum design which provide for each pupil, and sometimes member of staff, a basis for disenchantment even when this is not positive disaffection.

A starting point for much of this is in the way pupils become marginalised into learning groups (classes we call them, sometimes special), which in outcome make pupils feel outsiders, determine their success at school, and pervasively erode self-esteem — the basis of all effective learning. Sometimes the system of marginalising is a structural process within schools, arising from ways in which pupils are grouped, and how facilities are made available for some pupils and not others, but sometimes pupils are marginalised out of normal schooling altogether, into units and special institutions. When the latter occurs there is a plethora of professional administrators, peripatetic support services, research and inspection, all of which support the marginalising process, but in doing so, offer a bewildering array of approaches and practice on how to educate such pupils once they are marginalised. This is not to say that a proportion of our school population is not without an educational approach that requires action to be taken to minimise disaffection where it occurs. However, it is the contexts, the aims, and the practices that come into play that determine whether disaffection is part and parcel of the learning (and making mistakes) process, or whether it is a self-determining creation of the way we organise our schools which in outcome secures certain pupils in modes of alienation that they can do little about. The aim should be that all pupils feel normal, valued, and achieving.

Disaffection is, however, a normal experience for both adults and children. It has a positive aspect when it acts as an incentive for self-appraisal, for it can be a spur towards setting new goals. Yet there are circumstances when for certain pupils the strong feelings of disaffection can be damagingly pre-occupying, adversely affecting learning and a sense of accomplishment. If this occurs during the time a pupil is at secondary school then its effect may be heightened as pupils cope with the turmoils of adolescent growth. A peak in disaffection is also noticeable as young pupils begin to approach school-leaving age, appraise their circumstances, and reflect on prospects for work and a career.

The response of a pupil to disaffection can vary considerably, depending on past experiences, the manner in which these have been coped with successfully, and the nature and extent of existing precipitating factors. How well a pupil is able to cope with new frustrations is very difficult to predict. The need, however, is for an awareness of those school experiences which place pupils under extra strain and which some pupils find intolerable, leading to a devaluing of the self and lower self-esteem.

If a pupil feels devalued then there can be ample opportunities during a school day for this to be reflected in disaffected behaviour which becomes pervading and entrenched. This is more likely to happen when the pupil discovers there is no resolution to feelings of disaffection either through personal effort or the efforts of others. Pupils then begin to look away from support by parents and teachers, seeking friendship and mutual support from peers or experiencing various forms of social isolation. It is at this point that feelings of disaffection become translated into characteristic patterns of disaffected behaviour either of active or passive forms.

In the active form pupils behave in ways that have a tendency to exacerbate their feelings of disaffection. These behaviours are usually categorised according to the style of management or resources available to cope with the disaffected behaviour. These categories of behaviour used to have their roots in medical typology: now they are administrative descriptions. The behaviours are disruption, vandalism, maladjustment, absenteeism, and truancy. In the passive form the characteristic behaviour is that of educational underachievement and simply opting out of ordinary school activities. The active form of disaffection creates more problems for teachers while the pupils are in school. The passive form is possibly more insidious, having implications beyond school life, maybe throughout the life of the pupil, and can be overlooked by teachers. Both active and passive disaffection may be part of a matrix of home and family conditions. All carry implications for recurrent family cycles of resistance to schooling. For whatever the cause of pupil disaffection, whether arising from home or school factors, there is always the risk that the pupil, finding no solution to problems, may become educationally alienated.

Although disaffected pupils are open to negotiation about their problems, alienation becomes a state of mind where a pupil is highly resistant to help or support, believing that there are no solutions. For such pupils this legitimizes aggression, aggravation towards teachers and other pupils, and sometimes the vandalism of school property.

Research in recent years has revealed the extent to which pupils, not always wittingly, negotiate their own learning. They do this with their peer group and often with the class teachers as part of trading off work and obligations. In one sense alienation can be seen as a breakdown in these negotiations with teachers, and maybe with peers. Where there is conflict there is in the majority of schools no 'ACAS facility' to bring the conflicting sides together. Indeed, where there is significant alienation in a school this can highlight the absence of 'ACAS-minded' teachers! Alienation becomes symptomatic, when the maintenance of discipline and dignities have to be upheld and other channels of resolving conflict are closed.

Alienated pupils increasingly find themselves in a position where negotiable options have ceased to exist either as a process of learning or as negotiation out of difficult circumstances. Where this has happened pupils have crossed a threshold of acceptable or non-acceptable behaviour. These thresholds are not always clear either for pupils or staff. They become activated when problems arise but are always present as 'hidden' factors of the ethos of a school. It is usually the case that it is the staff who have the prerogative in deciding whether to maintain a threshold or not. They may be related to pupil–teacher relationships but also can be a function of the administrative procedures like class streaming, setting, and banding, or the existence of special classes or units within a school. Sometimes the thresholds centre round such issues as school uniform, the use and maintenance of lockers, and homework. Thresholds differ considerably from school to school, within staff within staff groups, and in classroom practices. Every child has to learn the threshold matrix of every given staff member and there are no lessons or tutorials to help. Because of this the extent to which an alienated pupil can engage in negotiation about his or her feelings of disaffection is often not clear. This is part of the problem that makes management and restitution so difficult. Yet thresholds need not be constant factors but can be open to review from time to time. Indeed in some schools such review procedures involve pupils as part of the progress of re-negotiating thresholds. In these circumstances pupils can take a part in creating the ethos of the school in which they are to learn and grow and the risk of alienation is thereby reduced.

By definition, disaffected pupils invariably feel in some respect devalued persons. Not all devalued pupils express their sense of worthlessness through disaffected behaviour nor become alienated; sometimes there is passive acceptance of the status quo. However expressed, devaluing processes are both historical and endemic in state education. Indeed ordinary education is occasionally defined by such practices.

An example is where schools practise discrimination by virtue of categorising ability. Many schools systematically group children for learning purposes according to some criteria of ability. This happens in nursery and primary schools as much as in secondary education, though in secondary schools the procedure may be formalised in methods of streaming, setting and banding. It is not the exercise of grouping pupils that is at fault so much as the criteria used for determining how the learning group shall be constituted and the style of relationships which this engenders. What is beginning to be questioned is the appropriateness of always having pupils in age-related groups for learning purposes; that classes should be of given size irrespective of the subject matter being taught. The notion of a school 'class' is an educational concept whose validity rests on administrative convenience rather than effective education. There is no special requirement that all learning has to take place in classes or even an institution or building we call a school. A school intent on doing something about pupil disaffection will take a hard look at the way it groups its pupils especially if this is related to some criteria of deficiency.

Attitudes and prejudice are rooted in discriminatory policies and practices in three other areas of school management: firstly the issues of sexism both in respect of female staff and pupils, secondly, the growing recognition of widespread racial attitudes, thirdly, attitudes that in outcome discriminate against class groups in society. In all these areas there is an assault on personal status and self-esteem, accompanied by feelings of devaluation, but these are all part of what is currently regarded as the normal fabric of our education system.

Neville Jones
Director, Disaffected Pupil Programme
Oxfordshire
1989.

Introduction

Gill Barrett

The purpose of this book is to explore the nature and appearance of disaffection in young children in schools and to seek to understand the significance of it. This exploration leads us to both the micro contexts of classroom interactions and adult expectations of children and macro contexts of historical and policy related perspectives on schools as they relate to the under-eights.

Within the book a number of practices, theories and assumptions we have about children of this age are re-examined. This leads us to question our interpretations of their behaviour, the appropriateness of predominant practices in the classroom, teacher education, policy levels and the social value that is placed on the schooling experiences, thinking and knowledge of children.

Defining the Parameters

What is disaffection and what does it look like? Who is disaffected and why? Where does school come into the picture? The answers to these questions depend to some extent on who is answering them, and in what context. This book seeks to present a number of the perspectives needed to provide a multi-dimensional answer to these questions.

This introduction examines notions of children and their relationships to adults and society at large. Perceptions of disaffection are set within an analysis of the contexts in which they occur — adult created environments and expectations. Through examination of adult responsibilities towards children, notions such as the 'needs of children' will be examined, showing how these ill-defined ideas underpin much practice related to the early schooling of children. Analysis of the role of teachers and the theories and policies which create that role will show some of the inherent problems for teachers and children in school. This leads to a synopsis of the perspectives, practices and ideas to be examined within the chapters.

Children in the Early Years at School

Although the statutory age for compulsory schooling is five, the focus of the book includes children of four because they are increasingly being admitted into school (see Chapter 9). The upper age limit of eight relates to that of many first schools but these ages are arbitrary. Those with an intimate experience of children will know that age tells little of the reality, either in physical size, or in terms of how children cope with intellectual and social challenges. All it tells you is how long they have been alive in the outside world and the sort of situations in which society and adults in their immediate environment may be expecting them to function. Thus at five years children are expected to start school. At the age of seven plus, children will be expected to move school and to move from a class labelled an infant class to one labelled a junior.

This analysis of the focus group of children for this book also makes explicit the relationship of children to adults. Children between 4 and 8 years are essentially powerless in societal terms. They largely depend for food, shelter, stimulation and emotional maintenance on adults. However, when they come to school they are also dependent on them for the environment in which they learn and socialise as they are virtually powerless to withdraw themselves from it. The only power that children have is to withdraw their willingness to engage in tasks set by adults. At home, for example, children may stop eating at mealtimes, or washing, while at school they may show their power to disaffect through crying or hiding under a table when, for example, PE is due. They may simply attempt to avoid doing work set. This limited power that children have is nevertheless effective in illustrating how the power of adults has to be used in negotiation with children, particularly in school, because many children will already have learned to use the withdrawal of goodwill in order to assert their negotiating rights. Others will already have learned that with some adults at least, frequently the mother, they hold many of the negotiating cards and they learn to use them with force. This book is focusing on the children in their first phase of schooling and analysing the withdrawal of goodwill to engage in and learn from the adult world of compulsory schooling.

The Nature of Disaffection

What is disaffection? Fundamentally the word implies a negative state of something that was once positive. Thus affection for something has been reversed to become disaffection. Here we are concerned with disaffection in the early years of schooling. Thus, instead of affection for the activities of schooling, disaffection implies a dislike and hence a turning away from the activities and learning expectations of the classroom and school. This is the understanding we have pursued in this book. It is crucial to examine this disaffection in the early years of schooling because they are vital to the formation and use of intellectual and attitudinal ways of thinking of the children, about themselves and the world of people and ideas. In other words it is crucial that children become confident learners and holders of knowledge in these early years at school.

Children are thinking, knowing and feeling people. But the reasons and purposes of disaffection may not be overtly stated, or even consciously known by the child. The child may not, therefore, be able to articulate feelings or reasons for behaviour, but in a variety of ways children show us through their behaviour that they do not want to engage in the learning situations which are presented to them. In trying to understand disaffection however, the behaviour of disaffection has to be examined, not only how it might look or sound or the context in which it occurs, but the understanding of that behaviour by those around. All these factors are examined in the book.

The Context of Disaffection

Adults create the learning environment for children in schools, and the theories of adults create a form of reality within which children have to operate and from which they learn. Within the environment are people with different roles, artifacts with different purposes and symbolic forms with different functions. As an example of the latter, consider the symbolic form of spoken language: imagine the class teacher taking a mat session first thing in the morning. The teacher uses language for the bureaucratic function of taking the register and then may invite some pupils to tell their news: the children have to feel they have something to say and to want to share it, to know how to do it, and thus to volunteer. The teacher may play a sounds game using instruction and asking questions about discrete words which need a different way of thinking to make sense. There is an expectation that each child will work out how to think about these words and give an appropriate 'answer' to the teacher. The expectations and their complexity are continuous but different depending on the individual creating the environment. Thus within any environment that is created for children are embedded assumptions about the adult role, about children and how they learn, and theories of knowledge. For instance a student of mine was doing some research about the role of art in the curriculum and learning of primary children. He asked some 7-year-olds whether they ever did junk modelling: 'No, I think our teacher thinks it would be babyish to do that'. Indeed, the teacher did have a very definite idea about what were appropriate forms of art work for his class and the role they should take. The pupils had made meaning out of the expectations just as they do about maths or English subject expectations.

As adults in society we create contexts of learning in schools which are underpinned by the history and policies of state schooling, and apparently a fundamental belief that adults have a responsibility towards children because of their powerlessness and dependence.

Adult Responsibility To Children

What are adults' responsibilities to children? Beyond the responsibility to nourish them physically and emotionally, a simplistic answer would be 'To provide them with a safe environment in which they can learn'. This begs the question about concepts of safe or value positions about what would be included in the environment from which they could learn. People may well ask how this takes into account different personalities or abilities and disabilities, or indeed the things which we as adults think children 'should' learn to fit in with society.

These are all significant elements in trying to conceive of adults' responsibilities to children. However these responsibilities are frequently thought of in terms of answering children's 'needs'. Considering children's needs however does not provide us with just one answer as Woodhead (1987) illustrated when he identified four different categories of 'needs'. These are used in writing about what adults should do or provide for children in order to respond to their needs. Only one of these can be perceived as purely intrinsic to children, the others are extrapolations from what appear to be psychologically good experiences for children, or are social constructions based on a particular culture.

(a) Needs in Children's Nature
Kellmer Pringle's four basic needs — for love and security; for new experiences; for praise and recognition; for responsibility — come under this category.

(b) Needs and Psychological Health
... particular experiences in early childhood are being judged according to their consistency with later mental health, and projected on to children as their 'needs' e.g., close bonding with a mother figure.

(c) Needs and Cultural Norms
... While the general principle underlying statements related to love and security in the early years may have universal validity, detailed prescriptions for children's care are normative, and depend on a judgement about processes of cultural adaptation and social adjustment. This conclusion could have important implications for any inter-cultural generalizations informed by Western culture and research.

(d) Needs and Cultural Prescriptions for Childhood
Many educational 'needs', such as children 'needing' to learn physics, or pottery, or parentcraft, are largely a cultural construction. They are neither a quality of the individual nor a pre-requisite for psychological well-being, either in absolute or relative terms. There is a weak sense in which children in Western society deprived of educational opportunities may be culturally maladapted. But arguably the major reason why this framework is employed by educationalists is in order to project their judgement about what children should learn on to the children themselves, and thereby direct attention away from the value position from which it is made.

Where does the teacher's role lie in this spectrum of needs? Or is the teacher's role a social construction as well? It would seem that this is likely when the Press is considered, or the received view of teachers' role is taken into account. The following reflect received views from the Press and educationalists, so there are differing though potentially complementary views of the role of the teacher in relation to the child. Appended are questions that make apparent the problems.

(a) To enable children to achieve in society . . . achieve what?
(b) To make individuals able to follow societal rules and expectations so that they can become part of a community . . . which community?
(c) To enable individuals to be happy, to develop their potential and self in all dimensions and thus think for, and be in control of, themselves . . . for what purpose?

The questions indicate the diversity of pressures from parents, government, and Local Education Authorities that may be exerted on teachers which will affect the environment they actually produce (Berlak and Berlak, 1981).

System pressures have traditionally affected the learning climate in the early years of compulsory schooling. Thus societal pressures for an appropriate curriculum may neglect questions about what is important at age 5 to 7 and instead focus on what will count as success at 16. This leads to expectations of the teacher that s/he will prepare the children for the next phase of schooling. It can be argued that this has led to the dichotomy between the curriculum of nursery schools or playgroups which is essentially child centred, and many infant schools where the curriculum is focused on symbolic forms in preparation for later schooling. Woodhead (Chapter 9) spells this argument out in more detail.

In reality this is too simplistic. There are conflicting theories and practices concerned with the education of 5- to 7-year-olds. Thus the contexts in which they learn or become disaffected will vary. The questions we have to ask of their experiences reflect the theories policies, and values that underpin the answers:

What will they learn?
For what purpose?
In what process?
How will they learn?
Who pays for their education and how much?
Who notices and values what is achieved in the early years of education — and why?
Who values the learning of young children, and how?
Why is disaffection from early years schooling an important issue?
How can we understand it?

The chapters in the book address these questions from perspectives which are represented by the four sections: the child; the teacher; parents and community; and an overview which takes in both society and the individual.

In Part One the first chapter attempts to present the perspective of the child. From an adult perspective this is not easy but the use of a wide range of data from children demonstrates how aware they are of their learning experiences in school and the feelings they engender.

In Chapter 2, Annabelle Dixon looks more specifically at curriculum from the point of view of a child and addresses a fundamental question about the purposes of curriculum. She illustrates the dangers of mismatch between the teacher's experience and the child's if we are concerned with children learning rather than becoming disaffected from learning. The chapter includes an analysis of the inadequacies of traditional record-keeping which tells us nothing about the child's relationship to the curriculum and learning expectations of the classroom.

Part Two focuses on teachers' perspectives and theories and practices of education and learning in classrooms. Chapter 3 presents teachers' understanding of children's responses to classroom expectations which emerged through a year of research. Their observations and subsequent analyses of children focus on children starting school, but their understanding is relevant to all the age group under consideration. The chapter begins with an explanation of four major factors they identified which lead to understanding of this behaviour. Observations led them to recognize four major categories of response behaviour; knowing, not knowing, being involved, not being involved. However, the chapter outlines how the teachers, in coming to understand the context in which the children were responding, were able to manipulate the learning environment even for children who had many learning needs and strong responses to situations they found difficult.

This analysis is pursued more specifically in Anne Saunders' chapter in which she examines the meaning and practice of 'creativity' in infant classrooms. She identifies two types of infant classroom which have distinct cultures, roles and purposes within them. As the children grow older they move from one to the other. The curricular activities of children which are related to creativity change from the child-centred 'play' culture to a group-, teacher-directed, work-centred, culture. Through having to abandon the creative thinking involved in play activities in the former, the child also loses the expectation of making 'work' personally meaningful. The writer argues that in order to maintain self esteem in the group- and 'work'-centred culture, the child has to opt for what the adult approves of, so denying the value of his or her own thinking. This would seem to be highly significant in terms of disaffection.

In Chapter 5, Clem Adelman examines disaffection and the behaviour that frequently goes with it, in relation to the moral basis of children's learning and action. This historical perspective on classroom practice and curriculum leads the reader through theories about children, learning and moral reasons for teaching and curriculum. He speculates on the significant influences of these theories and practices on schooling today and their implications for disaffection. He leads the understanding of issues related to disaffection away from the direct context of the classroom to that of the community and society from which the child stems.

In Part Three the focus changes to consider the perspectives that emerge when the continuity or discontinuity between home, school and society are examined. John Schostak brings a parent's perspective to the question of disaffection and describes and analyses the schooling experiences of his eldest son from his first experience in school to subsequent less positive classroom interactions. The chapter concludes with a plea for schools to provide parents with genuine choice to engage in the education of their children through sharing the process of educating the whole person with teachers, instead of being forced into a position of having to bolster the thinking and personal qualities of a child alienated by narrowly defined schooling.

Ian Menter places disaffection in the context of one of the major issues relating to it in schools — racism. He points out that many of the problems he outlines are also relevant to sexism and a whole spectrum of gender-based issues of disaffected behaviour. His analysis emphasises that any form of disaffection cannot simply be seen in terms of the immediate context in which it occurs, but must also be seen as part of a system which maintains the values of the classroom in which it occurs. As a result of this analysis he makes a case for seeing racism as a white problem at a societal level because it is a power structure that maintains it rather than simply individuals with prejudice against black people. He illustrates how discussion of race and disaffection in education has frequently focused on 'disruptive black children' rather than the racist context in which they acted. Thus he argues that it is the racist disaffection of white children which must be as much our concern as that of black children in school.

Val Wood looks at the way schools may respond to being part of a working-class community in order to counter disaffection of children and parents from schooling, and to counter any disaffection teachers may feel about children and parents. This chapter is based on her own experience of working in and being head of schools in areas of social and economic hardship. She illustrates and analyses the ideas, structures and practices that promote a working relationship between the people of the community and the school. She concludes by pointing out that none of the changes that occurred at her current school would have been possible without the policies, commitment, financial backing and support through extra teachers and advisers, provided by Leeds LEA. This again emphasises that the wider context of policy makers, society values, etc., is crucial to an understanding of disaffection.

In the final part, three issues are examined in a broader context giving perspectives provided by an examination of policy and societal values. Martin Woodhead examines intake policies of primary schools in relation to the apparently arbitrary entry age of 5. He shows that despite the history of the statute and subsequent parliamentary discussion of entry age for early years education, succeeding governments have failed to provide recommended nursery education to complement entry at 5. He goes on to consider current policies and practices for entry to school and the context of demand in which they are made. The author questions the value of early admission, particularly when the organization, curriculum and staffing are inappropriate to pupils' interests and curricular needs. He is fundamentally questioning the rationale for intake policy decisions, and asks that educational questions should be considered.

Peter Heaslip makes a similar plea when he re-examines teacher education for early years teachers. He outlines the growth of early years and particularly nursery teachers' courses and the continuing shortage of higher education tutors who have experience in this area of teaching. He points out the significance of this as their inability to help the students to understand fully the practical implications of aspects of their job. In the second half of the chapter he highlights significant elements which he feels should be included in the education of early years teachers; not the least of which is the opportunity for teachers to learn to articulate and assert the arguments and practice of the experience-based approach, usually referred to as 'play', to curriculum.

Finally, I look at disaffection, and its opposite, in terms of the two apparently opposing perspectives, 'the needs of society' and 'the needs of the individual'. I argue that the two perspectives do not have to be polarities if we shift our understanding of knowledge towards one that has been argued strongly for many years. The chapter concludes by relating to each other the curricula of schools, societal growth and individual development to show how ability to learn and change at a societal level depends on the experience of individuals being able to value, evaluate and develop their own understanding of the world. The form and process of curriculum becomes the key to understanding both these possibilities and much disaffection in schools. Research would suggest that the actual content, despite the National Curriculum, is not as crucial to the well-being and willingness to learn of the individual as the beliefs about knowledge held by the adults holding the power. Given the 1988 Education Act, these adults may now be the parents and not the teachers.

References

BERLAK, A. and BERLAK, H. (1981) *Dilemmas of Schooling: Teaching and Social Change*, London, Methuen.

BRIERLEY, J. (1987) *Give me a Child Until He is Seven: Brain Studies and Early Childhood Education*, Lewes, Falmer Press.

DONALDSON, M., GRIEVE, R. and PRATT, C. (Eds) (1983) *Early Childhood Development and Education*, Oxford, Blackwell.

WOODHEAD, M. (1987) 'The needs of children: Is there value in the concept?' *Oxford Review of Education*, 13, 2, pp. 129–39.

Part I
Learning to be Disaffected

1
A Child's Eye View of Schooling

Gill Barrett

This book is seeking to present a variety of perspectives on disaffection from school in order to gain a broader understanding of it. An essential element within these perspectives is that of the child as a learner in school but it is inevitably difficult to represent. In this chapter we explore this problem and seek to find a solution through recognising that children as thinking people make meaning of their experiences. School is recognised as a place in which children constantly have to face and respond to adult expectations. We conclude with pupils' comments about their school experience and consider some questions about learning situations for young children.

Problems in Presenting a Child's Perspective

As parents or teachers we are constantly faced with children's understanding of the world particularly when obviously dissonant with our own. Children's interpretations of how old their teachers are provide an explicit example of the differences between child and adult perceptions. What it is easy to forget is that children appear to have a complex understanding of schooling which adults have no immediate access to except through observing how they behave. Children's perspectives, including their reasons and intentions, are important however. A number of educationalists have attempted to show how essential it is for adults to put aside their own conceptions in order to understand children's experience and enable children to learn effectively. But to a large extent they have been ignored, misunderstood, misrepresented in action, or simply applied to one section of the school population. Montessori's work for example is only seen as relevant to preschool children and Pestalozzi's pioneering work became limited in application to younger children.

An implication we may draw from this is that adults do not find it easy to know their own perceptions of the world, and thus cannot readily put them aside, because they assume that their perception is the reality. We must question, therefore, adult theories of children which in effect create a particular reality of children.

It follows that in this chapter we cannot roundly assert developmental ages, stages and associated children's behaviour, as if they were representing children's perspectives. Such theories have been created by adults who derived their ideas from disciplines or perspectives which are not based within the experience of the child, although they would claim to be based on it.

If in this chapter I am seeking to avoid those interpretations and descriptive analyses of children which make generalisations easy, I am left in a void of exploration to a large extent. This may sound rather dramatic but what I am trying to emphasise is that we still don't know very much about the thinking and interpretations of the five to seven year old child, though we are beginning to realise this and are now devising methods that lead us forward. For example, child abuse cases have led to further development of interview techniques with children, and researchers and teachers are learning methods to enable children to communicate classroom experiences (Barrett, 1986b). This chapter reflects the tentative nature of the claim to present children's perspectives while at the same time asserting that the child's thinking and experience is vital to any appreciation of the issues of disaffection in classrooms.

Towards an Understanding of Children

One of the problems we have in understanding children in the early years of schooling is that we largely see them *behaving*, i.e., doing things, and we do not assume they can also talk to us about what they are doing. We are not taught within our education system to perceive behaviour as cognitive or higher order activity. Having taught Physical Education early in my career, it was not hard for me to make the shift of understanding to see that there are thoughts and intentions behind all the consistent actions of very young children.

During a period of research in schools (Barrett, 1984, 1986a) I was led to understand that regardless of age, no consistent changes in behaviour happened by chance and children had knowledge of what they were doing and why they were doing it, in their own or social terms. An example of such change in behaviour emerged when I was asking some six-year-olds what they liked about school because I had discovered that 'like' was akin to knowing, the thinking of something.

> Nicky told me she now liked writing as well as reading and sums. 'I used to write big', she added by way of explanation for her change in attitude. 'How did you manage not to write big?' I asked. She thought for a moment. 'I thinked to make it little. Helen (her friend) did little writing and I thinked to make mine little. Cos they wouldn't understand if you did big writing up at the junior school would they.'

Similarly, an infant school child I had observed in the playgroup told me as I watched her drawing a cat (in response to a television story), that she knew how to do cats because her mum had taught her. She, looking across to her friend Kathy who was involved in drawing an apparently amorphous set of lines, said 'Kathy hasn't done cats yet'. In fact, as Kathy was responding to the task I think she was 'doing cats' but was drawing something of the quality of cats, i.e. the fur, rather than the stereotyped shape of cats. In these two examples the children were able to explain their changed behaviour and how they were able to do something that adults could see they could do. Other examples of pupils thinking which involved apparently little change in behaviour emerged in the research.

Individual children continued to engage voluntarily with a number of activities over a period of time, and in some instances over a year, and I came to recognise that this signalled a growing understanding even though to untutored eyes the behaviour or outcome appeared the same. I saw five- six- or seven-year-old pupils choosing to repeat work cards and remaining engaged in the task until they finally abandoned it and were just bored. I tested my understanding that they were thinking about and mastering different elements, when I observed another six-year-old still drawing space pictures after a year. To me they looked essentially the same. I asked him, 'How does your thinking about space grow?' He thought for a few seconds without showing any signs of not understanding the question.

> 'Well! From the news and things like that . . . Like there's going to be a comet in 1986 — err when I'm eight — (he does a mental calculation) yes in 1986.' He appears to have an awareness of me as an audience and asks, 'Do you know what a comet is?' I confess I don't and he proceeds to tell me — and about a meteor and a meteorite.

It would have been so easy to dismiss his drawings as pure fantasy until I discovered that most voluntary representations of knowledge, through words, drawings or actions, represented much experience and a great deal of re-thinking and structuring. For example, I watched a four and a half-year old in a playgroup and later at school. The only things he ever became intellectually absorbed in were cars and making things, preferably using tools. He frequently got told off in other situations. When I interviewed his mother I discovered he used to spend hours watching the next door neighbour repairing cars and spent long periods of time at home finding out how things were put together and frequently taking things apart when he couldn't see how they worked. What I'm emphasising here is the fact that children are thinking, observing and listening, and making meaning in relation both to themselves and their experiences. They have preferred ways of thinking and relating experiences, which may or may not match up to those of the adults around them. Adults in school may create situations in which children cannot, or are not expected to, demonstrate what they know but they will in turn make meaning from this. This meaning, and the way that the child responds to it, may be one clue to disaffection and the behaviour associated with it.

What I am sharing here is a range of insights about children's thinking which have been triggered by studying young children in classrooms. These insights have been expanded by reading such innovators as Donaldson (1978), Bruner (1984) and Bruner and Haste (1987). My research over the last six years has helped me to develop a new awareness of young children, both because of some very special teachers, and through the children themselves. I have listened carefully to children who have been put into the position of 'experts' rather than learners which enable them to express thoughts and feelings that otherwise remain unexpressed in words. The extracts that follow are comments of children about their education, derived from research about children's learning and understanding children's responses in classrooms.

Children's Perspectives on School

At the beginning of this book I am trying to represent the experience of being a child who has knowledge of her/himself as a relatively powerless person in an adult society. We are, therefore, looking at the experience of school through the perspective of a child facing the shifting sands of adult expectations. We need to see children as essentially thinking and feeling people whose behaviour is affected by their experiences and the sense they make of them.

The rest of this chapter provides a range of children's perspectives on the experiences of school and seeks to represent some clues to the meaning they make from adult expectations. Interpretations or ways in which these may be seen as significant are suggested in places; but otherwise they are left for you as reader to reflect on and think about in terms of the experience of children who have their learning environment structured with inbuilt adult and societal values which may or may not value children and their thinking.

When children start school they have usually had five years experience of living and learning at home. Home does not mean the same thing to all children and their pre-school learning experiences will differ considerably. School is not the same as home so the move to a school context requires a conceptual shift for children not least because there is a change in the value placed on the individual child. The concept of a school as a different place from a home is something that young children develop by recognising their erroneous thinking. One four-year-old, thinking that the teacher must sleep somewhere in the school asked, 'Where do you keep your jamas?' What is school if it is not a home? What is it for?

The child's view of the purpose and meaning of the school experience is significant in considering disaffection and it is possible to gain some insights into this by considering the way parents introduce their children to the notion of school, and by listening to pupils as 'experts'. Many parents prepare their children for entry to school over a long period:

> We used to walk past the school most days on the way to the shops and I used to say to her, 'That's where you'll go to school when you're a big girl'.

Children soon become aware of reasons why they come to school apart from the fact their mothers tell them they have to. These have implications for the future as this group of seven-year-olds showed. We come to school:

- To learn to write and do work cards;

- To learn about all the countries and about all the things we do;
- To learn to work;
- Not to mess about;
- Not to wet your pants (a boy who still did);
- Well, when you're learning you haven't just got to do it for nothing. You've GOT TO — cos you can't get a job if you don't learn.

These quotations suggest that learning in schools is multi-dimensional and not all of it to do with personal growth: above all it is to do with adult expectations. These reception year children from different classrooms recall personal memories of starting school and show both the variety of expectations made of them, and also their awareness of them and how they felt about them.

- I didn't like sitting on the floor. There were no carpets.
- Sometimes you get tired of working. You need a rest and a drink.
- I couldn't cross my legs. My legs were too little. Look they can fit now.
- I didn't like getting into line when I came to school. I wanted my mummy to hold my hand.
- When I first came to school I painted and readed and doing my book — my colouring book and I do some colouring — like scribbling.
- When I first started school I drawed a picture and it was horrible (long pause) I forgot arms and legs.

Children learn that school learning has adult defined purposes, models and action which the child identifies as expectations are made of them by adults through tasks or the classroom context provided. However, many children appear to want to learn when there is some intellectual stimulus and they have the chance to find out and work things out for themselves, though are aware of boredom and reluctance when they haven't.

- Sometimes all this work is boring.
- Sometimes you want to stop writing and talk to your friends about something that comes into your head.
- Sometimes you aren't bored — cos it will be all new (in a new class). And I found that when I came here — (I was) so pleased I couldn't really sit down cos — I had to find another place in the room to see what was going on there. I could see the people doing number — and they had scales and I had to see what they were doing with the scales — then I noticed people carrying books around the class and so I went and asked them what they were doing with the books.

It appears that children are well aware of their feelings about school activities, and about the imperfections of their own confidence and efforts when they are expected to do things that they don't know how to think about or do perfectly. Children know the feelings involved, and it would seem they recognise the behaviour associated with them when they see it in others — as these responses to the following pictures show. It is interesting to note that although there is a similarity in

7

response to these pictures, individual differences emerge and serve to remind us that it is hard to generalise about children's thinking or behaviour.

- He might be bored or upset, I don't like playtimes, being pushed about.
- The little boy would like a turn but he is too shy. Matthew (a twin) was shy when he came to school. He wouldn't do anything. Mark (his twin) was not shy, he did things.
- Matthew why were you shy?
- I am the shy one.
- No — you do things now.
- But I didn't know what to do when I came to school. There was too much of everything. The twins had never been to a nursery school or playgroup.
- There's a boy standing watching.
- He doesn't know how to do it. He's scared.
- One's thinking what to do.
- He's sucking his hand because he doesn't know what to do.
- The boy is feeling sad because she won't let him play.
- I let anyone play except fighters: (Teacher's note. This child often 'fights'. Two boys did want to talk about this picture and turned away from it.)

- They are writing in their busy book. They are writing about their lego model. You must make sure you have clean hands and have finger spaces.
- Girl can't do it. Perhaps she's drawing a ship.
- One's putting her pencil in her mouth cos' she's thinking what to draw. I like drawing mummy, daddy and me in a house with curtains.
- A boy doesn't know what to do. He is sucking his pencil. He cannot do his work. He must tell his teacher. I didn't know how to do it. I didn't know how to paint or mix the colours properly.
- He's thinking about his mum and dad at home.
- I didn't like to write when I came to school. I couldn't make a snail. I couldn't draw a picture. It was too hard. I was too little.
- I feel miserable when I can't do it.
- I'm frightened I might get it wrong.

The learning process is stressful and the 'harder' the work the more tiring it is. 'Hard' related to teacher expectation and the extent to which children had the opportunity to find out what had to be done prior to doing it. Some seven-year-olds explained, when telling me how work in their new class was harder, because it was 'put on the board for everyone to do and you didn't always know what the words meant'. Reception children too also found some work hard.

Chris and Nicholas are doing a 'writing sheet' on which they have to do some vertical lines and then fill in some horizontal lines on two ladders. Nicholas comments to Chris who has almost finished, 'I don't want to do

9

anymore'. The teacher comes over and encourages him to complete the second ladder. I asked Nicholas why he hadn't wanted to do anymore? 'Cos I wanted to sit down there', pointing to the carpet. 'I will do some more tomorrow'. They had both been very intense and totally silent while doing these sheets and I asked Chris, 'Did you have to think a lot when you did that?' pointing to the sheet. He looked and thought. 'I had to think about doing — that — ' and he gestured a horizontal movement of his hand, 'and I did it all by myself'.

Committing effort to learning activities is both stressful and tiring, particularly if many of the expectations in the classroom are concerned with public symbolic forms, which in the early stages may have very little meaning. Children in many different schools reflected on a picture of a young girl (aged 5 +) asleep at a desk with her head on her arms.

● The little girl is tired. She wants to go home and watch T.V.(5)
● She's crying because she wants to play.(5)
● One girl's sleeping because she's tired and fed up of drawing.(5)
● They're thinking what to draw. He's tired because he's fed up of drawing.(5)I get tired at dinner time because I want to go and lay down.(5)
● That little girl has gone to sleep. She went to bed too late. (5)
● No! I always get tired at school. Jason always went to sleep at story time.(5) School is very long. School is big.(4 +)

These provide us with examples of personal expectations when children are learning and the emotional and intellectual energy that is expended in trying to make sense of them. When expectations about the curriculum are increasingly controlled or structured by the teacher then the engagement of pupil thinking and learning is affected in other ways too.

● Daniel and Carl have found a book on New Zealand (Carl's homeland). They start to read when the teacher calls, 'Time to put them away'. Daniel's face and comment show disappointment. 'But I've only just got it'.(7 +)
● There are always too many people in school to make things properly. You have to stop too soon. Someone always spoils it.(5)

These comments seem to be showing us that some disaffection by children may well be due to misunderstanding of them and their learning by adults. If we want them to engage with learning and thinking they need time and space in which to do so. Adult expectations not only apply to the content of learning but clearly also affect the process. As a result of close observation of a vertically grouped infant class over a period of a year I saw the teacher make allowances for different approaches to learning. This did not happen in many of the classrooms I was observing and had known in my years as a teacher. For example, two reception boys had totally different approaches to learning maypole dancing which other children in the vertically grouped class could already do. One wanted to have a go at the first opportunity he was offered; gradually over a period of a few weeks he learned the movements of the dance and for his feet through engaging in doing the dance. The second did not want to join in at the first or next few sessions. He sat out for a number of weeks, watching, listening and obviously learning — because eventually he said he did want to join in. When he did, he could already complete the moves of the dances as learned by the 5-year-olds.

In this same classroom pupils were encouraged to pursue their own interests as well as engage in the curriculum of the school. They also had the opportunity to choose their own teacher, and many younger children used older or more experienced children as mentors. Frequently children used more appropriate concepts and language with which to explain what was needed. For example, a 5-year-old child had been asked to draw 'x' circles on a number of lines in his maths book. The circles were meant to represent beads. He drew them sitting on the line. The teacher asked him to 'draw the next lot of beads ON the line'. A six-year-old watching this said, 'You have to draw them on the string', thus illustrating for the child the experiential context of what was being represented. He nodded in comprehension and went off and did what was required. Many of the expectations of classrooms are associated with the translation of experience into symbolic forms. But as the example above illustrates the language used to convey the task, and indeed the experience required may be inappropriate to an individual and therefore not give access to appropriate thinking. Thus the seven-year-olds cited earlier found the work of their new classroom 'harder' because the language used initially prevented them identifying the thinking and experience they needed to complete the tasks. In subject terms the tasks were conceptually easier than those they had been doing in their previous classroom. Even in classrooms where role play, talking, models and drawings are recognised and encouraged as expressions of organised experience and knowledge, the degree of familiarity with the specific symbolic form will affect the ability of pupils to translate their experience into that form until it too has been learned.

At the beginning of this chapter the potential differences in perception between adults and children was highlighted. We need to emphasise this as we question some of the traditional expectations of children in the early years of school in the context of disaffection. What happens to children's self esteem when their thinking and knowledge, or lack of it, is ignored or misunderstood by adults? What happens when the learning strategies they have developed in the early years of home life are denied them in the school? What happens if one expectation constantly replaces another before the first has been mastered? Children have very little power because they are dependent on adults for emotional and physical sustenance and are largely uncritical. Socialisation of children into particular behaviour, and the thinking that goes with it, is therefore easy. But this puts tremendous responsibility on teachers and leaves us with an important question. In trying to see the learning experience from the perspective of the child, rather than through adults' theories about children which evolved in a different social context, we need to examine our expectations if we want to avoid disaffection and encourage effective learning across a broad range of subjects in the National Curriculum.

References

BARRETT, G. H. (1984) 'Getting it in your brain', in Schostak, J. and Logan, T. (Eds) *Pupil Experience*, Beckenham, Croom Helm.

BARRETT, G. H. (1986a) 'Learning in the Schooling Process: Ways of Thinking, Learning and Knowing in Classroom Interactions of Pupils from 4 to 16, Unpublished PhD thesis, University of East Anglia, Norwich.

BARRETT, G. H. (1986b) *Starting School: An Evaluation of the Experience*, London, AMMA.

BRUNER, J. (1984) *Children's Talk*, Oxford, Fontana Paperbacks.

BRUNER, J. and HASTE, H. (Eds) (1987) *Making Sense: The child's construction of the world*, London, Methuen.

DONALDSON, M. (1978) *Children's Minds*, London, Fontana.

SALZBERGER-WITTENBERG, I., HENRY, G. and OSBORNE, E. (1983) *The Emotional Experience of Learning and Teaching*, London, Routledge and Kegan Paul.

2
Deliver Us From Eagles

Annabel Dixon

No one should be surprised in a society that sees nothing odd in collecting old jam jar labels or used bus tickets, that the collection of *mistakes* has a certain popularity. Not just any kind of mistake; these are specialist mistakes. They are not visual, to be hung in art galleries or stuffed into disused barns. They are not tangible in that way. That they are a very particular kind of mistake can be judged by the fact that no one publishes books on collections of knitting disasters, cooking failures or withered plants, yet there is a sufficient readership of these specialist mistakes for publishers to sell collections of them from time to time.

Can one tell from the readership of such books the nature of these specialist mistakes? To say they would probably be of a certain educational background, possibly middle class and above a particular age, would seem to tell us nothing exact or helpful. In fact, it not only tells us a great deal, it raises some fundamental questions about the nature of education, appropriate curriculum and the process of learning itself.

Can all this be gained from what would appear to be a light hearted collection of childish mistakes? For the common name for these particular kinds of mistake is nothing more than the familiar 'howler'. Can such claims be made for what appears to be merely amusing trivia? Nothing is more unfunny than the joke explained; can 'howlers' bear the weight of such analysis?

Howlers are not limited to young children. There is an annual crop from the various examination boards, e.g., from a biology paper, 'The difference between pollination and fertilization is that fertilization takes place in a moment of confusion'. However, many more familiar and frequently quoted howlers have a religious basis, a fact not without significance as I hope to show. The Lord's Prayer provides rich pickings: 'Our Father which chart in heaven', 'Harold be thy name', 'Lead us not into Thames Station', 'Deliver us from Eagles' and 'trespasses' seen as a new kind of cornflake that was somehow delivered along with the 'daily bread'. Prayers and hymns are another good source: 'Praise the Lord in his hard vest', 'Pity mice implicitly', 'Sadly my cross-eyed bear' and the happy transformation of 'Let us with a gladsome mind' to 'Let us with a glass of mild . . .'

To students of humour, it is not hard to see the origin of the appeal of such howlers. The unexpected shifts in meaning, the familiar made unfamiliar, and, for some, the frisson of a sublimely innocent near-blasphemy. For most though, the appeal is left unanalysed and rests simply on the attractiveness of children's artless sayings.

Many authors (Loukes 1963; Goldman 1965) from the early 1960s onwards have been trying to alert teachers in particular to the real meaning of such mistakes with regard to religious education. Children have been making such errors because they have been misunderstanding. They have been misunderstanding, not because they have been inattentive or unintelligent but because the material they were supposed to learn was entirely inappropriate to their understanding of it.

Religious education conveniently provides us with a neat model of what can happen when children cannot make sense of what they are being taught. At first, they will try to make sense of it in terms they can understand. None of the howlers quoted above makes nonsense if you read them from a child's point of view. Each one represents a child who has listened intently, feeling he or she has not quite heard or understood and yet sensing some kind of obligation to do so. If they are lucky they won't admit until they are adult what they made of the 'difficult' part in case it is wrong. If they are unlucky an older child or adult will overhear them and will be doubled up with unkind mirth. This will merely serve to hasten what I think is a general pattern of behaviour among young children and for which, as I suggested, religious education provides such a telling model. There seems to be a comfortable assumption that children, having got over making such amusing little mistakes, will get back in line, as it were, and somehow start to understand what they are being taught. Some children presumably do so, but if R.E. is a good example of what can happen, then many give up the unequal struggle and simply disassociate themselves from it altogether — they become disaffected.

Generations of children who were taught a didactic form of R.E. that introduced them to abstract notions before they could possibly understand them, demonstrated the outcome in a highly measurable way that is sometimes difficult with other school subjects. Presumably one of the main aims of R.E. in Great Britain was to ensure a new generation of church/chapel-goers and committed Christians. Other factors undoubtedly also influence such an outcome, but the observable drop in church attendance over the last fifty years has been quite dramatic. Surely the nature of R.E. in schools must bear some of the responsibility.

What are the characteristics of this disassociation? Are they temporary phases that some careful explanation will soon sort out? For the fortunate children with a perceptive and patient teacher, this can sometimes be the case, but I would suggest it would have to happen at the early stages of such disassociation. There seems to be an identifiable progression, a combination of intellectual and emotional responses that culminates in the kind of disassociation commonly called disaffection, and once it has reached its final form it may be so intractable as to be virtually impervious to any but the most sustained and sensitive treatment. (A useful analogy here might be that of the process of de-sensitisation, for example, in relation to a phobia about dogs). All these seem to be implying a largely emotional response to what seems to be, initially, an intellectual confusion.

In one of the key books on disaffection, *How Children Fail* (Holt 1964), the author maintains that children are confused because the 'torrent of words that pour over them in school makes little or no sense. It often flatly contradicts other things they have been told and hardly ever has any relation to what they really know, to the rough model of reality that they carry around in their minds'.

It is sometimes cosily assumed that such disaffection is only discernible in the later years of schooling, from middle childhood onwards, but the critical years are from when children first enter school up to 7 or 8. This is the age when children learn to distance themselves from schooling, when the under-achiever learns how to scrape by, when the 'lazy' child begins to be so described, the over-anxious to give up easily. It is the age when the importance of the right answer is established and panic reactions begin their insidious growth so that for some, for example, all things mathematical start to provoke the same kind of phobic response that might equally well be achieved by sitting in a snake pit. This is when many a non-reader becomes adept at comparing him/herself to others and gives up the unequal struggle. These are the years when the emotional response to learning is established; from eager, interested and passionately involved at one end of the continuum to fearfulness, hesitancy and straightforward antagonism at the other.

It seems to be generally assumed that this is a natural polarity, but were children like this when they first learned to walk, when they first played in the snow, picked up their first ladybird? That children by the age of 7 to 8 don't all belong to the first category is very largely the fault of schools, a fault which could become exacerbated beyond belief if future testing is handled clumsily and without understanding. Holt even goes so far as to claim that 'to a very great degree school is a place where children learn to be stupid'.

My own experience of teaching young children from 4 to 10, over twenty-five years, has served to convince me that for many children, 'it's too late by eight'. Their attitudes towards themselves, learning and school have become set, and with a class of thirty or so for only one year, the most willing teacher can do little more than lower the antagonism slightly. It should be noted that such antagonism is not always obvious; it manifests itself as a passivity, listlessness, or dreaminess, a reluctance or awkwardness, as much as straightforward non-conformity and/or anti-social behaviour, although it is the latter that often receives the most recognition. Of course, some children enter school as more tentative or more aggressive than others, but this only goes part way to explaining attitudes towards learning by the time they are 8 years old.

Some nations, sensibly in my view, do not admit children to formal schooling until they are six or even seven years old. Much of the problem, I think, lies with the fact that younger children appear to think and feel so differently from adults or indeed older children, that a very specific curriculum has to be designed to suit their characteristic intellectual and emotional response. A curriculum would thus be so foreign to their teachers as to be totally unlike any other kind of provision in a child's school career. Piaget and Bruner may no longer dominate teacher education as they once did, but this reflects political trends, not an assessment of the most profound contributions to the education of young children. This is not to say that because younger children are less experienced, they should just have a simplified version of the older children's curriculum, e.g. 'We'll do "water" for our topic but the little ones won't understand displacement, so we'll just do floating and sinking instead'. I can quote this example, as I did it myself when I began teaching. The children showed me that things *didn't* obligingly sink or float. Out of the window went the attempt to capture the world of sinking and floating into two neat categories: some of the objects the children tried out did much more interesting (and exasperating!) things: they fell over on one side; they sank all except one little bit — but if you put them in at a different angle to start with, they did sink, and with a satisfying gurgle. What else made a gurgly noise — or any kind of noise? There lay the true excitement of the following fifteen minutes but there will be increasing pressure for teachers to stick to the National Curriculum programmes of study and ignore this kind of feed-back that is their vital tool for understanding what is really going on in their children's minds and hearts.

Feedback, such as noting the responses children make to various experiences, seldom seems to be given the high priority that is necessary if teachers are to become truly effective. It is not just a matter of noting the responses but reflecting upon them and very possibly altering one's own behaviour in the classroom as a result. It is learning what the children are *really* saying — and it may very well be in the form of non-verbal responses. At a simple level the following might serve as an example: you are reading an exciting story about pirates (*you* think it's exciting . . .) to the class, when an insistent hand goes up. Full of the milk of human kindness, you stop and ask Donald what he wants, even though he is actually stopping the flow of your exciting story. 'My Nan's cat's got three kittens'. End of *non-sequitur*, 'Thank you, Donald, now perhaps we can get on with the story . . . ', but is it a *non-sequitur*? Donald is telling you something about the story, himself and the important things in his life. The story is far removed from his own experience — What are pirates and anyway, has he learnt to listen to stories yet? There's a chance he may never do so if all stories are beyond his understanding and vocabulary. Stories, he may well conclude, are not for him and he becomes the perfect nuisance as a six year old at story times, pulling girls' hair, tickling his friends and simply not concentrating. The roots of disaffection are being established but of course it's Donald's fault for being naughty — not what we did to him as a 4-or 5-year-old.

There are, or should be, many questions to ask oneself constantly in a classroom and many would seem unanswerable without this knowledge of children's learning. Indeed without it, the children's responses must be like semaphore signals. You can see that some fairly urgent messages are being signalled, but you don't know the semaphore code. You know lots of other things, such as curriculum design, classroom management skills and evaluation techniques, but how young children develop emotionally and intellectually isn't considered (exactly) irrelevant but not the essential knowledge that illuminates everything else. Not for nothing do Blenkin & Kelly (1981) in *The Primary Curriculum* when discussing education as a process, state quite unequivocally that 'A major part of the expertise of all teachers, therefore, whatever the age of their pupils, is an understanding of the fundamental processes of child development'.

What other ways are there to assess children's behaviour? Keeping records? Do records exist that tell you a a six-year-old has switched off writing because he finds filling in word blanks beyond either his interest or understanding, and anyway he's not allowed to sit next to his friend (who used to help him with the right words) any more because they were silly when they worked together? The majority of records may tell you the topics or workbooks covered in a particular term. They may inform you as to which mathematical concepts have been introduced. Certain skills may be identified as having been learnt; the stories and poems that have been read and the visits undertaken may be recorded. They may try to inform you as to the relative degree of success or otherwise that has been achieved. Some records even have a place for 'attitude' but few seem to see the irony or information contained in the word 'poor'.

There is much confusion over record keeping and many records are less than informative when trying to assess children's real attitudes to learning and themselves as learners. This is partly a confusion about the function of records and partly a misplaced optimism that they will nail down the reality of a child's response and achievement. Where is the place in a conventional record sheet for noting that Sarah was so excited when she finished her first woodwork model, with nails banged in by her and her alone, that she wrote a whole page about her achievement, and this from a child who can hardly stagger through a line of writing without great labour. The chatty note about this in a teacher's diary seems ingenuous, cosy and disorganised compared to the many available systems of tick lists and record sheets. It will nevertheless have a certain ring of truth about it; something a list of ticks doesn't always engender. When teachers want to learn about the way children really respond to schooling, they don't sit down with a satisfying heap of old school records to read. They choose books about people closely observing children as they go about their daily lives in school. Ashton-Warner (1963) may have written a good many years ago but her book still has more recognisable validity than many a detailed record matrix.

The reality of children's lives and responses totally permeates Armstrong's (1981) *Closely Observed Children*. What characterizes both books? They give accounts of the process of education as it actually happens. The record sheet could undoubtedly be devised that requested information about individual children's degree of disaffection or otherwise and may indeed have a degree of helpfulness in focusing attention on such matters. It will not record Darren's discomfiture at getting all his sums wrong for the fourth time in a week and his subsequent reluctance to engage in things mathematical. It will not enable us to track back and see what kind of maths Darren was doing that allowed for the possibility of his getting them all wrong. Without that kind of information, such a record sheet will tell us little beyond the fact that he has (mysteriously) become disenchanted with school. That is not to say that record sheets are untruthful or that, in a strict listing sense, (books read and topics introduced) they are not unhelpful as an aide-mémoire. What cannot be extracted is another kind of truth, one that may have a far more vital bearing on young children's future educational progress — how they feel about themselves as learners in the context of school.

The young horses being led to the running waters of curriculum objectives are not necessarily going to feel all that thirsty when they know what happened last time they drank from them. Such children may make us feel frustrated, annoyed and exasperated with their ingratitude, their time-wasting strategies and lack of concentration. If we are to make a different kind of record it is also our response we need to find a place for. Teachers will often add a delighted exclamation mark in a reading record, for example, when some breakthrough has been achieved. Maybe a reverse one should also be used, for it is diaries and notebooks that offer the widest opportunities for more personal reflection and responses.

A Closer Look at Curriculum in Action

For those who feel that something more structured helps them personally, a set of queries might act as a guideline to their observations. The reception and infant class teachers have more responsibility here than maybe any other teacher in the primary school. What happens in these classes may well affect all future responses to a very wide range of educational experiences. For example, the queries should be about individual children. 'Does X hang back at the edge of the group? In what way? Interested but not confident enough to push forward? Not interested and hoping to be ignored? Does X only manage to write the minimum number of words about news, topic, story, anything? What does X show most enthusiasm for: sport/P.E., music, writing, maths, topic, painting, anything, nothing?' How does this enthusiasm show itself? Class teachers have a remarkable knowledge of their children which is rarely mined. Few would not be able to answer such questions about their children and probably even more detailed ones than that. The most telling and informative queries though, should be the following: what is X's response to difficulty/failure? Gives up straight away, distracts self/others, cries, needs normal/disproportionate amount of encouragement, sulks? The possible responses are more extensive than this but they serve to give an idea. Answers to such queries do not tell us how intelligent a child is or what maths/reading book he or she may be on, but they do give telling information about attitudes and motivation — in other words, how particular individuals actually feel about themselves and school.

It would be easy to be dismissive about thinking such things important, that this is merely another manifestation of the 'warm-glow' approach to education. It would not be hard to find psychological evidence to refute this but even common sense and our own memories of school or even more recent learning experiences, should point to the crucial part in learning that is played by both negative and positive attitudes. Our curriculum may be elegantly designed. It may have breadth, consistency and continuity. If it switches off half the class these qualities are not going to count for much. Indeed can these qualities be recognised and appreciated by the children? The missing word is 'appropriate'.

Now for the next set of queries. How do I, as a teacher, feel about child X, for example, (not necessarily how I respond, but how I honestly feel) in relation to the behaviour shown when X is having problems? Do I feel exasperated, pleased that X is tackling it without fuss, puzzled, frustrated? How do I evaluate those who give up: lazy, unintelligent, lacking in application? Such value judgements are just that. They evaluate the children's responses and do so from a given viewpoint. If we add 'bored' or 'disheartened' to the list, the viewpoint subtly shifts. It is no longer the viewpoint of the adult but that of the child.

The Curriculum

This is where attention turns more closely to the curriculum. It may not necessarily be the whole reason why young children can become disheartened but the chances are that it plays a very great part. Teaching style and the way in which the curriculum is delivered, can also be effective determinants of whether or not a child becomes disaffected with school, or a particular aspect of it, e.g. maths. Such aspects will be considered later after looking at the nature of the curriculum in the first years of school. In practice, many infant schools have a shorthand way of referring to most of the curriculum on offer to their children; in the interesting way that language evolves, reference is no longer made to centres of interest or projects, but topics. There are certain skills areas of the curriculum like learning to read, write and perform what one teacher remembers being told as a bemused infant, were 'operations', i.e. addition, subtraction, division and multiplication. There may well be provision for play activities which are used to a greater or lesser degree, but they are rarely referred to as part of the curriculum. Nonetheless they may be very important to the children themselves and they form an integral part of the 'hidden curriculum'; a viewpoint that Pinder (1987) takes in her valuable book *Why don't teachers teach like they used to?* Provision of any kind indicates to the children what is, or is not, considered important.

Are their box models thrown away or construction models broken up at the end of each day? Their work books are not. Are there plants, flowers or living creatures? How well they are looked after gets over a powerful message about caring for the environment. Is there provision for music making in the classroom or is that what you get on Friday afternoons? It tells them something about the place of music, for example.

What then influences the choice of these topics? To a greater or lesser degree, they are those things which are considered to be of interest to children in general, within which may be information or skills that are presumed to be suitable for children to learn. This suitability is influenced consciously or otherwise by a number of identifiable pressures. It is particularly important that teachers are aware of these pressures in today's political and economic climate, in order to be able to assess them professionally. For example there would seem to be a re-emphasis on the importance of factual knowledge, without any apparent reference to its appropriateness for the children themselves. Even Skinner (1988), a psychologist who is not viewed with any distinctive warmth by educationalists in Great Britain, had this to say in April 1988 ' . . . teachers still nourish some notion that they can impart knowledge, and this flies in the face of all we know about teaching'. He was referring to the fact that teachers punish children in various ways when they show no wish to learn, i.e. they are no longer interested. This method quite naturally reinforces the dislike. What subtle ways do infant teachers employ to punish children who do not seem to want to learn? Usually by giving them unintended social pre-eminence amongst their peer group by selecting them for a special place in the classroom and telling them they are silly or babyish.

It is also becoming clear that rewards as well as punishments play a significant part in, surprisingly, making learning less rather than more attractive. The rewards are the familiar ones of giving marks; several researchers have found that although what was to be learnt was initially attractive to children, giving marks or grades to the subsequent work lowered that interest. Butler's (1988) recent research supports this, indicating that comments do not have the same effect as marks do, except in the case of the high achievers. In classroom terms and in terms of a nationally tested curriculum it is fairly evident that motivation by competition will be attractive only to the few and the casualties will not only be the less able in school or societal terms, but even learning itself. As the intrinsic interest in learning for its own sake becomes diminished this will affect all children.

To return to the choice of topic; it is often dictated by television which has unwittingly imposed a form of its own national curriculum upon the country; by the head teacher; the seasons; sometimes because it has been successful in previous years or maybe because transport or dinosaurs are topics that have not been covered for a while. It could reflect a school curriculum policy or that the whole school will in its own way be looking at shops or colour. Within each topic there may well be information or activities that are of interest to individual children, but the choice of topic must seem to be of an arbitrary nature to many children.

Within the more sensitively thought out plans there are places for unintended outcomes, which means what happens when children get carried away by a particular aspect and the teacher doesn't teach what she or he intended to teach. Unintended outcomes do not mean that children are not interested. They are an aberration and can be and often are ignored. It may very well have been because there was a significant mismatch between the children's understanding, the teacher's expectation and the choice of topic.

This mismatch is particularly significant in areas such as maths or science and has been of very particular concern to Harlen (1982). She also makes the important point that it is not always a lack of understanding in a child that can make for disaffection, as intelligent children can become equally bored and uninterested if what is presented to them is too easy and predictable. The matching then has to include a fit between appropriate knowledge and activities on the one hand, and the form of intelligence, experience and interest of the children on the other. The former is ensured by a personal knowledge of the matter in hand on the part of the teacher and the latter by an equally good understanding of the individual children in the class, an understanding that, once again, can only be based on a thorough knowledge of how children develop intellectually, socially and emotionally. An awareness of their social development will also include the matter of gender, class and race. Is equal attention paid to the interests of both boys and girls and to their respective achievements, enquiries and problems? What about those of differing backgrounds and cultural experiences? Health education, for example, can very quickly be thought of as 'girls' stuff' and history, with its emphasis on kings and battles, more suited to the boys. These are places where disaffection can find its roots growing easily.

If this matching is to be carried to its logical conclusion, the class teacher will soon be aware that children need to develop their own self-chosen interests and investigate their own lines of enquiry in maths and science. Is there any provision in the day's timetable that allows for this? For children to discover the limits of their own knowledge and understanding they need to have the opportunity to make choices and decisions. This is what can confirm them in the belief that they are learners and the world is then full of uncharted fascination. If a teacher allows you to make choices, that must tell you that there is a belief not only in your ability to do so, but that it is important that you do so for yourself. King (1978) in *All Things Bright and Beautiful?* takes a unique look at the reality of infant classrooms and makes the following observation in one classroom. Children are making collage fruits and vegetables from sticky paper. Teacher calls out 'Cabbage people, here are yours' (two shades of green), 'Tomato people, these are yours' (red). There are $5\frac{1}{2}$-year-old children who can equally well say, (as one did in another school) 'I've found out something: some flowers have got five petals and some have got four. I'm going to collect all the flowers I can and I'm going to see if they're all like that and stick them in a book'. She was not only able to articulate her new-found knowledge, she was able to think of taking it on further, following a personal hypothesis; she also had a clear idea of an effective means of recording her findings.

Thus the implications for children and schools of the implementation of a national curriculum and testing are obviously very serious. If a national curriculum for young children is going to be based on a narrow set of skills to be learnt and facts to be stored, then the potential for disaffection beginning in these early years of school will be enormously increased, so what should an appropriate curriculum look like for these children? Not unlike one we already have in a number of schools. Not, as many have misunderstood such a curriculum mountain, the abandonment of learning new skills and facts. Challenge and difficulties are not eliminated; if anything, there is probably an increase but of a particular kind. There is probably a greater diversity of topics and an introduction to a far wider world than that envisaged in a narrow impoverished set of national curriculum objectives.

It is a matter of deciding what intellectual capacities one wishes to encourage and what emotional responses and social skills should be fostered, resulting in competent, interested learners who can get along with each other. They may not all have the same experiences or form of intelligence as each other but they will not be muddled or dispirited whatever their capacity. Where there are grades, tests, right and wrong answers, this competency simply will not be achieved, as research suggests and the experience of test-obsessed systems like the United States' have demonstrated.

The production of the alternative curriculum depends very largely on appropriate provision. This alone will not produce the learners I have described, but it is the essential background. The provision is already familiar to many and includes such items as sand, water, clay, dressing-up clothes, paints, books and practical mathematical equipment. It used to be said that there was a minimum of sixteen areas of provision if children's intellectual and emotional growth was to be adequately provided for. These establish the necessary conditions but are not sufficient in themselves. A popular view of such classrooms is that children play all day and achieve nothing. There can indeed be a danger that children will do this where it is not understood that there are very different levels of play. Low-level play is characterised by aimlessness, lack of involvement and concentration. Children can then become bored and unmotivated. To raise the level successfully, the children's play activities with such provision must have sufficient interest and challenge for them to become totally absorbed.

For example, a group of children playing in the home corner decide to change it into a hospital. They know that when they have finished, they will give an account of their story to the teacher. It is very likely that they will then record in some way what they have been about. According to their age and/or ability, they will either write out the story for themselves or dictate it to the teacher and then copy underneath. This may well be prefaced by a drawing, painting or map of the hospital. The teacher may decide that the hospital interest is worth developing as a vehicle for maths, language work and social awareness, to say nothing of a golden opportunity for some health education. She will act fast, because as an experienced infant teacher she will know that such interests have to be caught and developed quickly for this age group. Even by the next day the children's interest may no longer focus on hospitals but have been directed to crocodiles. It means the teacher has to be flexible and quick thinking but the extent of the children's involvement and interest are such that the quality and depth of their learning is beyond dispute.

A second example might be that of children using construction toys to make two large aeroplanes. This is no mean feat in itself as there are many technical problems to solve and they have to act as a cooperative team. They have decided to undertake this task themselves so the motivation is high. The teacher's role, supportive and encouraging but still in the background while the children are actually making the aeroplane, alters when they have finished it. This is the point where a teacher might well provide the group with a roll of blank wallpaper and suggest they record their aeroplane by drawing round it. This raises a whole new set of technical problems and much discussion. The second model is also drawn round. The opportunity for maths is extensive and exciting. Which is the longest or widest? How can you tell? What are the units of measurement? Why is the longest aeroplane 'two Stuarts' but only 'one and a half Rickys'? The children's findings and solutions are later shared in a whole class lesson time which gives further opportunity for using new vocabulary and demands no small degree of articulacy. The re-telling of news which is the more common and often the only activity in similar group sharing times, may have its place but creates few such intellectual challenges for young children.

There is no rigid timetable which insists that certain facts are learned by a certain date. There is time though, and time allowed deliberately, for asking questions; for involvement in explorations and observations and for sharing such work with other children. Allowing time in its widest aspect is one of fundamental importance in such a curriculum. The curriculum aims to make sense of the children's experiences in terms they can understand and perceive as relevant. It will point them to the way of increasing their understanding by responding to their needs and interests. The choice of topics will now be less arbitrary and will reflect and respond to children's interests in that particular class.

The link with learning skills such as reading and recording is that they develop naturally out of such activities and are perceived as having a real meaning. Learning to read can be, and is, a minefield of fear and unexpected traps for many children and is made so by a timetable for learning this skill that doesn't allow some children to read six books of their own choice in a day because they have just discovered how to read, or another child to read the same 'Spot' book that was read last week because he/she is still feeling shaky about the whole exercise. Slow readers may always be with us, but the strongest indictment of an inflexible and insensitive approach to the teaching of reading is the reluctant reader.

Long-term planning will not look so neat in such circumstances but the sensitivity in meeting that particular group of children's needs will make for more real efficiency. 'Match' in all areas of the curriculum is deliberately sought. Lack of interest, lack of progress and misunderstandings in such classrooms are no longer the children's responsibility. That shifts to where it has always belonged, to the teacher. If the teacher is constrained, however, by a national curriculum which does not reflect an understanding of children's development and worse, by consequent and meaningless testing, opportunities for creating the 'intelligent classroom' will be further and further reduced.

Can all this be achieved in the context of an infant classroom organised by a teacher with any style of teaching, e.g. a predominantly 'formal' style? It would seem less likely than with a teacher using an informal or mixed style of classroom management, in that the former seems to suggest a very low degree of autonomy on the part of the children. It would be far less likely to find a child initiating its own research in a setting within which such activities would have to be strictly timetabled. Children's interests, like their needs, have their own timetable and only if there is sufficient flexibility in the day's arrangements and the curriculum, are these likely to be met. Until they come to school, learning has not been parcelled out into set times and even subjects for infant children. They need time for observation, reflection and activity if there is to be continuity between home and their first years at school. If their needs are not properly understood or accommodated in their curriculum, then it would hardly be surprising if the most profound lesson school has to teach such children is that it is not for them. 'Pity those who had music in them, to die without knowing what it was to sing'.

References

ARMSTRONG, M. (1981) *Closely Observed Children*, London Writers and Readers Publishing Corp.

ASHTON-WARNER, S. (1963) *Teacher*, London, Secker and Warburg.

BLENKIN, G. M. and KELLY, A. V. (1981) *The Primary Curriculum*, London, Harper and Row.

BUTLER, R. (1988) 'Enhancing and undermining intrinsic motivation', *British Journal of Educational Psychology*, 58, 1.

GOLDMAN R. (1965) *Readiness for Religion*, London, Routledge and Kegan Paul.

HARLEN, W. (1982) 'Matching', in Richards, C. (Ed.) *New Directions in Primary Education*, Lewes, Falmer Press.

HOLT, J. (1964) *How Children Fail*, New York, Delta.

KING, R. A. (1978) *All things Bright and Beautiful? A Sociological Study*, Chichester, Wiley.

LOUKES, H. (1963) *Readiness for Religion*, London, Friends House.

PINDER, R. (1987) *Why don't teachers teach like they used to?* London, Hilary Shipman.

SKINNER, B. V. (1988) 'Interview with B. F. Skinner, The Psychologist', *British Psychological Society*, Leicester, 1, 4.

Part II
Classrooms as Contexts for Disaffection

3
Teachers' Perspectives on Disaffection

Gill Barrett

This chapter examines the learning context created by teachers. It is based on research teachers carried out to evaluate the behaviour responses of children to starting school.[1] They identified more explicitly the complexity of the classroom and pupil behaviour within it. Despite the focus on four- and five-year-olds there is evidence to suggest that many aspects of the understandings and consequent practices they arrived at are relevant to teachers of all age groups. This is so not only because we may see similar behaviours in parallel situations at ages six, seven or eight, even sixteen or in teaching adults, but also because the understandings of school that children learn in their first year of school are likely to affect their view of themselves as pupils and their subsequent behaviour in later years.

The research began with the concerns of an infant teacher who felt there were increasing numbers of 'disruptive' pupils starting school. Her Union, the Assistant Masters and Mistresses Association followed this up with a local, then national survey.[2] Following criticism of this design they commissioned the Centre for Applied Research in Education, University of East Anglia, to follow up their concern. When I took over as research officer I negotiated the following basis for the research:

1. An evaluation of children's responses to starting school must build on teachers' understanding of behaviour and classroom organisation, and seek to understand that behaviour and organisation from the child's point of view.
2. Behaviour is based on experience and knowledge, or ignorance, and therefore has potential for change over time: this makes some element of longitudinal study essential.

You may ask why 'disruptive' children are not referred to and why the research was not focusing solely on their behaviour. There were two major reasons for this. Firstly, it was important to understand all responses in classrooms and not simply disruptive ones as the latter only occur in the context of other responses which are not disruptive and in the context of overall classroom expectations. The second concerned the difference between labelling behaviour disruptive because it disturbed other people and on the other hand, the assumption that there was intention to disrupt on the part of the child. As one appeared to be related in peoples' minds with the other I thought it best to avoid the label if we were seeking to understand rather than pre-judge the children's responses to classroom situations.

The research took place over the period of a school year with teachers who were interested in developing their understanding of children's responses in their classrooms. Thirty six teachers were involved for the whole or most of that time; others withdrew during or following the first period of observation.[3] Most teachers analysed their classroom expectations and observed children's responses to them for the first month of each term. Following each period of observation there was a group meeting of teachers to discuss the process and findings of the research. Over the period of the year understanding of the task and children's responses grew and questions changed. In the third period the research built on the awareness the teachers had reached. They chose research tasks according to their situation and/or interests from a range which included:

(a) Further observation of children observed in September and a summary of their major developments through the year and how they coped with learning

(b) Focusing specifically on a child who had particular difficulties and whose responses were difficult to handle, recognising in what situations these occurred and trying to manipulate the classroom situation to alleviate the problem

(c) Interviewing reception children about the experience of starting school through the use of pictures which I had taken in schools during the year

(d) Keeping a research diary about the experience of having reception children starting in the summer term compared with other intakes.

These research tasks gave the teachers new dimensions to their work in that they had to become more overtly analytical of their understanding and interpretations. At the final meetings in May the discussions focused on the renewed awareness that the observations and interviews with children had created. Teachers commented on how aware the children were of what they were doing, on how much they appeared to know, think and feel about their experiences. They were stressing that children were thinking and learning young people and not simply young children 'doing' things. This emphasised the importance of trying to understand the factors that influenced how and what they thought and learned, and also what influenced the knowledge they were able to use and develop in classrooms. Four main issues which feed our understanding of children's response behaviour in classrooms emerged. These were:

● The continuity/discontinuity between home and school;
● The relationship between the individual and school expectations;
● Concepts and practice of work and play in the classroom; and
● Theories and beliefs about child development and learning.

These four themes were explored further in inter-professional workshops[4] because prior agreements with unions had limited the project's meetings to four. Teachers, including some of those involved in the project were central to these discussions. The following understandings about children's behaviour are derived from project teachers discussions and the work of the workshops.

Continuity / discontinuity between home and school learning

It may be stressed that children do not start learning when they come to school. One teacher commented . . . 'they have learned to do a lot of things before they come to school without any systematic programme, just at their parent's elbow' . . . This means that they have learned through experience and with the support and guidance of adults, particularly parents, ways of seeing, thinking about and interacting with the world about them.

> But as teachers, we give the impression that once the child starts school there are certain things you don't do as parents and so a lot of natural support that children have been given has actually been taken away because of the school's attitude . . . so I honestly do think we've got to re-think our ideas.

However, as teachers realised, at home children are learning about many different things, including beliefs about and attitudes towards themselves, others and actions they should engage in. So when children come into school they bring with them knowledge, experience and attitudes which may or may not match the expectations of the school.

> I said, "Don't you have to clear up your toys at home?" and they said, "No! They're in the playroom". And you see a lot of these children too had not even been involved in the family because they have a room upstairs where you go and play . . . They ate separately from father because he came home on the 7.00pm train.

The teachers believed these experiences affected the knowledge the children had of themselves and their role in the family:

> You can walk into a lot of these big houses and you will see no evidence of children at all. I mean the quality of life in a lot of these houses I'm going in now is a lot better. I mean I'm going in houses where the filth, the dirt, the ragged furniture is revolting, but there is evidence that there are children there and that the children have a place within that home which there is not in a lot of the others.

These differences affected what the children learned and how they gained adult approval:

> Last year I saw a child I taught fetching a bottle of whisky for his alcoholic mother.

> One of my new children, both mother and father are teachers, has come
> in — she's on the equivalent of *Through the Rainbow Blue Books* — and
> not 5. She can read stories — self taught — she's incredible.

Not all the learning that children had done matched up to either the values of
particular schools or to the constraints of the classroom. One head reflected on this
problem in relation to class differences:

> I would say that when a child comes to us we have to accept what that
> child is — no it may not conform to what we consider to be norms of
> behaviour, it may not conform to what we consider to be norms of
> manners but what we've got to do is be sensitive in getting it to the stage
> when we can communicate because I'm a middle class mother with
> middle class standards and these children are working class, perhaps one-
> parent families. I've got to understand what their standards are and try
> and encourage them to form a code that is suitable to their home and is
> suitable to me.

The values and beliefs of parents, learned by the children in terms of what activities
they should engage with, also affected which activities children would engage with
at school and their response behaviour to alternative activities. For example, a
number of teachers commented on children's reluctance to play or to create ideas
for themselves, because this was not seen as educational by parents. Others could
not organise themselves, or play with others, or could not engage with symbolic
forms, because of lack of experience and expectation of this learning at home. All
these factors affected what and how children could engage with the social and
intellectual curriculum of school.

But home experiences do not stop when the child starts school. There were
ongoing factors which also affected how they could engage with school curriculum.
For example, if children are thinking about, or trying to make sense of something
that has happened at home, then they will not be able to focus attention on school
learning. Unless we as people, and that includes children, are feeling secure, we are
unable to function effectively with other people, or in a formalised learning
context. We cannot learn and reflect if we are uncertain about basic securities and
do not know how to value ourselves.[5]

The actual experiences of pre-school life may not have provided opportunities
for learning those things required to fit comfortably into the school setting. Perhaps
the most significant of these is learning how to learn and knowing that failure and
the feelings that go with that and 'not knowing' can be worked through and
expressed in a number of ways. If the experiences have not helped the child to be an
effective learner, able to work through fear or frustration when faced with
something new, then school, with all its new expectations and people, is likely to
provoke strong responses such as crying, hitting other children and removing
oneself from the source of the frustration. If the child knows that these strong
responses have always been responded to by an adult in the past, and the cause of
frustration removed or dealt with, then it may cause even stronger response

behaviour in school when the initial crying or attempted withdrawal fails to remove the expectation. Many children learn these differences between home and school expectations. A number of teachers commented on the different responses children had to their parents, particularly mothers, compared with their behaviour at school. A number felt that mothers had given in to their children in order to keep them happy or because pressure of time made it easier. As the children grew older it became more difficult to alter their responses as they learned to manipulate a situation to get what they wanted.

> New Parents' Evening is revealing isn't it? You get parents who say 'Does she scream, does she kick out? She does at home'. You really think they are talking about a different child don't you?

> And yet we shouldn't blame everything on parents.

> No, of course not. I think it just makes our job quite difficult sometimes.

This is both true and difficult because family, financial, cultural, societal, health, environmental, historical, political, pre-school education and personality factors can influence the experience, thinking and behaviour of children starting school. Given the possible permutations is it surprising the children are so different and some have not had experiences that make them confident learners in school situations?

The comments of some teachers at meetings implied that parents needed to prepare their children for school in a particular way; but one teacher responded:

> But it's a different situation, you can't compare home with school. The relationship you have as a parent with a child, is totally different and I don't think you can expect parents to produce perfect children for school — I think you've just got to accept them as different.

This leads to the second major issue identified by teachers which affected our understanding of children's behaviour in school.

The Individual and the System

One difficulty that reception teachers have at children's entry to school is the proliferation of individuals who arrive on their first morning. Given the proliferation of home experiences described above this is hardly surprising! Whatever the experiences of children before starting school they have usually had access to an adult who they have shared with few other children. Even in playgroup or nursery school the ratio is around one adult to eight children. They have, therefore, had the opportunity to learn as individuals and as such arrived in school with a myriad of different experiences and some belief in their own ways of learning and being effective. These ways may be very different. For example, children might be effective through knowing how to go to the shops for their mother, or to keep out of her way and make entertainment for themselves, or through manipulating situations to get what they want, or through being able to sit quietly and read a book. All these things need learning and in doing them, and being given space or encouragement to do them by adults, the child's thinking, forms of effectiveness and concept of self is validated.

In reception classes there is only one adult, the teacher, in the vast majority of classrooms. Occasional help by parents or an ancillary helper may be available but this depends on the staffing and policies of the school and local authority. The child, therefore, has to learn about themselves, and their effectiveness in this new situation, in relation to an adult who has responsibility for maybe thirty or more other children. If that adult is making totally new expectations of knowledge and associated behaviour then the child's concept of self is also under threat.

> The girl's fine but the two boys just have no idea whereas the children I get from the nursery are into a routine like being able to line up or being able to sit at a task for a few minutes and these boys just haven't got that.

> . . . they don't know how to cope with them (expectations) — they don't know what they are. You're asking them to do things that perhaps nobody's ever asked them to do before and it's getting used to your expectations that shows over time in the observations.

All these organisational expectations that they are learning are ones which make them able to do things at the same time and in the same way as other children. These are largely for the benefit of the teacher who must cope with large numbers of children. This conformity appears doubly difficult for children who for one reason or another have learned that they have the right to ask for something, or to take it, and expect to have it. This can apply to children who (a) are demanding of teacher's attention in order to be given 'work' and who cannot mix with other children or chose an activity for themselves; (b) want to engage with 'play' activities or in wandering about, or to have a particular toy or all the bricks, and (c) do not find it easy to wait for adult attention, or do an activity like sitting on the mat, or other language based activity that the teacher directs them to.

Through the research the teachers began to recognise the amount they did not know about individual children's experience and knowledge. They also began to question some of the practices taken for granted in the school which required conformity rather than responding to the learning needs of children. One such which teachers recognised through children's comments was playtime. For some children it was a release when they could run and play with friends in different ways. For others the noise and hurly burly were simply frightening and others seemed to need calm, stillness and quiet in order to recoup their energies for the classroom. Some schools already had changed their policies and practice in relation to playtime.

The classroom regime itself was also recognised by some to be requiring conformity rather than enabling learning. One teacher had a particularly difficult child in her third reception group of the year. Brian was a diabetic[6], and his older brother had died at the age of eleven. He had difficulty with a number of situations in the classroom and exhibited quite marked anti-social behaviour which frequently made it difficult for the teacher and other children. However, through the research and specific attention to analysis of the contexts in which his behaviour grew worse (e.g. mat sessions), the teacher was able to modify what she did and the difficulty of the learning expectations made. For example, during mat situations she shortened sessions and used body language and pictures to make her words more accessible. She also secured help from the Welfare Assistant to be with Brian at that time and help him focus on what was going on. She was able to anticipate situations he might find difficult and thus help him to engage in the learning of the classroom. Throughout the term she maintained her expectations of, and insistence upon, social behaviour, i.e., not abusing other people or their work. She commented that she had learned she did not have to fit them all into the same mould — because by changing the learning environment for Brian, she was also changing it for the other children and making it better for them. What she, and other teachers who came to, or had similar understandings seemed to be saying, was that they were not removing their expectations of curricular, social or personal learning, but they saw that it was important to meet the child half way and understand what they knew and how they expressed it. If the child knew this was being taken into account they had freedom to adapt and develop the under-standing of themselves and to learn to act as socially responsive individuals, within the classroom and school.

Concepts of Work and Play as Curriculum Activities

You may ask how these ideas relate to children's behaviour. Let me explain. Although children's response behaviour could frequently be interpreted to mean that they appeared to know what to do, they did not always move on to the message that they were involved with an activity over a period of time in a cognitively active way. Involvement appeared to mean that the child's thinking was engaged with the activity. There were two distinct forms of involvement. One responded to teachers' expectations or tasks; the other to a child's questions. In all circumstances involve-ment meant thinking and re-thinking something in order to make further sense of it. These two forms of involvement appeared to relate to what was frequently called 'work' and 'play' by children. Play however was much more likely to involve 'doing' their thinking in some form and was more likely to involve creative thinking.

The teachers recognised the significance of these differences through obser-vations and recognised that many children would more willingly go to, and become involved with, an activity they chose to do (a 'play' activity) than one they were directed to (a 'work' activity). One teacher found through observing a child who was under the guidance of a psychologist and doctor, that although he found it difficult to become involved in most activities offered, he became absorbed by cars or things mechanical and technological. During these times he did not bestow kisses, but would hit or lie on other children, wander away from the activity, or otherwise display lack of interest, knowledge or involvement with the expectations of the classroom.

It must be stressed however that the actual activities classified as work or play would not necessarily relate to those perceived by adults. One child for example told me that work was doing drawing; while others perceived that as play. Others would choose to write as a fun activity while one boy explained to me (while tackling some writing) something that I've often felt myself, 'Hard work makes you sweat'. These understandings of work and play and the related feelings, stress and behaviours were recognised by teachers through the observations.

They also recognised the expectations that were made of them as teachers that children would 'learn' and engage in 'work' when they came to school which affected the curriculum they provided. These expectations sometimes exerted pressures that were potentially anti-educational. One teacher told of the ex-head who expected a particular approach to reading and writing which limited the use of either her own or the children's experience and understanding. The new head devolved more responsibility to her staff and in turn the teacher could devolve more opportunities for problem solving, learning and thinking to the children. Not all pressures came from head teachers however. This teacher expresses the effect of parent pressures in some schools:

> I don't think I talk to them enough about what they are reading because I don't have time when the parents expect the children will have read to me every day.

The teachers, therefore, had a particular function with associated 'work' expectations of children, which was significant to children when they started school. This had to be learned, however, when children were moving from a play situation, where they had been able to have more autonomy in developing their own thinking and knowledge, to a regime which had specific guidelines or timetable attached to it:

> So going to see the playschools, I've gone in and I've thought — well those children must come in, having been at playschool completely confused by it all. The fact that there is going to be suddenly a working atmosphere which makes expectations of them.

> And Prudence was saying, 'I can't do that', 'I don't know how to do that'. No matter what it was, she couldn't do it. But they soon cotton on. But I thought (about playschool) there is this play situation the whole time. (When they come here) they really do need a few days to get to know the building, get to know who this body is who's telling them to do this, do that and the other . . . It made me see from the child's side — you see, I think I probably go from the days when children, most of them anyway, would not have been to playschools and were not used to choosing what to do.

'Choosing what to do' carries with it understandings of the pupils' activities concerned, and of their own ability to make decisions and create their own learning agenda. This is important to bear in mind and concepts of work and play that are used within school or the home are crucial to the expectations made of children and consequently the response behaviour they make. If play activities (i.e., those which allow children to try out new experiences, to develop new or enhanced concepts of things they know well, to share with others through activity and language the ideas they are formulating and the language they are learning) activities are devalued by parents or teachers, then the child too learns to devalue the knowledge they have in their head and their ability to think and develop ideas. If work is seen solely as those activities which relate to the Three Rs and teacher time is spent trying to enable children to learn these symbolic forms, separated in purpose and meaning from their own ideas and experiences, then children will learn where the value lies within the school or home setting. Disaffection is inevitable when children cannot make sense of activities and where judgement of success of the activity is thus in an adults hands leaving the child out of control of the situation. The response behaviour to not knowing and feeling out of control varied from retreating under a table for the first week of school, to crying (with one child for almost a term), to apparently aggressive behaviour towards other children, simply withdrawing or expressing frustration through a tantrum of some sort. Behaviour which indicated non-involvement might be apathetic 'doing' of the activity, or more decided withdrawal in order to create an alternative activity.

From the teachers' observations and discussions it became clear that many children, given the choice, would choose activities that they had some under-standing of, knew how to think about, but would also give them opportunities for developing their understanding and knowledge. Many teachers built on this knowledge to enable the children to express language in spoken, and written form about ideas that interested them. Thus 'work' as conceived by parents and many adults was assosiated with 'play' activities in terms of the child. These cognitive links appeared crucial to counteracting disaffection.

Through recognising these differences and the significance of experience that created them, the teachers became doubly aware of the questions this raised for elements of their theories of development.

Development: Theory or Reality?

We have so many pre-conceived ideas about what a child ought to be able to do when coming into school and very rarely do we actually admit to school — I've never admitted to school — a 'normal' child, a child who is totally ready for school (in every way) and yet normally we are aiming our teaching at the normal reception child.

Through the research, teachers were able to articulate this fundamental problem that they had to live with in classrooms. The different experiences of children make concepts of 'normal' development hard, even impossible, to sustain as a reality. It was also difficult to decide exactly what development was meant to mean particularly when trying to understand pupils' behaviour. How did it relate to other concepts that teachers used when analysing children's response behaviour in classrooms like maturity, growth, experience, or expectation? We did not have time to pursue these questions in great depth at the original teachers meetings so this was explored by one of the groups of the inter-professional seminar.

The understanding of development arrived at through small and full group discussion raised major questions about its use at all. I wonder whether effectiveness might not be a suitable alternative in relation to school? The analysis drawn up by the group and plenary sessions stressed the child's self awareness and knowledge of her/his socially given right to have knowledge and to make it effective. Thus the social, emotional and physical context in which children were expected to learn and to know is crucial to their cognitive growth.

The group also stressed the relationship between cognitive, emotional, social and physical areas of learning because they, and the project teachers, recognised that all forms of effectiveness, or competence[7], were based on thinking and learning processes and were therefore cognitive. This understanding ran counter to the understanding of development theories many teachers had been exposed to which treated development as normative behaviours which simply happened at particular ages.

The group went on to stress how children's responses to starting school, and the manifestation of their effectiveness or competence, depended on their pre-school experiences. These affected what they knew about themselves and their world and also their maturity. This latter was defined as the ability to handle different situations appropriately. The term flexibility was also mentioned and this seems to suggest the breadth of experience and self knowledge required to be mature particularly in those situations which are constantly expecting you to be a learner and therefore somewhat out of control of the situation. It would seem that this relates to development of self esteem. I wonder how many of us can always claim to be mature, or to maintain our self esteem, when in circumstances where we perceive ourselves to have no power and those in power keep giving us the message that everything we know is inappropriate? In gender terms women have certainly failed to do that over centuries. In person terms, many of us have been in new situations where the people apparently fail to value our existing experience and knowledge and simply expect us to become socialised into the new culture and knowledge. We might also ask whether it is more mature to stay in a situation where you feel abused, or to leave it for more congenial surroundings?

Finally, the group outlined the difficulties within the school and classroom situation of developing individual effectiveness through learning situations in school which traditionally are geared to the group or the class with normative expectations. A number of teachers recognised this as one element of the problems they have as reception teachers; however, many were working with what has been called a developmental curriculum[8] which builds on experience and understanding of the child in a number of dimensions.

The research carried out by the teachers gave them the opportunity to re-evaluate their understanding of both the classroom environment they created and the meaning of children's responses within that context. The issues above were the culmination of the understanding to which they came. However, over the period of research the teachers themselves were going through a learning process as they developed understanding of the dual role they were taking as teachers and researchers. They also had to come to terms with shifts in understanding that arose through the research process and to unlearn some assumptions they had operated on for some time. These were at times uncomfortable and led to feelings of disaffection. I am including the following insights into the process of the research to provide the reader with a view of the complexity of learning processes and the feelings engendered by them. These underline the significance of the previous issues as relevant to any age group who are prepared to take on learning processes that have real relevance in terms of change. The chapter concludes with a re-iteration of the teachers' major findings and examples of specific responses to them.

Developing Through Research: Teachers Learning for Change

At teachers' meetings following each month of research, and during individual discussion with teachers at their schools, I invited comment on the process of doing the observations because one of the important aspects of the research was the development of a research tool for teachers. This had been spelled out at the first meetings but the difficulty of the task had not been fully anticipated by the teachers or myself. One group meeting did not take place because the teachers had decided that the research was too time consuming. Most of the teachers who had done the observations etc. expressed some anxiety about not knowing what to do, and felt they were doing it wrong. Some of this uncertainty was due to possible inter-pretations of the language I had used:

> What I got confused over was when you talked about expectations — my understanding of 'expectations' seemed to differ slightly from what you were expecting . . . but I've worked it through in my own mind now.

> My biggest problem was deciding what you meant by categories — because I wasn't able to sort out what was required even by talking to other people . . . I wasn't sure what a timetable actually meant.

Others were to do with deciding when to make an observation:

> Some people seem to have studied one activity throughout the work — but I decided to try and cover something of all aspects.

> The thing is I didn't know whether I recorded the right things. I wasn't sure whether to observe at the beginning of an activity — in the middle — or at the end — because they change. At the beginning they might be hesitant and not wanting to do it — but once you've sat them down and explained . . . they could see what they had to do . . . they were either

then happy to do it or they weren't . . . so I decided I would observe when I'd got them and explained what they were going to do.

If you're talking about stressful situations it's when I'm getting them ready for P.E. but I'm so busy then there's no way I can do an observation — your hands are so full of shoe laces and shirts and things like that!

Others were concerned with the inappropriateness of the categories for observations that they had identified at the initial meetings:

Did you find a lot of the Face categories we decided on at the beginning didn't fit the children we were looking at? A lot of them seemed to verge on the happy/excited/joyful rather than on the sullen/sulky/negative side. They all seemed to enjoy it.

Others were aware of methodological issues as they took on the role of researcher in the classroom:

T1   There's another thing — when the child sees you observing it changes instantly — doesn't it.

T2   That's when a quick observation is better.

T1   As the weeks have gone by mine have cottoned on I'm writing something down.

T3   Mine haven't — I can observe and write down without them seeing. We have a very large room with lots of plants and screens!

The teachers experienced new expectations and ideas and responded to the consequent demands for learning in different ways. I was not able to support teachers by visiting schools in that first period of observation as the project, and funding, did not start officially till the October. This meant that teachers could only be supported by each other through the support groups set up at the initial meetings, and by the Primary Advisers who had given the project their backing. Some teachers dropped out during that month as they felt overwhelmed by what they didn't know or couldn't make time for, others came to the second meeting and showed their frustration through anger and alternative suggestions:

I have found it a bind — perhaps just watching one child at different times of the day might be a good idea — that's why I think three children is too much.

Others were fearful that they had done it wrong and were afraid to share, while others appeared to put aside their feelings and focus on the professional development aspect in that they were finding out new things about their practice and their children:

T1   I haven't found it a bind — I found the initial preparation hard — doing all the background information — that took hours and hours — almost to the point of tearing my hair out — just trying to think it all out.

But once I'd started I found it fitting into place. It will still be a relief not to do it mind . . .

T2 Actually this observation has made me consider the difficult ones more — and the provision I'm making for them — that I should be making more individual provision for them than I have been doing because although I want him to attempt to sit down at times and settle to a task — he's not able to do it — so it's made me think more about the provision the individual needs. It's helped me in that.

So the teachers were aware of their own learning and feelings about doing research which expected and valued their individual experiences and understanding of them and did not give them precise formulas which ensured conformity. They also began to learn about, and thus to intellectualise, their own classrooms and curriculum; and the constraints or benefits of buildings, headteachers, external curriculum expectations, previous experience in other areas/schools/age groups, or lack of it. They began to understand the learning environment they created for children starting school. In doing these things they began to understand the behaviour of children in more specific terms as they learned to relate it to the experience, understanding and thinking of the child.

Recognising and Understanding Disaffected Behaviour in the Classroom

The teachers explored in more depth the responses of children to school situations during the second period of observation at the beginning of the Spring Term. Some teachers were observing the same children, having taken all the year's intake in September, others chose children from the new intake to observe and were not limited to the oldest and youngest as in the first observation:

I enjoyed making the choice. It was much better than being restricted . . . so I chose a little boy who cried on the first morning — he cried for a fortnight — and a little girl who came in dead (very) chatty — she's the one who asked you to read her a story this afternoon[9]. And then I chose a brother of an older boy in school, really just to see what an older and younger brother were like together . . . so it's been quite interesting and I've enjoyed being able to choose.

This same teacher went on to explain how she used the observations differently which led her to more insight into the significance of change over time:

I've done my observations sort of tightly. I've looked at just a small number of activities, last time I did a different one every time and I didn't see continuity but this time I've seen more continuity so I've found it more helpful this time.

During the first observations teachers had found that when a child was crying or behaving in a way that might cause damage or disturbance to themselves or others, they frequently did not have the opportunity to observe. They were emotionally, intellectually and physically involved with responding to the situation. Similarly, teachers perceived the behaviour as needing, or not needing their attention, or sometimes in terms of good or bad behaviour. In attempting to understand behaviour, whether disaffected or not, we wanted to avoid these prejudgements and so from the start of the project had used a method which looked at three elements of how people demonstrate what they are thinking and know.

The observations therefore focused on:

the face,

the body, and

the voice.

Teachers identified categories of response for each of these at initial meetings[3]. At the meetings following the first and second observations the significance of these responses was explored by teachers:

> There's a difference between what they can do when they come into school and how they can cope with it. I feel we are looking at how they approach things — not whether they can do it or not. We don't expect them to be able to do lots of things but you give them the experience anyway — but by writing down the responses we're not writing down whether they can do it or not.

These observations led to recognition of similar responses between children as this discussion between three teachers reveals:

> T1 The children I'm watching seem to respond in the same way whatever they're doing. No particular facial expression. By the same token I've been surprised by what an independent, confident group of reception children they are — I wouldn't have expected a lot of the responses to be as they have been. I certainly think they are unusual — certainly in the children I have come across — in that they are so confidently independent and as if they've been at school for years. Perhaps I'm forgetting the responses I would have expected.

> T2 I've had a limited number of responses. Nearly always the faces have been serious and concentrating or smiling — I think they're still interested and keen on everything aren't they — *you don't get that later so much* (my emphasis).

The observations also led to new understanding of how to 'read' children's responses when thinking and feelings were not made explicit through facial responses.

> One boy I was observing his face never changes — I don't know why but you have to tell by other ways how he is feeling. I don't think he is

unhappy — you can tell by his body movements — but his face doesn't move.

I had a boy who always had a blank face. So when I was doing my observations I felt very limited because I was saying — He has a blank look — but I know he's taking in what I'm saying and it's not disinterest, it's just blankness because he's the sort of child who doesn't give much facial expression. And when he's excited I realised, after the first week, that I could tell by the voice. So if he was being loud . . . in the playhouse, there's this loud voice but if I look over the top his face is quite blank. And when he's, say in a maths situation with me, he's again fairly blank, he's interested but his voice is very quiet. That's how I'm registering with him — it's a different pattern. So it may be face or body language with some — with him it's his voice.

The teachers made it clear that it was not always easy to interpret children's responses even though we may have assumptions about the category of response that had been identified:

T1   One of my girls came out smiling all the way through . . . no matter what she just smiles.

T2   That devalues the smile doesn't it!

Add to this smile totally contradictory body or voice responses, such as one teacher noted when the child was apparently 'aggressive' in her body response yet smiling, and the difficulties of interpreting the messages of children's responses are thrown into relief.

Teachers recognised that over time the responses they were observing fell into patterns. These could then be interpreted in relation to the individual and in relation to the classroom expectations she or he was engaged in. Thus change, or stability, of response began to reveal something of how the observations could be interpreted.

Short term changes in response were noted very early on by teachers as they tried to write down a child's response to an activity. One teacher who observed these changes investigated further. She found that when the child she was observing was able to continue with what he was doing his facial response was interested or even smiling but when he apparently got stuck his facial expression became serious, blank or even frowning. This observation led her to re-interpret other children's responses in relation to their degree of understanding of what they were doing. She found her understanding and her consequent response to the children to be appropriate.

These changes in children's understanding and consequent response were also observed in relation to 'changes in the behaviour as they settle into school'. Short term changes were also noted when children were not involved or became disengaged from the thinking of the task in hand.

GHB   Are you still finding the observation a useful activity?

T   Yes, because it's what I do anyway when they first come in. The only thing is — how long do you actually observe them 'cos even in just a minute you're looking and the expression changes. One moment they look happy and the next they're miserable and you think 'Why?' Is it because a child's came up and said something or is it actually the work they are doing?

GHB   Have you explored that?

T   Well sometimes it's obvious, someone has snatched a toy away — but not always. It could be a thought that's passing through them, it's difficult to say when it's a sudden change. And also whether they've just started a task, in the middle, or tidying up and being a bit bored with what they are doing. It does make a difference and I didn't think about that the first time I did it (the observations). The more time you've got to do it the more things you've got to think about.

GHB   But does it make us question how they are responding?

T   Yes — and the same task on a different day gets a different response. Even the weather . . . Or if they didn't really want to do a sitting down task, yet that is what you've timetabled to do and planned for — that makes a big difference.

Long term changes were also observable and they too had similar interpretations in relation to knowing what to do or involvement, but were frequently situation specific e.g. changes over the month, and eventually the year, in leaving mum; sitting during class discussions on the carpet. Over time withdrawn facial expressions became serious or smiling; aggressive or contorted body responses became fidgety or appropriate, or indeed appropriate body responses became fidgety or withdrawn as children lost interest in an activity which ceased to stimulate or failed to involve them; or voices that had been silent or quiet became loud; or loud voices became quiet. Thus there were signs that children's understanding of what they were doing, or of involvement of themselves within that activity changed over time as they had more experience from which to learn.

To sum up, therefore, the teachers recognised response behaviour as related to what children know, or don't know; and also related to their intellectual involvement or non-involvement with the thinking of an activity they were engaged with. They recognized through the observations that:

(a)   different children expressed this knowledge or involvement in different ways e.g. some children used themselves or 'real' artifacts as symbolic forms which intellectualised and made abstract the real experience they were representing — language became part of that experience rather than the expression of it. This was particularly so for children intellectualising technological or social understanding which is not easily reduced to language forms. Others engaged in playing with symbolic forms could be totally absorbed intellectually but have bodies that fidgeted;

(b) there were many facets to what children did or did not know about any activity which might prevent them from engaging with it. A number of teachers commented how they were much more able to ask children pertinent questions about what they were thinking, feeling and doing in order to find out how to help children since coming to this specific understanding.

Despite this understanding and the subsequent development of alternative responses to children's behaviour to help them engage in classroom activities, there were still some children for whom special observations were needed. This was because of their extreme learning needs and the way they expressed their difficulties in the classroom.

In the final period of research some of the teachers chose a task which meant focusing observations on one of the children whose behaviour responses were more difficult to cope with in the class situation. Having identified the situations or context which she/he found particularly difficult, the teachers were to outline the action they took to change the context, and thus behaviour, in an appropriate way. This last section reflects on this relationship between context and pupil behaviour and shows how two of the teachers responded.

Teachers recognized that behaviour is not something that a child's body does that can simply be changed. It is part of a whole child and occurs in a context. Extreme disaffected behaviour, for example prolonged crying, withdrawing, becoming aggressive or passive, is related to what the child knows of themself both outside and within that context. Clearly when teachers are expected to be dealing with thirty or more children such behaviour presents problems. However, as these teachers showed, it is possible to respond by simply attempting to understand the difficulties being experienced in the context in which the behaviour occurs. This can be carried out even when making it clear, through what is done rather than words, that the behaviour is not a necessary or appropriate response and not the best way to express feelings. Let me leave the final word to two of the teachers who finish this chapter with examples of some of the problems that they have to cope with in their classrooms on a daily basis.

The first describes how Penny had come to pre-school sessions and cheerfully started school. Owing to high numbers and shortage of staff the two vertically grouped infant classes had to make use of two part-time teachers, one the male headteacher, to give all age groups a little extra individual attention. This included some movement of the reception group twice a week. Penny became distressed when the class teacher had to go elsewhere or when she (Penny) had to go out of the classroom even with the teacher:

> . . . In the afternoon when I asked her group (Reception) to prepare for craft she began to cry. I explained they were going to do 'clay' with Mr Milton next door and she became quite distressed. I took her with the group explaining further what they were going to do. She settled quickly and became involved . . . Similar response on Friday when I asked the class to change for P.E. . . .

ACTION: I have therefore decided to assign a middle infant (not too removed from experience of being new) to be Penny's friend and to be available when I am not. Also I'm trying to explain more closely what is involved in any change ...

The second example describes the medical and family history of a boy who has been referred for brain scans and had not appeared to accept the arrival of his younger brother. The teacher describes the problems she identified following observations:

Tim is a physically big boy who lacks co-ordination and tends to be clumsy. He behaves aggressively (physically and verbally) towards his peers in uncontrolled situations e.g. play, free choice and practical activities .. This didn't happen in the nursery where the ratio of adults to children was 1 to 10. It's now 1 to 29!

Although I hope to get help from the psychologist I need to do something now.

I therefore decided to:

a) ask an older child to help Tim get ready for P.E. etc. when he got stuck;

b) monitor more closely 'free situations' so that I can step in quickly should aggressive behaviour occur and remove the child to a different activity;

c) set smaller, attainable tasks where success could be gained relatively quickly;

d) have an older child or parent, or myself step in to support when concentration lapsed during 'formal'-type work.

At all times the emphasis was to allow Tim the freedom to respond positively in each situation — but to be ready to step in more quickly when difficulties arose.

Postscript

It seems to me that in understanding and responding positively to disaffected behaviour, even in these cases, the teachers were not only creating opportunities for learning and change for the individual concerned but were also providing a model of enabling acceptance of individuals. They were embodying an understanding of behaviour at a person to person level, not simply either ignoring the behaviour believing it would go away, or responding to the outward manifestation of it alone through labelling it in a particular way. Although these were two of the extreme cases teachers are responding all the time to the messages that children are apparently giving through their behaviour. These observations and group discussions had helped the teachers become aware of both what they knew intuitively about children, and also the things that they did not really know, or had conflicting understandings about. Through these renewed understandings teachers came to be more aware of children's experience and implicit messages in the behaviour manifested in the classroom.

Notes

1. Barrett, G. H. (1986) *Starting School: An Evaluation of the Experience*, London: AMMA. This includes a full report of the teachers analyses, a case study of one group of children's pre- and post-school experiences plus Appendices of the research design and procedures, background information about the schools and classrooms involved, an examination of policy related to early years schooling, and a report on Hyperactivity.
2. AMMA (1984) 'The Reception Class Today', *Report* 7, 1, pp. 6–9.
3. A full account of the research procedures can be found in Appendix 1 of the research report, referenced above. This includes reference to the categories of activities, organisational structures and face, body and voice responses of the children. I think it should be noted that the teachers extended the observation categories over the period of the research and wanted to change the organisation categories at the end of the research because they no longer felt they were entirely satisfactory. These were the categories they used during the research:

   Activities / Expectations:
   1. Listening; 2. Talking; 3. Reading; 4. Writing; 5. Social; 6. Maths; 7. Physical; 8. Creative / Aesthetic; 9. Science; 10. Personal. Each teacher then created lists of specific expectations under those headings which were pertinent to them.

   Organisational and Social Structures of Activities
   Unstructured (or Free Use); Structured (Directed); Formal (all class); Self Help; Free Choice; Group.

   Face Responses
   Smile; Grimace; Serious; Frown (worried); Sulky; Sullen; Withdrawn; Blank; Interested; Accepting*; Relaxed*; Expressionless*; Enthusiastic*.

   Body Responses
   Appropriate; Withdrawn; Contorted; Fidgety; Aggressive; Enthusiastic; Apathetic; Still; Thumb sucking*. (Teachers realised at the end of the research that they had not included non-verbal communication categories for the body which were particularly significant in some schools and for some children.)

   Voice Responses
   Loud; Quiet; Aggressive; Unintelligible; Crying; Silent; English*; Not English*.
   *Added to list by individual teachers as need arose then subsequently included on shared list.

4. The inter-professional workshop was held in London at AMMA headquarters and a range of professionals attended. They came from relevant associations and institutions (e.g. Hyperactive Children's Support Group, and the National Children's Bureau), education, medical and social services or were concerned with research about 'disruptive' children or early years. The workshop was divided into four groups who were allotted one of four tasks for the day. They were asked to consider and identify:

   (a) the ways in which home experiences may affect the starting point of school experiences;
   (b) the significance of the individual within the school setting;
   (c) the meaning and significance of *work* and *play* for children starting school;
   (d) the significance and meaning (and relationships) of concepts like development, experience, learning and maturity.

   During their final sessions they were also asked to make recommendations for policy and practice.

5. See Donaldson, M. (1981) *Children's Minds*, London: Collins/Fontana. Particularly Chapter 8 'Why Children Find School Learning Difficult', examines the difficulty of the reflective process when language is involved in making real experience abstract and in a form when control of thought and interpretation becomes possible — for some. This a helpful though somewhat limited analysis of the intellectual process with which school learning engages children.

6. Many of the children who teachers experienced as difficult were under medical or psychological care for a variety of reasons. These included food allergy and consequent hyperactivity; disfunction of brain rhythms; speech disorders; and problems apparently stemming from sibling births. The majority, but not all, of children who apparently found school difficult to handle were boys.

7. Blenkin, G. M. and Kelly, A. V. (Eds) (1988) *Early Childhood Education: A Developmental Curriculum*, London: Paul Chapman Publishing Ltd. See particularly a section on the growth of competence, pp18–22 which stresses the role of education in enabling the child to become more reflective, self conscious and 'thus increasing their control over their actions and thus over their learning' (p. 20).

8. Blenkin and Kelly (see 7.) argue for a developmental approach to education rather than one which assumes a body of knowledge which children must absorb. Underpinning the two sides of such an argument are differing psychological theories of children and learning, and epistemological differences. The development approach does not assume that children are empty vessels waiting to be filled with knowledge created by other people; instead it assumes, as indeed the teachers research found, that children are thinking, making meaning and knowledgable, even before they come to school and that in order for school experiences and expectations to make sense they have to link them with existing knowledge or way of thinking. The book makes

worthwhile reading for those interested in a theoretical basis for learner-centred schooling.

9. During the two weeks following the January observations I visited twenty of the research schools to interview the heads and teachers about the research process and more specifically about the view they had of parental expectations of schooling and education. This also gave me opportunities to support the teachers in their work, to see the classrooms and talk to children.

4
Creativity and the Infant Classroom

Anne Saunders

Introduction

Creativity as a concept has invited a variety of definitions (Vernon, 1970). Behind these wide ranging categories we can often see simplistic assumptions based upon prejudice, for example, the notion that artists are creative while scientists are not, that naivety is creative, and that neurotic eccentricities are the hallmark of a creative individual who then has a passport to non-conformity. There is also the assertion that creativity is the same, at all times, for all individuals. Embodied within these assumptions, there are two discernible trends. On the one hand there is the notion that creativity leads to a *product*, which has to be judged by the constraints of its own discipline. This view links creativity to an élite. Set alongside this, there are those who view creativity as a *process*. This perspective offers an egalitarian view of creativity inherent in all individuals.

The role of creativity within the classroom has equally stimulated much debate. Whether or not creativity has a part to play within the classroom depends upon an individual's understanding of the nature of creativity, and the purpose of education. In most infant classrooms, creativity appears to be most frequently linked to an artistic product for example, a painting or a model. This type of creative activity clearly has a specific task focus, not dissimilar to that found in basic skill activities, which involve following instructions, for example, make a butterfly, make a Mothers' Day card. The result of such activity is a measurable outcome or product.

As we have seen, however, creativity can also be viewed as a process. Such an understanding would encompass deductive thinking, problem solving imagination, and flexible thought manipulations, as key elements. Research into this area of the infant classroom revealed that both types of creative activity were apparent, but that processes were not defined by the teacher as creative, whilst involvement in artistic production was perceived as being creative (Saunders, 1987). In addition, it was evident that as time in school increased for the pupil, so the preoccupation with products increased, not just in relation to creative activities, but to all learning experiences, whilst the opportunities for deductive thinking and flexible thought manipulations decreased. In order to understand this situation, we need to consider the *purpose* of the infant classroom. This in turn sheds light upon the role which creative activity assumes within the infant curriculum.

The Infant Classroom

A classroom is a physical environment, housing common features such as desks arranged in groups, shelves, cupboards, nature tables, play areas, book and wall displays, a carpet area, teacher's desk and blackboard, but, classrooms are much more than either equipment in a room, or topographical organisation. There are socially constructed worlds of interaction between the participants and the environment. Routines, rituals and roles are basic elements in the construction. Routines organise the timing of activities and structure the day. Rituals form part of the daily routine and include registration, standing in lines, and putting hands up. Rules transmit the do's and don't's of classroom life, which include the transmission of pupil and teacher roles.

In trying to understand the meaning of the infant classroom, a model of the infant curriculum emerged:

Figure 1: The Infant Curriculum: A Centre For Cultural Transmission

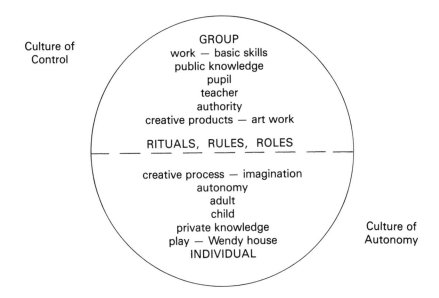

This model of the infant curriculum was developed from practice. Inevitably it does not do justice to every aspect of classroom life. Like all models it falls short. However, it provides us with a starting point for considering the purpose of the infant curriculum, which enables consideration of the relationship between creativity and learning. The findings from practice are purposefully enclosed within a circle, which represents the boundary of the classroom, whilst also suggesting that the classroom is a contained educational culture. By culture I refer to

> A concept used by social scientists when they attempt to explore a social struture of knowledge, skills, customs and beliefs, in order to understand how they came about, how they relate to society, and how society handles them.
>
> > (Stenhouse, 1975)

So that,

> In the concept of culture we can catch the idea of a multiplicity of traditions, public in the sense that we can learn them by joining the group which shares them.
>
> > (ibid.)

> Schools make cultures available by providing pupils with an opportunity to take part in learning groups.
>
> > (op.cit.)

These learning groups take place in classrooms (and ability groups within classrooms). Each classroom transmits a given content of knowledge, skills and roles. The culture of the classroom is one of many available for individual participation.

Within the classroom culture, the teacher has a clear sense of meaning, purpose and intent. The child entering the infant classroom has little or no idea of the rituals, rules and roles which structure the life of the classroom. However, the child quickly assumes the role of a pupil — queueing at the teacher's desk for attention, learning to congregate in a group for registration, and standing in line. These recurring events enable children to become pupils. They cement the culture. Nonetheless, it is clear that the child's extensive skills in fantasizing permit escape from what is recognizably a classroom, for substantial parts of the day. For example, counting heads can become conkers; spaceships on the blackboard can really fly, and monsters can be found at the local beach. The recognition of the classroom no doubt looms and fades in the child's perception as he/she moves in and out of fantasies. Perhaps at this age (nursery and reception classroom), the classroom is a chimerical thing; less so for the teacher. For the teacher, the notion of institutionalised routine and role is more fixed, more compulsive. Pressures exist reinforcing his/her task and priority. He/she is accountable. Yet, within all the classrooms studied (Saunders, 1987), play was accommodated as part of the classroom experience. Thus, not only does the child fantasize and imagine as an individual, but the culture permits this activity by providing a variety of equipment and opportunities, for example, sand tray, water tray, dressing up box, and desk activities, all of which are regular features of the infant classroom. The activities offered graded difficulty from basic play in sand, water, and the Wendy house, to more complex play activities requiring skilful dexterity and coordination, for example mathematical puzzles. Such displays of equipment transmit a notion that play is equally important as more formal work activities, such as writing and reading.

Work and Play: The Infant Curriculum

Both work and play are offered in infant (and nursery) classrooms. Increasing age and time spent in school reduces opportunities for play. Perhaps the moments of freedom in play which gradually diminish as more formal work activities predominate, emphasise the inescapability of constraint. If we look at three different stages in the nursery and infant curriculum, we can see how classroom activities and pupil involvement begin to change over a period of time:

Nursery

9.00 a.m.	10.00 a.m.	10.45 a.m.	11.30 a.m.

Free/Play Activity	Outdoor Activity	Organised Activity

Reception Class

		12 noon			
9.00 a.m.	10.30 a.m.		1.30 p.m.	2.30 p.m.	3.30 p.m.

English	Maths	L U N C H	Art or Free Activity	Story or Mime or Concert

NB Children played until basic skills were acquired or when tasks were completed.

3rd Term and 2nd Year Infants

		12 noon			
9.00 a.m.	10.30 a.m.		1.30 p.m.	3.00 p.m.	3.45 p.m.

English	Maths	L U N C H	Project Work or Busy Books	Free Activity or Story

As we can see, in the nursery classroom free or play activities take priority over organized activity, for example, participating as a group for a radio broadcast. By the time the child arrives in the reception classroom, basic skill activities precede play activities, and this trend continues into the second year of infants – suggesting the priorities of the culture being transmitted.

However, play experiences contribute to the purpose of the classroom, partly in that, as is widely recognized, children learn through playing, and learning is meaningful to the child if it is translated into an accessible experience (Dearden, 1968); also play is utilized by the teacher as a starting point for teaching basic skills, to initiate the child into the culture of the classroom.

Several types of play are offered to children:

(i) *Basic Play* — such as Wendy house, sand, and water. Children first entering the nursery or reception classroom engage mostly in these types of activity.

(ii) *Complex Play* — including desk activities such as jigsaw puzzles, bead threading, word games and mathematical puzzles.

In the first instance, teachers do not appear to become involved. In more complex play, the teacher uses the experience to introduce basic skills. As basic skills are acquired, play becomes a reward for the completion of work and a stop-gap after one piece of work until the next.

It is interesting to note two features at this point. Firstly, the teacher's expressed aims and actions begin to change, as the pupil becomes more adept at basic skill activities. Most teachers express the desire to enable the child to achieve his/her maximum potential. In the nursery classroom, the activities considered to promote this are play and free activity. Maximising individual potential becomes linked to basic skill acquisition, as soon as basic play is abandoned. Secondly, in conjunction with the teacher's changing aims and perceptions, the pupil's response to play and work begins to change. As the work load of basic skill activities increases for the pupil, play appears to diminish in interest. Even if pupils are given time to play, their desire to do so seems to decrease. The child who engaged actively and enthusiastically in processes of discovery and exploration, becomes pre-occupied with the number of sums he or she can complete, or which grade reading book has been reached.

Authority of the Teacher and the Autonomy of the Child

If we refer back to the model of cultural transmission, we can see that both the authority of the teacher and the autonomy of the child represent major features of the nursery/infant curriculum exemplified in work and play activities. The world of play constitutes the culture of autonomy, where the child explores the classroom and its contents as an individual. The child's world and way of understanding is accommodated.

The world of work where the teacher is the authority, exemplified in the culture of control, offers the child access to the world of public knowledge, through basic skill acquisition. Certainly the culture of control is given priority. The timing of work and play activities suggests the priority — which pupils are aware of. What is problematic, however, is that the processes of thinking available to the child in the culture of autonomy (available on initial entry into the classroom), are replaced by a pre-occupation with products, which fail to translate learning into meaningful experiences for the pupil. If the culture of control fails to acknowledge processes as key elements in learning, then not only does creativity become product-based, but by implication all other learning equally assumes this emphasis. Publicly shared knowledge is transmitted in such a way that learning and creativity are restricted.

Creativity and Learning Within The Primary Classroom

Research conducted in relation to this issue prompted over-exposure to art work in a number of classroom settings (Saunders, 1987). One teacher informed her pupils that someone had come to see their art! Children were sent into this classroom from other areas of the school, to show crowns they had made for Valentine's Day. In another school, children followed instructions to make two butterfly wings identical, the basis of mathematical symmetry. Art displays showed a uniformity of subject. The measurable and comparable product appeared to dominate. Another teacher who actively encouraged problem solving and deductive thinking did not perceive these as creative. Play activities were not described by any teachers as being creative, but they were seen as offering a starting point for basic skills acquisition. The message transmitted to researcher and researched was that creativity is an artistic outcome. When instructions are followed it is a foregone conclusion. Stories relating to a child's imagined sighting of a shark at the seaside were regarded as evidence of a 5-year-old's immaturity and wasted imagination. Thus, creative activity becomes part of the purpose of the curriculum, which is to move the child from an active involvement in his/her own learning exemplified in play, to a situation where the individual is controlled in such a way as to preclude under-standing of the private use of public knowledge. This knowledge is given rather than applied. Learning and creativity become part of the socialization into educational norms which are measurable, if they are comparable. Some examples from practice illustrate this point. They demonstrate the change that was found between expectations of younger and older children.

A Reception Classroom: Excerpts From a Day

Mrs. White's classroom was full of things to do. Every area was used to its fullest potential. Mrs. White explained that it had taken her a long time to plan the layout of her classroom. It appeared a very rich environment — with possible exploration everywhere.

When Mrs. White's class returned from assembly they went into free activity, because they had sat for quite some time in assembly. A group of children approached Mrs. White from the nature table, excited by the growth of a parsnip and carrots. Then a larger group gathered to look at some seeds. Mrs. White produced a magnifying glass for the children to look at the plants. She later commented that she had carried the magnifying glass around in her handbag for weeks waiting for the right moment to give it to the children. One girl was so intrigued with the magnifying glass, that she spent about ten minutes, after the other children had moved on, looking at everything on and around the nature table, including the sand in the dry sand tray. During this free activity period Mrs. White asked one or two children to read to her. Apart from this all the children involved in free activity were allowed to choose and structure their own activity, staying with it for as long as they chose.

After free activity the children went to the library to watch the television. Mrs. White took the opportunity to count the seconds on a clock face before the programme began. All experiences seemed to be used for learning. During the programme a spider was shown. Mrs. White informed the class that they could make spiders that afternoon if they would like to. Eleanor expressed a positive interest, and it was agreed that they would be made. After the programme Mrs. White took four children of various sizes out to the front of the group — they were the body of the spider — their arms were the spider's legs.

Returning to the classroom, the children stopped to look at the frieze which they had made. The frieze showed a local beauty spot. Mrs. White had put up signs like 'No Cycling' and 'Dogs on Leads', so that the children could work these out for themselves. Mrs. White saw finding out as an integral part of the learning process. Similarly she left mistakes in the classroom. Incorrect letters were placed in front of objects e.g. 'f' in front of 'phone. Jonathan corrected this to 't'.

After lunch, one table had been prepared for the spider activity and all other activities, including painting, were available. The children were asked, 'How can we fasten the legs on?' Various children offered suggestions, for example glue, staples or sellotape. Staples were agreed by the majority. The day ended with a concert. This was the children's idea. Lindsey started the concert off with a song. She asked everyone to join in, which they did, then Lindsey had to choose a boy. She chose Robin (who suffered from muscular dystrophy). He acted out a mime and the children were allowed three guesses as to what the mime might be. Eleanor pointed out that they were usually allowed five guesses. Mrs. White told Eleanor that if there were only three then more people would be able to take part. A number of children took part. They concluded with a story about a grandpa and his magnifying glass.

Third Term and Second Year Infants: Excerpts From a Day

When these children left their reception class at the end of the second term in school, they moved into Mrs. Bailey's class, where they were grouped according to ability, with second year infants. Mrs. Bailey taught an integrated day. Each day a timetable was prepared for the various groups. The children were expected to work through appointed tasks, according to whichever group they were in. Work cards related to ability were collected by each individual child. At the beginning of the day all the children were told what each group should be doing.

The new children, third term infants, began their day with English (after assembly). This they did from an exercise book entitled 'I can write a story'. When Mrs. Bailey introduced the work she asked, 'What is a sentence?' A second year infant replied, 'Something about one thing'. He had this the wrong way round, and Mrs. Bailey pointed out that it was 'One thing about something'. Then the children were asked what a sentence contained. Several of the older children explained that a sentence had a capital letter and a full-stop. Mrs. Bailey asked the third term infants to try and remember this. When the books were collected in, it was noticeable that many had remembered; one child had put a full-stop after every word. For the brightest group of third term infants, their activity was to complete a sentence by filling in a missing word listed at the bottom of a text book page. The sentence described an accompanying picture. No explanation was given as to how to carry out and complete this activity. All of the bright group encountered difficulties. A variety of strategies were attempted by the children, from counting dots to working numerically down the sentences and word list. The first sentence required *making*, the second sentence required *in*. Coincidentally these followed each other in the word list. The girls in the group then thought that you had to keep working down the list for the right word. The next word in the list was *put*. This did not make sense in the sentence (i.e. - - - puts flour in the cake). Finally Jane said, 'she', which was the word at the top of the list. When asked how she knew this, her reply was, 'I just know'. She did not get the word from the list.

Stephen, also in the bright group, had completed all but one of the sentences, the last one which was 'Jane and Mummy - - - the cake'. This missing word was *eat*. Stephen asked how to spell *ate*. He did not appear to be working from the list but seemed to be putting his own words in. It was suggested that he looked at the list to find out what word he needed. He looked at the list and stated that '*ate*' was not on the list. This was correct but *eat* was on the list. Stephen was apparently thinking in the past tense, rather than the present. Again it was suggested that he looked at the list. This time he pointed to *eat*. Antony and Ben re-affirmed this by reading out their completed sentence, i.e. Jane and Mummy *eat* the cake. Stephen then wrote this down. When the children had finished the sentences, they were asked to draw one of the pictures from the text book. Jane copied the picture of putting the sugar into the cake. She noted all the details, and reproduced the picture. When the children had finished their English work, they then went on to their Busy Books. After the break the children returned to their number work, which was 'count on', and 'count back' addition and subtraction. Donna turned to Jane and said, 'On Friday we won't do any work, no number, nothing, we play'.

What we can see from these examples is that when the children moved from their reception class to their second class, a number of features relating to the classroom experience changed. Firstly the teacher's strategy changed; Mrs. White encouraged the children to be actively involved in processes of thinking and decision making, whilst Mrs. Bailey had definite set tasks for the pupils to complete. As the teacher's expectations and actions changed, so the pupil's role became more clearly defined. In Mrs. White's classroom the children were regularly given opportunities to explore, ask questions and intervene, whilst in Mrs. Bailey's classroom, children were regularly asked to be quiet and to get on with their work (Saunders, 1987). The process of involvement with Mrs. White changed to an emphasis on task completion for Mrs. Bailey. The product rather than understanding assumed importance. Let us now consider the effects of the infant curriculum's purpose upon the child.

A Process in Mind

We have seen that the child is gradually introduced into a culture which appears to reduce choices and opportunities for decision making, problem solving and active involvement in the classroom. The world of the child, which was initially accommodated in a variety of play experiences, is replaced by the world of the pupil who engages in a number of task-focused activities. In assessing the effects of this situation upon the child, it seems that the learned role of the pupil appears to exclude the desire to ask questions (in Mrs. Bailey's classroom the bright group did not ask the teacher for assistance, they turned to each other and the researcher), or to engage in exploration. The child who enters the classroom with a desire to play and explore gradually begins to change. Some children quickly adapt to the expectations and knowledge of the classroom. Others find themselves confused and are judged accordingly. For example, Mrs. Bailey described several of the third term infants in her classroom as being slow, lacking in confidence and unwilling to help themselves. These descriptions were attributed to children who appeared to be finding it difficult to make the adjustment from Mrs. White's classroom. Amanda, who had explored Mrs. White's classroom with a magnifying glass was placed in the second brightest group (of third term infants) in Mrs. Bailey's classroom. She had become withdrawn in Mrs. Bailey's classroom and was perceived as lacking in confidence. Other children however, realising what is expected of them, manage to acquire a number of strategies which, whilst appearing to conform, in fact allow the child opportunities for deviation. Those who appear to conform have the opportunities for creative rebellion. Sitting-up and looking busy, the hallmarks of conformity, can often be assumed, so that autonomous action is possible.

In one classroom Jonathan regularly misbehaves, yet his teacher Mrs. Bradley saw Jonathan as a child who tried hard. Jonathan regularly brought books and other educationally desirable artefacts to the new periods. He was regularly praised for his contributions. Jonathan, however, had worked out how to play the system. He regularly instigated disruptive activities, for example on one occasion he instigated a game during P.E. Jonathan suggested to a group of four boys that they should swing from a beam and see how far they could kick their plimsolls. The game went unnoticed by Mrs. Bradley for five minutes, as Jonathan and his friends tested out the flying capacity of their footwear. When Mrs. Bradley noticed the group,

Jonathan smiled, dropped from the beam and started to straighten the safety mat. His friends were reprimanded. On another occasion Jonathan was working with a group of three boys making clay pots. Jonathan was the first to finish, but he informed his friends that he would pretend to be busy, so that he would not have to work on his reading scheme. Jonathan spent the session squirting water at the other three boys whilst smiling at Mrs. Bradley if she looked in his direction. (Saunders, 1987). Jonathan had very quickly learned the behaviour, knowledge and values of the classroom. He utilized this to his own advantage, and secured the privilege of choice, which supports a point made by (Jackson, 1968). He suggested that when children 'sit up nicely', and wave their hands in the air, with an aura of knowing the right answer, they may be feigning both interest and knowledge. They have certainly learned about *Life in Classrooms*, (Jackson, 1968), but what are they actually learning?

When the child starts school he/she enters as an outsider, who has to gain inside knowledge. Part of the process involves accepting new behaviour, such as standing in line and sitting at a desk. These rituals offer the child a structure or routine which gradually, for most children, becomes automatic. The child has also to adopt a new role, that of a pupil, which involves not only new behaviour, but also new values and attitudes, such as not wearing jewellery and being willing to work. This role in turn comes with it certain cognitive tasks based upon basic skill acquisition — linking words with objects, accurate representation of reality (trees have green leaves), and the quantification of objects. Thus the role of the pupil involves acquiring new knowledge. The regularity of events helps to cement the whole experience (Berger and Luckmann, 1966). Whilst routines enable us to grasp a structural understanding of events, then roles transmit a set of imperatives which carry with them emotions and attitudes. Roles eventually shape both action and actor (Berger, 1969). The child who played in free activity gradually finds his/her activities becoming increasingly task-focused. As this occurs, the child expresses a preference for work activities. Competition begins to occur, and the world of fantasy is abandoned for the world of fact. Skies are blue, rather than green. Perhaps at this point we begin to see the role of the child being abandoned for the role of the pupil as the child becomes increasingly aware of institutional expectations and purpose; the culture of control replacing the culture of autonomy, work replacing play, products replacing processes.

The role of the teacher shapes the role of the child. Her/his evaluation and assessment introduces the child to a world of behaviour where as she/he controls the classroom, the individual complies, not because there is no choice, but because of the desire for approval, a desire for enhanced self-esteem which is socially bestowed. The world of spontaneity evident during play periods appears to be replaced by a world of inauthentic values, calculated to please authority figures. Most pupils are aware of teacher expectation, and respond by either conforming to what they understand the teacher's expectations to be, or by appearing to conform. The teacher's watchful eye controls. The pupils, aware of this, regulate their action, so that the institution, (in this instance the school),

regulates agency, channelling human action into grooves — these grooves
are offered as the only possible ones

(Berger, 1969)

Individual internalizing roles, respond as if there was no choice. But does this relate
to the infant classroom? The infant classroom appears to have a definite movement,
or process in mind, which is to introduce the child to a world of educational knowledge, values, attitudes and behaviour. As the child becomes a pupil, his/her role
becomes recognizable, which in turn shapes the individual's action. Not all
children conform, but by and large, most are aware of what is expected. We see
children gradually abandoning autonomous play activities and flexible thought
manipulations. We see an increasing awareness of a culture which co-opts the child
into replacing private knowledge by public knowledge which is presented in such a
way as to preclude meaningful learning. Perhaps we also see the abandonment of
self for other (Berger, 1969), where external acclaim becomes more important than
internal motivation and comprehension.

What is also apparent is that creativity like all other learning experiences in the
infant classroom becomes part of the purpose of the infant curriculum, where all
become orchestrated into group activities, and where the soloists' opportunities for
meaningful learning begin to diminish. The hungry keenness of the pre-schooler
very rapidly becomes the dissonant teenage recipient of an education system. By
failing to give pupils opportunities to use and engage in applying public knowledge, we greatly reduce their opportunities for independence; we simply increase
the controls and alienate pupils from meaningful learning processes. Notions of
creativity in the infant classroom play but a small part in this process.

References

BERGER, P. L. (1969) *Invitation to Sociology*, Harmondsworth, Penguin.
BERGER, P. L. and LUCKMANN, T. (1966) *The Social Construction of Reality*,
Harmondsworth, Penguin.
DEARDEN, R. F. (1968) *The Philosophy of Primary Education*, London, Routledge and
Kegan Paul.
JACKSON, P. W. (1968) *Life in Classrooms*, New York, Holt, Rinehart and Winston.
SAUNDERS, A. (1987) *A Process in Mind*, unpublished PhD thesis, CARE, University of East
Anglia.
STENHOUSE, L. (1975) *An Introduction to Curriculum Research and Development*, London,
Heinemann.
VERNON, P. E. (Ed.) (1970) *Creativity*, Harmondsworth, Penguin.

5
The Context of Children's Learning:
An Historical Perspective

Clem Adelman

Educationalists, philosophers, clerics, psychoanalysts, paediatricians and law makers have, in their various ways, propounded their theories of the realm and development of learning and moral action in young children. In these respects we might contrast John Wesley with Dr. Spock, or the Plowden with the Newcastle Report, but we create our own misunderstandings if we do not take account of the historical context in which ideas were propounded. For instance, we cannot understand the idea of child-centred education out of the fragmentation of the present. We have to compare the views of educationalists and psychologists at the turn of the twentieth century to see the contest there was between those who thought they knew what was right for all children and those who thought that nurture of *naturally good impulses* would lead to morally good children. Both groups claimed that their interests were centred on the child's innate interests.

From the various theories of young children's moral propensities have come different sets of principles for discipline and schooling of children. Wesley believed that children were imbued with original sin. The teacher (and parent) had to watch out for sinful tendencies and punish these on the spot. From Wesley comes the saying 'Spare the rod, spoil the child'.

> Let a child from a year old be taught to fear the rod and to cry softly; from that age make him do as he is bid, if you whip him ten times running to effect it. If you spare the rod, you spoil the child; if you do not conquer, you ruin him. Break his will now and his soul shall live, and he will probably bless you to all eternity (quoted in Southey, 1925).

To elucidate the moral bases for the schooling of 4 to 8-year-old children, we have to take into account the differences in educational philosophy of the founders of early childhood schooling and their influences. This chapter focuses specifically on the creative ideas of Pestalozzi, Froebel, Fichte, Owen and McMillan and briefly sets these in the context of schooling today.

Pestalozzi (1746–1827) was the first to develop an integrated philosophy and practice for the education of young children. His schools were mainly for 5 to

12-year-olds and partly for this reason he, along with Robert Owen (1771–1858), is considered a founder of infant schooling, as denoted in the United Kingdom. However, Pestalozzi's writings treat education as extending from birth, emphasising the form and content of education nurtured by the mother in the home prior to the age of 6 years. Robert Owen's New Harmony (Indiana) School, founded with William McClure in 1824, modelled on Pestalozzi's school at Yverdun, took children from the age of 3 (Lockwood, 1905).

Pestalozzi grappled with the theory and practice of education and especially with the themes of individuality, community, agency, work and moral educability. Pestalozzi argued against the Augustinian doctrine of original sin, enunciated in A.D. 400 as a response to the 'free-will' heresies of Pelagius (Winslow, 1973). The doctrine of original sin held that the child was imbued with propensities which might, if they were not suppressed and re-trained, be expressed as wicked acts which might cause disturbance in the wider society. This idea, reinforced at the time of the Reformation, of children's inherited guilt rather than innocence at birth, was accompanied by an idea derived from Locke, of children's minds being likened to blank slates (tabula rasa) on which knowledge was to be impressed by teachers and other adults. They were born with innate tendencies to indiscipline and being wilful, and had no way of learning useful knowlege except by being taught directly by adults. It is my understanding that the way to resolve the potential indiscipline of children whilst impressing knowledge on the 'tabula rasa', allowing for the paucity of books, was to use a pedagogy which required memoris-ation and repetition, rather than reasoning and understanding.

A description of this 'rote' pedagogy is quoted by Heafford (1967): it was against this pedagogy that Pestalozzi railed:

> Every day the first period was devoted to reading the Bible. We began at the place where we had left off the day before until we had finished the Bible. Thus we went through the Old Testament, the Apocrypha, and the New Testament; not a single word was left out. We really achieved something, for in about eight months we had got through. That is good going. It can be explained, however, when one realises that absolutely nothing was clarified, and that it was the 'done thing' to read away as quickly as possible without any expression or a single hesitation. For us the Bible was no more than a reader which was only of interest to us because with its help we could show how well and quickly we could read. The contents were mostly incomprehensible to us, especially to the children who spoke dialect; moreover we did not pay much attention to the contents. Of course, we knew the Bible was God's word, but we did not really understand what that meant. For us the title-page, the prefaces, and the chapter headings were equally God's word because they were in the Bible, and if the bookbinder had felt like binding another book in with the Bible, we would not have doubted that it was equally God's word (Heafford, 1967).

Contrary to this form of schooling, Pestalozzi developed his pedagogy with its emphasis on children's understanding of content, presented to engage children's interests; a pedagogy to nurture the process of a child's moral and intellectual development.

Pestalozzi was born in Zurich, Switzerland in 1746. His work and ideas have to be seen in the context of the French Revolution and its aftermath and the period of dominance of Napoleon Bonaparte in Europe. The wars resulted in a great increase in orphan children; a problem that Pestalozzi addressed by establishing schools for orphans who were usually paupers. They were, by the conventions on intelligence of the time, considered innately ineducable.

Pestalozzi was criticised in his time by both the philosopher Fichte and his former student Froebel for, they suggested, a lack of ability to express his theories in a philosophical form and for not building his practices on an a priori theory, as was conventional then. But Pestalozzi was in turn critical of the theories of the development of mind held by most of his philosopher contemporaries:

> I am not now speaking of those leading ideas which are from time to time thrown out, and by which science is advanced, or society benefited at large. I am speaking of that stock of intellectual property, which every one, even the most unpretending individual, and in the humblest walks of life, may acquire. I am speaking of that habit of reflection, which guards against unthinking conduct under any circumstances, and which is always active to examine that which is brought before the mind; the habit of reflection, which excludes the self-sufficiency of ignorance, or the levity of a 'little learning' — which may lead an individual to the modest acknowledgement, what he knows but little, and to the honest consciousness that he knows that little well. To engender this habit nothing is so effective as an early development in the infant mind of thought, regular, self-active thought....I, for one, would trust more in the experiential knowledge of a mother, proceeding from exertions to which she was prompted by maternal feelings — in that experiential knowledge even of an illiterate mother, I would trust more — than in the theoretical speculations of the most ingenious philosophers. Without troubling herself about the knotty questions, whether there are any *innate ideas* she will be content in developing the *innate faculties of the mind* (Pestalozzi, 1827). (Emphasis supplied).

By 'innate ideas' Pestalozzi was referring to Fichte's ethical idealist proposition that the child was born with innate moral, social and aesthetic ideas. 'Innate faculties of the mind' refers to Pestalozzi's view, which he shared with Kant, that the mind has innate potential for structuring sense impressions. This places greater responsibility on educators and the education of the child. In Pestalozzi's view, the mother, or mother figure in the form of the teacher, should nurture and educate that structuring propensity of the mind by providing a wide variety of sense impressions and drawing out the child's reflections of the experience of these impressions. Pestalozzi recommended that the mother figure should avoid wearying the child by her instructions but added that he did not wish to encourage the notion that:

> Instruction should always take the character of an amusement or even a play. I am convinced that such a notion, where it is entertained and acted upon by a teacher, will for ever preclude solidity of knowledge and, from a want of sufficient exertions on the part of pupils, will lead to that very result which I wish to avoid by my principle of a constant employment of a thinking power. A child should not be taught to look upon exertion as an unavoidable evil. The motive of fear should not be made a stimulus to exertion. It would destroy the interest and would speedily create disgust.

> This *interest* in study is the first thing which a teacher and, in the instances before us, which a mother should endeavour to keep alive . . . .I would go as far as to lay it down for a rule, that whenever children are inattentive and apparently take no interest in a lesson, the teacher should always first look to themselves for the reason (Pestalozzi, 1827).

As teacher, he acted as mother figure, engendering children's interest in the lesson, in contrast to contemporary practice on which he reflected 'that the children were punished, when really it is the master or the system that is to blame'. Pestalozzi's central concern with children's interests foreshadows those of John Dewey.

Pestalozzi objected to the 'indescribable tedium' which must oppress the juvenile mind whilst the weary hours are slowly passing away, one by one, in an occupation which they neither relish nor of which they understand the use. He suggests that the best means to prevent this boredom is:

> to adopt a better mode of instruction by which children are less left to themselves, less thrown upon the unwelcome employment of passive listening, less harshly treated for little and excusable failings — but more roused by questions, animated by illustrations, interested and won by kindness.

These conative concerns of maintaining interest, avoiding boredom, stimulation of the mind, and the expression of kind words and feelings to children run through the educational practice of Pestalozzi and are the basis of much current early childhood schooling. He objected to his contemporary philosophers' doubting speculations about educability, their lack of practical knowledge of pedagogy, to the notion of the *tabula rasa*, to the idea of original sin and to the incontrovertible nature of the poor — their lack of potential for improvement. Pestalozzi's objections are pertinent to our present times. The fundamentalist radical reactionary social and educational policies of the Thatcher and Reagan administrations have revived original sin, *tabula rasa*, and the incontrovertible but 'natural' state of poverty.

Pestalozzi's concern with self-active thought in the child was in part a reaction against the rote pedagogy widely employed in the schooling of the period. He expressed this thus:

> The second rule I would give to a mother respecting the early development of the infant mind is this — let the child not only be *acted upon* but

let him be an *agent* in intellectual education . . . .(Emphasis supplied). The child has a faculty of reflection independent of the thoughts of others. It is well done to make the child read and write and learn and repeat — but it is still better to make a child think (Pestalozzi, 1827).

However, Pestalozzi's concern to develop self-active thought through the development of the child's own agency as a thinker, encouraged through the kindness of the teacher, was fraught with difficulties in practice during Pestalozzi's lifetime. For instance, during his work at the orphan asylum at Stanz (1798–1799) (the first prolonged opportunity for Pestalozzi to practise his principles), the size of the class and the paucity of resources precluded a full implementation of his pedagogic aspirations.

'Three times a week after the evening meal there were meetings of the teachers. One of these was devoted to discussing the children, another to the more practical problems which the teachers had encountered during the week and the third to the 'method'. The principles of the *method* were being applied to various subjects by the assistants' (Heafford, 1967).

Pestalozzi was the sole teacher of a class of 80 pupils. In order to cope:

he had the idea of resorting to simultaneous teaching, all the pupils repeating in a high toned voice the words of the teacher. 'It was found', he said, 'that the rhythmical pronunciation increased the impression produced by the lesson'. Having to deal with pupils absolutely ignorant, he kept them for a long time on the elements; he practised them on the first element until they had mastered them. He simplified the methods and sought in each branch of instruction a point of departure, adapted to the nascent faculties of the child . . . .(Comparye, 1877).

This curriculum broke with the traditional memorisation of Bible and catechism.

Reading was combined with writing, natural history and geography were taught in the form of conversational lessons. But what engrossed Pestalozzi above all else was to develop the moral sentiments and the interior forces of the conscience. He wished to make himself loved by his pupils and to waken among them, in their daily association, sentiments of fraternal affection, to excite the conception of each virtue formulating its precept and to give the children moral lessons through the influence of nature which surrounded them and through the activity which was imposed on them (Comparye, 1877).

This context of fraternal affection, according to Pestalozzi, was essential as a conative means for engendering apperception in the child prior to its formulation in a propositional and language form.

Equipment and other facilities were minimal in his school. Everyday objects, the study of nature, formed the material for the lessons, along with mental exercises, mainly in mathematics.

Pestalozzi's method of intuitive pre-formation of concepts through the speaking out of the children's apperception of an object — what became known as an object lesson — originated not directly as an idea of Pestalozzi's but as befits his own principles, out of an observation by Pestalozzi of a child trying to learn.

One day, as according to his custom, he was giving his pupils a long description of what they observed in a drawing where a window was represented, he noticed that one of his little auditors, instead of looking at the picture, was attentively studying the real window of the school room. From that moment Pestalozzi put aside all his drawings, and took the objects themselves as subjects of observation. 'The child', he said, 'wants nothing to intervene between nature and himself' (Comparye, 1877).

This direct observation of the objects which serve as the material source for the lesson became a central precept of Pestalozzi and subsequently of Froebel and Montessori.

The first rule . . . is always to teach by the things rather than by words. That there be as few objects as possible named to the infant, unless you are prepared to show the objects themselves. If this is the case, the name will be committed to the memory, together with the recollection of the impression which the object produced on the senses (Pestalozzi, 1827).

Then, perhaps, as a reflection on the object lesson:

It is an old saying, and a very true one, that our attention is much more forcibly attracted, and more permanently fixed by objects which have been brought before our eyes, than by others, of which we have merely gathered some notion from hearsay and description, or from the mention of a name. But if a mother is to teach by *things* (emphasis supplied) she must recollect also that in the formation of an idea, more is requisite than the bringing of the object before the senses. Its qualities must be explained; its origin must be accounted for; its parts must be described; and their relation to the whole ascertained; its use, its effects and consequences must be stated. All this must be done at least in a manner, sufficiently clear and convincing, to enable the child to distinguish the object from other objects, and to account for the distinction which is made (Pestalozzi, 1827).

The psychological notion of apperception that Pestalozzi was working with includes the idea of evaluative reflection on incoming sense percepts. Cognition was originally synonomous with apperception but has now become identified as the process of concept formation. Pestalozzi was expressing what was later expounded as a cognitive theory of knowledge formation by, for instance, Vygotsky (1933) and Bruner (1968).

Pestalozzi was hailed by the German ethical idealist philosopher, Fichte, in 1807 with 'It is from the institute of Pestalozzi that I expect the regeneration of the

German nation'. In his *Address to the German Nation*, Fichte called for what we might now call 'moral rearmament' centred particularly on the upbringing of children, to reconstruct Prussia after Napoleon's victory at the Battle of Jena (1806) and the retributive Treaty of Tilsit (1807). It was Pestalozzi's ideas and what seemed to be his success in developing moral behaviour and sentiments in children, that so attracted J. G. Fichte to Pestalozzi's work. Although Fichte had never been a school teacher, he had a clear idea of what he wanted from a renewed education system, and this to a marked extent, was to inculcate moral behaviour which would lead to moral unity in a unified German nation. Fichte recommended that children be taken from their parents and placed in what we now term boarding schools (Turnbull, 1926). He attributed the defeat of the Prussian nation to a large extent to the demise of the moral condition of the family, particularly to the spoiling of children.

Fichte wished to see teachers fostering in their pupils self-responsibility and moral behaviour through self-regulation, rather than bribing and cajoling them through rewards into socially acceptable behaviour. It is noticeable here that Fichte was referring to those who had wealth, whose children were spoilt in the sense that clear distinctions between good and evil were not inculcated within them, whereas Pestalozzi's concern was to develop what he considered to be the moral sense and potential for intellectual development of even the poorest children. This is an important distinction, indicative of the differences in social philosophy and perspective of Pestalozzi as compared to Fichte.

Play, Childhood and the Curriculum — Froebel

Pestalozzi (1827) deliberately avoided the use of the term 'play' preferring 'work' or 'work for oneself'. Pestalozzi considered that as his pupils were inevitably going to have to work for their livelihoods, that to introduce them to play was to mislead them into the expectation that they would have time in their working lives for anything other than work. During the course of industrialisation and the growth of cities, play became associated with those who had wealth and time for leisure. Work was associated with the poor. Strict Calvinists and Lutherans (Froebel's father was a Lutheran pastor), believed that work was the duty of all people, including young children, whilst pleasure, which was synonymous with play, was to be deplored or severely limited. However, such extreme views were not prevalent in Great Britain and the U.S.A. where by the 1850's (Hobsbaum, 1962; McCann and Young, 1982) non-conformists, utilitarians and humanists held views as influential as strict Protestants and Evangelicals on the criteria for a good and worthy life.

By 1855 the concept of the child had reached the point where discussions were in terms of rights rather than duties. The philosophy of idealism, the influx of ideas based on Romanticism, and the increasing association of beneficent concepts of the child with American democratic thought, changed the prevailing view of the child's inherent impulses. In the thoughts of many, the innate tendencies of the child came to be viewed as good — as reflections of God's goodness. Play was then accepted as a medium for educational experience, and benevolent nurture came to be viewed as a right of the young child. This sweeping change took place in adult minds, yet it was so significant and far-reaching that we may yet recognise it as one of the great revolutions of history (Butts, 1955).

The kindergarten curriculum that Froebel devised was based upon the development of self-activity, which was premised on children's proclivity to play. Fichte, Froebel's tutor at Jena, had suggested that Froebel spend some time studying Pestalozzi's school at Yverdun. Froebel was observer and student at Yverdun between 1808–1810.

Froebel's observation of children at play in the home and the garden enabled him to realise the proclivity of children to persevere at, even to create problems, solving them in ways that were in part expressions of their own individuality. However, for Froebel, play in the house and garden was too haphazard, too indiscriminate in its objects of attention. Froebel was concerned that the child might not realise what he or she had been doing; concerned at the opportunity lost for learning by such play. Froebel wanted to wring out of the children's propensity to play not only their education but also his design for a curriculum. The objects of the kindergarten plays, the Gifts, were prespecified, as were the forms of teaching he considered appropriate to each Gift.

Froebel's observation of children at play in the home and in the garden are sensitive and rich in detail (Lilley, 1967). Froebel expressed his admiration for children's self-sufficiency and perseverance in play. However, the child's autonomy in play was not translated into practice in Froebel's curriculum. The practices that Joseph Payne (1876) (in North Germany) and Anna Bryan (1890) (in the USA) and others observed and criticised, were those of teacher direction of the children's activities, prespecified objects, rules and, indeed, roles that denied individuality. Froebel based his discussion of play on his close observation of children. The notion of the unity of nature and of God, Froebel states, is first realised by the child through play. Froebel, contrary to 'strict' evolutionary recapitulationists like Stanley Hall (1907) does not consider the stages of development as being increasingly superior one to the next.

Froebel, the reader will recall, distinguished play in the German homes of the time from the plays of the kindergarten. The kindergarten plays he devised as a sequence of tasks arising from the Gifts (or 'play things') (Lilley, 1967) which would induce in the child moral and intellectual realisation of a potential and foster self-activity. By self-activity was meant the child becoming the agent of his own development. For Froebel the plays of the kindergarten were serious matters to be closely supervised by the teacher (Froebel, 1907). The plays stimulated by the Gifts would induce a realisation of the unity of the 'inner and the outer' as the child's mind became relaxed. This ethical idealist subsumption of the material world through a striving to reach attainable moral perfection — 'God' (Froebel), the 'Spirit' (Fichte) — would, according to Froebel's theory, be accomplished by systematic teacher-supervised plays with the Gifts which would lead to realisation of desirable qualities of moral thought and behaviour.

The Occupations, which became a part of Froebel's programme for young children, were selected to offer an opportunity for controlling and modifying malleable materials. These included such activities as clay modelling, interlacing of paper strips and building forms with sticks connected by softened peas. They followed logically from Froebel's valuing of constructive activities. In the symbolic system of Froebel, Gifts for the child were manipulated in order to objectify the child's vague conceptions and thus lead him to a better understanding of himself and his world. The use of the Gifts depended on the urge of the child towards exploration. The Occupations of practical work were those that 'extended and fixed the impressions made by the Gifts'.

> Not only did Froebel devise the Gifts but he described with great precision the manner in which the children were to play with them. A large portion of Froebel's *Pedagogies of the Kindergarten* was devoted to this task. Each Gift was to be used to allow all possible means to be pursued, that they were to be employed in combination with other Gifts for expansion of ideas. The manipulation of each Gift and the study of its meaning might require weeks for completion (Weber, 1969).

As an illustration of the instructions Froebel provided for the teachers, there follows an excerpt from the use of the fifth Gift.

> Lay four times two whole cubes in an oblong before you; place perpendicularly upon them again four times two whole cubes. Over these two cubes place two half cubes, so that they touch in the middle of their sharp edges; with the last two cubes each of the two half cubes yet required is represented by two quarters. In the long hollow column thus made, sink four whole cubes. What have you made which now stands before each of you? A house with an overhanging roof, four cubes high and two cubes broad (Froebel, 1907).

Weber comments that by careful planning and ordering the plays of childhood, Froebel believed that he found the

> progressive course of the development and education of the child in the logical sequence. As the Gifts proceeded from solid surface, from mind to point, so the Occupations paralleled this progress from modelling to paper folding, from stick laying to pricking. The movement thus symbolised the unfolding of the universe from absolute unity to the multitudinous diversity of existence. For Froebel, this apparently logical arrangement of materials was also the psychological aim since it was in harmony with the growth of the child. It married the process going on in a child's development (Weber, 1969).

Whereas Pestalozzi's equipment and facilities were parsimonious, Froebelian Gifts and Occupations required construction of new materials and their manufacture as well as the recurring replacement of materials that were used in the Occupations.

The Froebelian curriculum included other activities apart from the Gifts and Occupations. Froebel placed considerable emphasis on the cultivation of gardens (Lilley, 1967) on games and playgrounds, drawing and story telling.

Froebel's educational scheme would engender a realisation in the children of the unity of an 'inner and outer' transcendent unity.

> Man is essentially good and possesses qualities and tendencies which are good in themselves. He is not naturally bad nor are his qualities evil, unless it is considered that the finite, the material, the transient and the physical as such are evil and that their necessary consequence, namely that it must be possible for the human being to fail if he is to achieve goodness and to be in bondage if he is to be truly free, is also evil. Yet this is inevitable since it is temporal and separate things that eternal unity is manifested, and it is man's destiny to become conscious, rational and free (Lilley, 1967).

Froebel developed his concept of unity from his religious convictions:

> He saw it stemming from God, thus encompassing the laws of both physical nature and the human spirit. But Froebel saw no dichotomy between the realms of the spirit and the realms of nature, or between the individual and society. The source of all pervading unity was God (Weber, 1969).

Froebel, following the ethical idealism of Fichte, believed that the material world was subsumed within the subjective mind in which a unity between innate ideas and natural phenomena was resolved. This belief, a precept of the ethical idealists, confused the process of reflection-on-doing with the presupposition of innate ideas — a distinction that Pestalozzi had clarified and transformed into practice with orphan paupers and the object lesson.

Whereas Pestalozzi had conviction of the goodness within each individual child, he did not specify the end moral state envisaged through his process of education. Froebel, by contrast, did specify the ends of the educational process that he advocated:

> Froebel insisted that the curriculum should be built around the 'inner urges' and 'native impulses' of the developmental stage of the child, in present day terminology, it should be 'child-centred'. Since, in Froebel's view, development proceeded from the connection between the child's inner strivings and his outward expression of them, the senses were involved in both an outward expression and inner ideas and the taking in of outer phenomena (Weber, 1969).

In Froebel's developmental scheme, the child was envisaged as being able to foster the process of unfolding of knowledge by 'his impulse to creative activity'. (Weber, 1969). Yet,

In the light of the kindergarten programme Froebel developed, which was, ironically, excessively teacher directed, Froebel's concept of creative self-activity needs careful assessment (Weber, 1969).

Weber suggest Froebel's writings are ambiguous about creative activity. Even the teachers of his day asked for clearer statements about play and pedagogy. Whereas Pestalozzi rejected imitation and direction in his concept of creative self-activity, Froebel included these two qualities, believing that the young child's productive imitation could productively help to establish connections between the 'inner' and the 'outer'. Froebel frequently claimed that imitation was an important aspect of creative activity . . . Imitative movement and production were said by Froebel to awaken subconscious thought and nurtured 'Universal Truths'.

> For the child this meant that his activities were creative in the sense that he created himself by producing objects that developed his own inner meanings. Thus imitation's true point of departure for nurture of subsequent independent production was not bound tightly to originality or divergent thinking as creativity is today (Weber, 1969).

It is questionable whether such directing of the child's thoughts would develop the child's agency as Froebel (and Fichte) desired. The 'plays' maintained the child's dependence on the teacher. An interpretation of Froebel's *Pedagogics of the Kindergarten* by the 'letter' did indeed deny the 'spirit' of Froebel's insights into children's minds and their play, as Anna Bryan pointed out at the International Kindergarten Union meeting of 1895. This literal interpretation led to a suppression of children's individuality, as did adherence to the sequence for presentation of the Gifts — indeed it would seem from the criticisms of the orthodox kindergartens the priority was on prespecified outcomes rather than, as Froebel had advocated, on the child's interests.

I am suggesting that play involves the child in making interpretations to the growth of self through reciprocity, to manifestation and reflection on another's response. Play, in Mead's (1896) interpretation, enables the growth of individuality by helping the child to realise the consequences of manifesting imagined transformations. The development of apperceptive learning and individuality is accompanied by the growth of agency. Play offers a process within which agency, individuality and apperceptive learning can be developed. Play in the context of social relationships, as with the kindergarten or nursery, provides the teacher with the opportunity to develop the sense of responsibility to the wider community, in the first instance to other classmates.

Play, Early Schooling and Community

The relationship between the nursery/kindergarten and the wider community and society was, and continues to be, a focus for differences in ideologies of early childhood schooling. Froebel hoped that his educational system would help children to transcend the conflicts in society and lead to a realisation of the unity of life and human affiliation within the oneness of God. Pestalozzi did not share these ideals. He sought to educate and train the children for a life of meaningful work rather than as subservient labourers or operatives. He educated the children to reflect on their own and others' actions, to become self-responsible and to play an active part in community life. For Pestalozzi only joint human action would begin to lead to a more just and compassionate society.

The source of children's moral acts and the extent and means by which teachers and parents could foster development, continue to be key questions for early childhood educators. For all their apparent similarity as co-founders of the English Nursery Association in 1923, Margaret McMillan (1927) and Grace Owen (Cusden, 1938) differed fundamentally in their approach to these key questions. Owen and McMillan campaigned for state Nursery provision to be expanded. Owen, like McMillan, was concerned with children's health and hygiene and behaviour. Owen promoted the English Nursery as a place where unkempt, unruly children of the working classes would be taught comportment, to desist from 'bad' language, to practise good manners and to keep themselves clean. For Owen the Nursery was a means to raise the standard of moral behaviour and personal appearance in the expectation that these qualities would persist into adult life and so transform the next generation of working class lives. McMillan did not believe that such an ameliorative function for the Nursery would have significant consequences. For McMillan the Nursery movement was a part of a wider socialist plan to provide equal access to national resources and institutions for all social classes. She campaigned for increasing state provision for working class children and their families, in their work, housing, health and education. The main sites for McMillan's radical reforms were the schools at Bradford and Deptford, the latter in what is still one of the areas of poorest housing in London (Bradburn, 1976).

Margaret McMillan established open-air sheltered gardens for children of the poor in Deptford, London, in 1911. In a way this was an early form of 'compensatory' education in what would now be considered conditions of extreme poverty and ignorance. McMillan encouraged the parents to visit the shelters and to learn ways of nurture which she was exemplifying. McMillan observed how, when children's physical strength and stamina increased, their play became more sustained and their learning was enhanced.

McMillan considered that nurture and good health should be prior to any attempt to bring about formal education. In her time she campaigned against and revealed neglect of the children in what was then the most prosperous nation in the world. She compared this neglect of children of the urban working class with the continuing Victorian romanticism of the innocence and beauty of childhood. McMillan placed actual nurture and nourishment above idealisations of the nature and spirit of young children. Bluntly: if children are undernourished and cruelly treated they will not have the interest or energy to learn. McMillan's pedagogic procedures, developed to nurture the children of the Deptford shelters, became incorporated into the curriculum for the preparation of teachers for nursery schools but to a lesser extent for teachers of infant and first school children.

The Boundaries of Play, Work and Labour in the Nursery and Infant School Today

Research evidence from sustained observations of nurseries and kindergartens reveals that very little spontaneous play (Sylva, *et al.*, 1980; Florio, 1978; King, 1977; Tizard *et al.*, 1982) takes place. Children do not 'naturally' à la Froebel's descriptions of outside school, autonomously conduct their own investigations into natural or constructed objects. The environment is constructed by the teacher who guides the children through learning materials. The teacher segments the time into activities over which the children have little or no choice. The locations where children may devise their own roles and plans such as the playhouse, are places where teachers do not try to teach but only intervene in the moral order of children's play by limiting noise, breakage, numbers of participants and even duration of stay.

It seems from observation and interview (Sutton-Smith, 1979; Silvers, 1975; Adelman, 1976 and 1984; and Barrett, 1986) that children regard play as activities in which they define the boundaries, initiate and conclude. Where teacher or adults define boundaries, initiate and conclude, the activity is experienced by the children as work. This distinction holds whatever the objects or materials in use. Doing colour matching or jigsaws, sand or water, may be play or work. The distinction lies in the moral relationships between the children at play and between the children and an adult's work.

About two thirds of play is preparation, making plans, devising rules and assigning roles (Sutton-Smith, 1981). In the eyes of the children, following the agreed rules fairly means playing properly. Infringements include taking too many turns, not sharing a role or object, not reciprocating, not following the agreed rules and plan. Children at play are essentially co-operative and fair. Latecomers to play ask for entry and more often than not, are allowed in and told the rules. Repeated infringements or deliberate disruption of play, may lead to shouted complaints or even to fights.

The moral relationship of work is that on request or command children begin and complete a task set by the teacher. The rules and roles and boundaries are set by the teacher. The task is assessed by the teacher. The child is thus constrained and his/her performance in the task judged not only on cognitive but also on grounds of good discipline and behaviour, i.e. not infringing roles, rules or boundaries. This is the regime of teachers and educational theorists knowing best what is in the child's interests or needs. It precludes the Pestalozzian insight that children learn best by being helped to reflect on what they are doing.

Labour relationships are literally not constructed in the children's interests. They exploit the children for their lack of power and physical strength. They do not offer alternatives in the activities and have no tolerance with children's reluctance or abstention. Whereas in work the teacher tries to make the task and relationships have personal meaning for the children, in labour the tasks are to be carried out willy-nilly. The teacher is not interested in how the children feel about the experience, only in getting the children to do the task. In labour relationships disaffection is easily visible to the teacher. It is 'off-task' behaviour: looking away from the task, partly about a topic unrelated to the task, going away before the task is completed and so on. This is the behaviour that has been cited as indicator of children's performance by Tikunoff *et al.* (1978), Bennett *et al.* (1984). They view the 'effective' classroom as one which embodies the moral relationships of labour rather than work or play. Indeed, much of the research interest in disaffection comes from such labour orientated studies rather than from studies which are set against a context of play and meaningful work; issues that arise most poignantly in early childhood and special needs education and were addressed by Pestalozzi:

> There is a most remarkable reciprocal action between the interest which the teacher takes and that which he communicates to his pupils. If he is not with this whole mind present at the subject; if he does not care whether it is understood or not, whether his manner is liked or not, he will never fail of alienating the affections of his pupils, and rendering them indifferent to what he says. But real interest taken in the task of instruction either in kind words, kind feelings — the very expression of the features, and the glance of the eye are never lost upon children (Pestalozzi, 1827).

References

ADELMAN, C. (1976) *The Use of Objects in the Education of 3 to 5 year old children*, London, Final Report to the Social Science Research Council.

ADELMAN, C, (1984) *The Institutionalisation of the Kindergarten Curricula: An Ethnographic and Historical Account*, Centre for Science Education, Chelsea College, University of London.

BARRETT, G. (1986) *Starting School: An Evaluation of the Experience*, London, AMMA.

BENNETT, N. DESFORGES, C. COCKBURN, A. and WILKINSON, B. (1984) *The Quality of Pupil Learning Experiences*, London, Lawrence Erlbaum Associates Ltd.

BRADBURN, E. (1976) *Margaret McMillan: Framework and Expansion of Nursery Education*, Redhill, Denholm House Press, National Christian Education Council.

BRUNER, J. (1968) *Towards a Theory of Instruction*, Cambridge, Harvard University Press.

BUTTS, F. R. (1955) *A Cultural History of Western Education*, New York, McGraw Hill.

COMPARYE, G. (1877) *A History of Pedagogy*, London, Swann Sonnenstein.

CUSDEN, P. (1938) *The English Nursery School*, London, Kegan Paul, French, Trubnew and Co. Ltd.

FLORIO, S. (1978) 'Learning How to go to School: an ethnography of interaction in a kindergarten/first grade classroom,' Graduate School of Education, Harvard University, Ph.D. thesis.

FROEBEL, F. (1907) *Pedagogics of the Kindergarten*, Translated by Jarvis, J. London, Sidney Appleton.

HALL, G. S. (1907) *Aspects of Child Life and Education*, London, Methuen.

HEAFFORD, M. (1967) *Pestalozzi: His Thought and Its Relevance Today*, London, Methuen.

HOBSBAUM, E. (1962) *The Age of Revolution*, London, Weidenfield and Nicolson.

KING, N. (1977) 'The Hidden Curriculum and the Socialisation of the Kindergarten School', University of Wisconsin. Ph.D. thesis.

LILLEY, I. M. (1967) *Friedrich Froebel*, Cambridge University Press.

LOCKWOOD, A. (1905) *The New Harmony Movement*, New York, Appleton.

MCCANN, P. and YOUNG F. A. (1982) *Samuel Wilderspin and the Infant School Movement*, Beckenham, Croom Helm.

MCMILLAN, M. (1927) *The Life of Rachel McMillan*, London, J. M. Dent.

MEAD, G. H. (1896) *The Relation of Plays to Education*, Chicago, University of Chicago Press.

PAYNE, J. (1876) *A Visit to German Schools: Notes of a Professional Tour*, London, Henry S. King and Co.

PESTALOZZI, H. (1827) *Letters on Early Education, Addressed to J. P. Greaves, Esq. by Pestalozzi*, London, Charles Gilpin.

SILVERS, R. J. (1975) *Starting School, The Children's Culture Project*, Department of Sociology in Education, Ontario, Institute for Studies in Education, September, mimeo.

SOUTHEY, R. (1925) *The Life of Wesley*, Vol 2. London, Humphrey Milford.

SYLVA, K., ROY, C. and PAINTER, M. (1980) *Childwatching at Playground and Nursery School*, London, Grant McIntyre.

SUTTON-SMITH, B. (ed) (1979) *Play and Learning*, New York, Gardner Press.

SUTTON-SMITH, B. (ed) (1981) *Fields of Play*, London, BBC TV. Producer: Michael Dibb.

TIKUNOFF, W. J., WARD, B. A. and DASHE, S. J. (1978) *Volume A: Three Case Studies*, (Report A78-7). San Francisco, Far West Laboratory for Educational Research and Development.

TIZARD, B. HUGHES, M. PINKERTON, G. and CARMICHAEL, H. (1982) 'Adults Cognitive Demands at Home and at Nursery School', *Journal of Child Psychology and Psychiatry*, 23, (2), pp. 105–116.

TURNBULL, G. H. (1926) *The Educational Theory of J. G. Fichte*, Liverpool, University of Liverpool Press.

VYGOTSKY, L. S. (1933) 'Play and its role in the mental development of the child' in: Bruner, J., Jolly, A. and Sylva, K. (eds) *Play*, Harmondsworth, Penguin Books.

WEBER, E. (1969) *The Kindergarten. Its Encounter with Educational Thought in America*. New York, Teachers College Press.

WINSLOW, D. F. (1973) 'Pelagius' in *Encyclopaedia of World Biography*, New York, McGraw Hill.

Part III
Home, School and the Community

6
Being a Disaffected Parent

John Schostak

In 1932 an American sociologist Willard Waller wrote that there was universally a conflict between the parent's and the teacher's wishes concerning the education of a child. This relationship between parent, teacher and child has always been two edged, never more so than when the State acts as the parent of all parents. In this chapter I want to try and describe the kind of relationship my family and I would have liked to have with the schools to which our sons went during their early years, how we became more and more disaffected but why we nevertheless let our sons continue to go to school. For reasons of space, the description will concentrate upon the experiences with the eldest son's schools, a description formed through consultation between all of us, raiding cupboards and boxes for old memories.

Our First Days at School

Looking back upon our very first days taking our eldest son to school seems like dreams of hopes that never materialised. We lived in a relatively modern estate. It was our first house — a terraced 'townhouse' — and across the park was the school. The school was also a 1960's product, its classrooms light, large and purpose built, its ethos progressive, child-centred, warm, caring. This seemed to us to be a good sign.

The first contact that my son had with the school was when the deputy head teacher (who would be his classroom teacher) made an appointment to come to our house to meet our son and so begin the relationship which she would develop in the coming months and years. This was standard practice for all teachers having new children entering their class. Let me explain further.

The school was 'vertically integrated', that is its classes operated a system of 'family grouping'. Each class contained children representing the whole age range of the schools: half-a-dozen 5-year-olds, half a dozen 6-year-olds, half-a-dozen 7-year-olds, half-a-dozen 8-year-olds — all together in the classroom. There were two new intakes per year, and as new children entered, they entered a stable classroom situation where routines and caring relationships had already been formed.

The new children were helped by the older children to settle in and to take part in the multiplicity of activities which were going on at any one time in the classroom. Children largely planned their own day's activities. Reading, writing, arithmetic, art and the basis of science all grew naturally through emulation of the older children's activities, the enthusiasm of the teacher, the help of parents drawn in to take part in classroom activities and the particular strength and interests of the variety of children.

At the time (1980) I recorded an interview with this teacher because I was just starting my doctoral studies and I had hoped that I might use this with other such interviews. As it happened the interview was never used because my doctoral studies changed radically. She told me the aim of the school:

> Well, the first aim really is to make sure the children are happy and feel secure before you, you know, try to do any work or anything with the children. I think they've got to feel that school's a place where they want to come and that they can choose what they want to do to some extent, that it's not something where they're going to come everyday and have something forced upon them that perhaps they don't want to do. I think the primary aim when the new children come is to make them feel secure and I mean that also means that they need to know where to put their coats, where uh, and a kind of routine. I think it's important to have a routine to give them that security.

That seemed to be borne out to the extent that our son settled in the first day without tears and I was able to leave him quite early (parents were allowed to stay as long as they liked) because he was busily play/working. During this initial period, the task as this teacher saw it was primarily observational.

> When they first come to school I try to watch them if I can to see what stage they've reached because they all come from such different back-grounds and different states of readiness to learn. But it's not very easy to spend the time just watching the children as much as we can.

This teacher was acutely aware of the complexity of the classroom with its many unique personalities. She had the approach not of the mass production designer shaping everything to fit the average, or to kit out the populace with some common set of clothes, but of the bespoke tailor who saw individualities, responded to choice and used her expertise, her knowledge, her intelligence according-ingly. Why? Because children, even very young ones, should be accorded the dignity of choice:

> I think a lot of the children if given the freedom will motivate themselves. I think if they come into a room where there's plenty to do, there are not many children who will just aimlessly wander around. Most of them will choose something to do that interests them and as a result of it will gain something from it, and obviously they concentrate for different lengths of time according to their maturity . . . We try to encourage them to find

out for themselves, to know where to go to find out things and also to know that they can go to one teacher or to another. They know that perhaps one teacher's more interested in something than perhaps another teacher is. I think also it's important to let them know that we don't always know the answer to things.

When this teacher speaks one gains access to a cluster of images, values, beliefs, accounts of ways things are done which together comprise a description not only of her beliefs and the way in which she sees the world but also her practice as a teacher. These images, ideas and practices are not unique to her. They are derived from a tradition not only of teaching but also of social philosophy which can be traced back over the centuries. When one inquires into this tradition one can find that it rests upon certain propositions, insights, knowledge, beliefs and assumptions about the nature of human beings and the way in which society ought to develop. As a parent, when I wave goodbye to my sons as they set off for school, I want to feel that the school environment into which they are being placed has within its belief systems, its philosophy of life and of action, the same kinds of ends or purposes that I believe will serve my sons best.

When we moved house to be close to the university for my doctoral studies, my son entered a quite different school. Its nature was prefigured in some comments by the teacher in the school we had just left when she expressed her worries about the children who left her to go to the junior and then the secondary school in the area. Their more traditional forms left little for the individual expressions of children.

At the end of the first week in the new school we knew it was going to present new problems. My son could not understand the obsessive need for competition, could not understand why his choices were not encouraged, and became bored with the repetitiveness of the work, but this was not a bad school. It was simply average. Its ethos was more traditional. It began to suffocate creativity. This was the first time that we began to discuss the merits of education at home. Was it simply that we had moved to a new area? We decided to allow a settling-in period. He began to make friends. A new year began with the same teacher, but a new approach emerged, a little more like the old approach. Things settled down. The teacher was learning flexibility — enough to understand that if our son was allowed to follow his own lines of enquiry, he could be bargained with and a mutually satisfactory deal could be struck, but the edge was there. Our credo developed an ironic sting 'All we ask of them is that they don't destroy his creativity'. At home we had to work upon his morale, and develop his ability to keep on doing what he wanted to do whilst managing the demands of schooling. In this way, we reasoned, he could guard his creativity, his curiosity and develop his interests without getting into trouble at school. If we reasoned thus, why bother with school? Because we felt it was important for him to meet people, make friends and deal with social situations.

Today we are still unsure we were right. His antipathy to school has grown. Crises occurred regularly. Serious discussions were had with him as to whether he should continue his education at home, but always, the need to meet friends and finally to have access to certain kinds of equipment for examinations decided him against opting out of school. If he were to leave school, we said, he must be prepared to contribute to detailed curriculum planning. It could not be a whim of the moment. These deliberations led him to the conclusion that he would continue on at school. Opting out has always been a serious option. His willingness to work has never been in doubt, either by us or by his teachers at every level. As a first school child his passions developed for reading, writing stories, studying animals and painting. His stories would fill exercise books. He always read voraciously and from 9 years old he was reading adult novels. What was interesting to us was the separation that was maintained between work at home and work at school. Work at school was considerably more childish, shorter and less thoughtful. Here is an extraction from his school book of September 1981 when he was eight:

> My story is Joseph and he helps you one day he had a baby cald baby Jesus.

This was followed by a small illustrative drawing of a stable scene and a teacher's tick plus one spelling correction. Towards the end of the book his stories were longer, about two pages, more developed, but always clearly provoked by some school work on say a fairy story. The following is an extract from a story of 27 pages written at home derived from his own interests and reading at roughly the same period:

3. *the Great battle*
Man that won the bet came to France he was called Caesar with 100 roman soldiers on Wednesday he came too David dminson and he said where is your king David said surprized 'I am' then Caesar said 'if yo do not let us have the whole of Gaul we will attack' David went up in smoke and landed on top of Caesar. David said in a feace voce that scard all of the roman soldiers 'Why on my Weddy day? then in his lord's voce he said We Will fight! caesar and all of the roman soldiers neerly jumped out of there skin! all of Fraces Wallys came rushing out but David went too a church and married the lady. back at the fight a roman sliped away and came too the church. David saw the roman so he finged out his sword and choped the roman's (–?–) then he brought it back and choped the roman's head of. then David daminson ran out like the wind . . .

(Extract 2)

5. *the Great idae*
John whated (wanted) to read one of David's books so he asked David he said 'yes' so he got up and chossed (chose) one that was called ideas John sat down and started reading then pop went David's brain David jumped up in a nise smiling face and said 'let's go up stairs' so both of them ran up stairs and sare (sarah) Was sitting down thinking What it would be like with a boy or a girl. When David and John got up stairs and sat down in a sitty David said 'I nid (need) you to come and see a roman camp will be and then will'll (we'll) take turns looking to see if the roman look out has

goin to bed then will'll rush two ways and put a fire and then you will sly around a corner and kill any body you like and I will hide behide a bush and fire arrows that way nobody will get out

No claims are made for these extracts in terms of grammar, spelling, punctuation or literary merit. They do, however, illustrate through the sheer quantity and effusiveness, a burning desire to write, to express thoughts, to see himself (like most young children) in heroic situations, with friends. None of this was expressed in school. Hence there was no opportunity for a teacher to help develop basic skills and expressive forms of writing as a natural accompaniment to his enthusiasm and developing sense of self in the world. We began to encourage him more and more simply to write — we took no notice at all of the formal aspects of writing. The task was to keep his imagination moving, his curiosity aroused, his desire to record his thoughts intact. Practice and persistence were the keywords. We decided we would not censor his reading or his writing. His choice of books at times worried us. For a period from 9 years old he read little but adult pulp war books with all their violence, swearing and appalling values. What we did do was to discuss the ideas of the books with him and to put forward our own view points. If education was about freedom, it was not about censorship. If education was about challenging, it was about setting ideas and values into contest with each other. Reasons should prevail. Here is an example of his writing from this period. It is an extract from a novella written at home which filled two exercise books:

Planet hopping
Anno kept on thinking about the battle that his space city had been destroyed, he also looked at different maps on the milky way, he kept on thinking how to take over the zxo1 space station and more: how to take the milky way because he was very greedy and liked the feeling of being a great hero. Suddenly he had a wiked idea, "why should I take the zxo1 when I can outwit them with taking planets" he quickly got up shaky on his legs because he was heavy with excitement. He thought again "I'm overworked so i'll be sensible and go to bed." He walked along the nnetwork of tunnels passing (sik) silken gaurds, silken robots, silken commanders. Anno felt happy as he strided along, thinking of revenge and capture of the milky way. He got to a cave and opened the door autermatekly and went in. He punched two nobs and a bed poped out of the wall with warm covers and a cold heater to cool him down and a cushion. He got into it and went to sleep. The zxo1 soard through space going to its secret base were all the ala rebals hide from Anno which sent space ships after them. He sent ships and pplanes after princess corgy and richard and foto the owner of the two droids, wanted: 303 and 030. The zxo1 had two space craft destroyers clinging to both sides of the zxo1.

This went on, without breaks, without paragraphs, only the occasional chapter heading, for 160 pages in the two volumes which survive (a third exists but could not be found). Of course, the story is derivative. Those who have sat through *Star*

Wars will recognise aspects of the emerging plot and characters. Compare it with a sixty page story carried out at his third school, a more progressive school than the second where choice again was valued, at much the same time:

> (Background: there's been a murder. Dave is a detective and he drives a computerised talking car)
>
> By now the only country which wasn't in chaos was russia, Dave went to check it out. 'Hmm, there's a police station over there,' Dave pointed out, 'I thought it would be more heavily guarded', said the car. 'It should be'. On the horizon was smoke and Dave heard gunfire. 'Hm,' said the car, 'I believe it's bace here', and a shadow appeared on a map. 'Yes and think I had come here to spy, I believe it's some craze Worwegon'. 'Then explain all the explosions and raids there?' 'So far I can't'. Suddenly as they neared the police station, a Norwegon ran through the door and into a car, two soviets came out firing their guns. The Norwegon slumped back onto the pavement. Next the windows shattered and the doors fell to the floor. there was an explosion and the building collapsed. In no time police cars were around the building followed by ambulances and fire-engines. Dave went up to a policeman, 'What was in that station?'

So it continues, an action, spy, mystery story. At much the same time he began to develop his interests in art, particularly via Asterix books and comic magazines. He would spend hours each day drawing, writing stories, reading. We were optimistic that by reinforcing his energies, persistence with creative work as well as his reading of fiction and non-fiction at home would carry him through. Then came secondary school. I include the following extracts because the seeds of his current disaffection with school can be seen from the earliest days at school. It is important to recognise this because there is a continuity of basic structure between all the phases of schooling despite the surface differences:

> *The thoughts Richard has as he rushes to school*
> Monotony has started already. I hate monotony, structures, mechanical learning operations. I have just described school. I like spontaneous creativity, inventiveness and developing fantasies and dreams. Wind and sleet slaps my face, children pass, light fading from their still laughing eyes. I've reached it, the rotting building for a rotten society.

The teacher's comments in red are: 'So good — but so sad!' It is immediately followed by *Parts of Speech*, a mechanical listing of the parts of speech with their definitions and so on for five pages until another little paragraph:

> Observing rythmless rythms of nature. Waves oscillating, gulls swaying and swooping. Nothing is rushed, nothing is conformed to prescribed thinking, or timetable. Fantasies invented by adults vanish, like need for law enforcement, poverty is your fault — when you were brought up to be poor. Light fades away, back to civilisation.

So it continued for two more pages — and that has brought us up to date, but this is now secondary school and while these thoughts constitute the development of the same story, thus complementing and providing some reflective insights into the primary years, I shall not dwell on them here. They seem to stand in stark contrast to the very first school where there was a sense of excitement, a sense of continuing achievement. How exactly did these changes from excitement through to indifference and then to a resigned hatred occur?

The Emotional Context of School

Some clues to the emotional changes were there even from the very first days at school. For a child, school (or nursery school as the case may be) is the first truly public event. It presents a stage for publicly observable action, where action is judged from a multiplicity of sources. The context is no longer the private family, the back garden, or the street as play area. It is a place where judgements are made by authorities. It is a place where one meets hundreds of others. As such it can be very exciting. It can also be very frightening. Having observed many first days at school (Schostak, 1986) I have seen the tears and the anxieties as parents leave their children with strangers. We remember classmates of both our sons often in tears as they approached school.

Our own anxieties were first aroused with problems of bullying. Next, it was an accident when a passing boy pushed our son's head (quite accidentally) and it smashed into the point of a water tap. Many years later he was asked by his secondary teacher to write about his earliest memory. He wrote:

> I was at school in the cloakroom. There was a surge and somebody pushed me. My head was rammed into a tap. Although I was nearly unconscious I had a crazy impulse to stay at school.

It seemed crazy from his later viewpoint. At the time he felt secure with his teachers and felt no need to go rushing home. Nevertheless, it was a nasty wound, the teachers themselves were frightened and it took months to heal. A little lower and it could have been fatal.

Schools are crowded and often dangerous places, even the very best of schools. Conflicts arise between pupils. There are so many children that there is not enough time nor enough people to attend to their real needs. As the first school teacher pointed out when speaking of a particular little girl in the class:

> They seem to want to share their experiences with other adults, which I think is a good thing as well . . . (. . .) it would be lovely to have a lot more time to devote to the child (. . .) you think of Lizzie (not real name) there, she needs a lot of individual attention . . . a lot. She could really do with somebody to spend, you know, be with her all the time.

For each child there is so much to know, some with long case histories already of medical problems or social problems. The teachers must know how to handle each.

My admiration for teachers who do cope so well cannot be over emphasised. Yet, it remains, we are not talking about individual teachers here, but about a particular social structure, an institution whose structures, whilst bringing people together, also come between them, preventing them from acting as they would wish. School is a crowded and potentially dangerous place. It prevents teachers from forming the kind of close relationship with each child that a realistic education demands. Crowds of children are placed into contact with each other. They have no prior training, nor experience of how to handle crowds, nor how to act within crowded situations. The underlying emotional feeling is that of anxiety, an anxiety which conscientious and kindly teachers clearly recognise when they insist over and over again that their first task is to make children feel secure and to create a safe environment. Think of it this way: we are ice skaters. The thickness of the ice makes us feel secure, but somewhere at the back of our minds we know that too many people, or someone acting stupidly, can break the ice, or somewhere there might be a patch of thin ice. Accidents do happen!

Illness also occurs. It has always struck me that schools are prime environments for the spread of disease: not only colds but measles, mumps, chicken pox, whooping cough and others. Our sons have had the lot, one after another. Childhood began to feel like one long illness. Ilness in itself provokes anxiety. Many children go to school ill. Some have that depressing condition called 'glue ear' which frequently renders much of schooling meaningless, because the ears are blocked and little can be heard. They have to learn to cope in such an environment where their pleas are not always heard, not always recognised as cries for help, and where many around couldn't care less even if they heard and recognised them. Such experiences arouse feelings which radically influence the development of the child. These experiences are not random, they occur in every school to most if not all children to some degree in their first experiences of schooling. The teacher is not omniscient, nor can she or he act without regard to the expectations of the job, and its organisational demands and limitations. Because the teacher's time and emotional resources are limited and her or his behaviour constricted by crises, lapses in care and misinterpretations are inevitable. There is then an economics of care, which distributes teacher care like a scarce resource amongst the consumers (i.e., the pupils) in ways which can never be adequate to all children all the time. Most first school teachers develop strategies by which to handle this in ways which they hope children will understand — 'Not every one can sit on my lap Melanie, therefore it's unfair to let you do it'. Reason and emotion do not always fit comfortably with one another. The feeling of lack remains.

Gradually, children learn to hide or to disguise their feelings. They learn, or at least try to learn, not to be a 'cry baby', they learn not to be babyish, the boys learn not to be 'sissy', they learn to be 'a big boy/girl now'. A certain hardness begins to develop and they learn how to 'get their own back'. From under the protective hardness, the hurt child shouts back in spite or punches out.

School presents children with a kind of structure they have not met previously. It is the first model of the kinds of institutions mass society generates. In it can be found all the parallels with government, places of work, and the institutions of the welfare and social services. Thus when they first go to school they are learning more than how to read and write and add up.

Learning to Live with a Stranger

At school, children are initiated not solely into the prescribed adult cultures of art, maths, science and so on. Schools are in the business of moulding characters both at intentional and unintentional levels. They are vehicles by which children are introduced to a whole range of personae, some ascribed to them, some they embrace willingly, and some which hover like ghosts above them, ghosts with names like 'governors', 'politicians', 'employers', and 'police'. They find out at first hand how adults operate within hierarchies of authority, what adults want them to respect and what adults want them to fear and abhor. It is like, but not exactly like, learning one's role in a play. The characters of the play are learnt through the various dramas that are played out day by day upon the playground, the classroom and in the head teacher's office.

Take for example, the kinds of play which we saw occur before our son's experience of school and then immediately after his first experiences of school. Before, play centred around using Lego-style building blocks, drawing, creating little townships with animals, people etc. After, play consisted in fighting, war games, using toy guns, tanks, soldiers and so on. School effectively taught violence. How? To be sure, not in any obvious way. Indeed, the school was itself philosophically opposed to any display of violence either in play or in its overt curriculum materials; it even discouraged any form of competitive activity which would reinforce the sense of winning or losing necessary to any war game. So how did it happen?

One explanation is:

> Children come all differently prepared and from different home background. I mean some children are taught to be aggressive at home (. . .)

Also:

> Children should retain their own individual characteristics and personalities. I mean obviously, sometimes it has to be, well some of their behaviour has to be modified to a certain extent to fit in so that they don't upset the other children. You know, you can't have a child who's pressing, um well, punching around and hurting the other children. At the same time, I think if you squash them too much you squash that (. . .) Some children are very, are going to be leaders when they grow up and they've got a certain, perhaps slightly aggressive and dominant kind of nature that you, you know, you shouldn't squash entirely. You know, you've got to get them to channel it so it's acceptable in society and the people they're with. You know, I think if you never let them be aggressive then they never learn to cope with it and the other children don't learn to

cope with it. I think you can't protect them too much. I mean they've got to learn to cope.

School is a stage upon which to act out a host of emergent personas and roles and also act out the dramas which arise as those personalities come into relationship. None of these dramas is arbitrary, even if they are not planned by anyone. They are culturally available. I asked our son about his memories of his early years; after a little talk I asked him to write about this:

> I never used to make friends easily as I didn't understand you had to endure being called names, and calling your friends names. I was also never brought up to fight, so I never fought anybody, in other words I was weak and cowardly. I've always hated school, now it's worse. I use to always look to the future as if it could be better. I've always been interested in girls, the only time I had girlfriends was at (second first school).
>
> I feel school is slowly destroying my ambitions and making me into some sort of dictionary.
>
> I never understood violence or the need for it in school. I still don't understand it but I'm slowly getting more violent.
>
> I always remember the 'bible bashing' and 'brainwashing' singing.
>
> The jump between Middle school and Secondary I remember.
>
> The teachers didn't work with you anymore, they worked against you. Many of the people I knew became more violent to put on a 'hard' image, including me.

When I went to (middleschool) I was really looking forward to it. I was put in a class which had a year older kids in it. They were excellent at messing about.

> I was horrified they were throwing chalk about (I do it without thinking now.) The girls teased me, I had no friends. It took three years to join a group of them, even then I didn't like them much, I was just with them for protection. Clothes were important, I didn't think so, so I was a snob. I liked writing and drawing so I was also a snob because of that.

What can a parent say in response to a child who asks what to do when other children want to fight? Fight back? What do you say when the child says, 'but I always lose'? Do teachers help? No, it's running and telling tales. Anyway, who can prove who hit whom first? Also a telling-off by a teacher is quite meaningless, their control and authority does not extend very far. We enrolled our son at Hapkido classes (a Korean martial art). He is now a green belt, enthusiastic and can take care of himself.

The Parent's Last Words

Currently, there is a fiction called THE PARENT which politicians of all parties use to support their various partisan views of what parents want. Robert Nisbet (1976) described in one of his books the gradual erosion of the rights of the parent and their usurpation by the state. One of the last of these rights was that of being able to educate their own children within the family. I am not trying at this point to set up the ghost of some dim and distant 'golden age'. I don't believe there ever was one. It is important, however, to bear witness to, and to recognise the gradual loss of rights that has largely rendered individuals and families powerless to take many major decisions vitally affecting their own lives. Equally, it is important to recognise the immense benefits accruing to modern life, made comfortable by technology, sophisticated forms of social organisation and liberated by the values of democratic politics and philosophies. Yet, within this cocoon of scientific and economic comfort, there is also much to fear, much to regret. I see education as having a vital role in all this and especially, I see the role of the parent as fundamentally educational. Let me try to explain what I mean by education.

Firstly, I mean by education an action which can only arise from the individual, and which happens to people or between people in ways which challenge their perception, augment their awareness of life and enrich their experience. In short, education is the key activity through which individuals grown stale with habitual ways of thinking and acting may recover a real power to act, to change, to reform, or to appreciate positively (not passively) the achievements of a society. Since it is an activity which occurs for people and among people it is also the key activity through which individuals meet and grow into a knowing and expressive relationship one with another. Hence, it is a relationship central to the parent-child experience. Yet, schools have traditionally kept parents out of the educational process. Why?

Jules Henry (1971) provides what I think is a major reason in one of his essays when he writes

> 'The history of American education in the last hundred years . . . shows that education has not considered the child's interest but that of industry; and I am not yet convinced that what is good for General Motors is good for our children. Even less am I convinced that what is good for the Pentagon is good for them.'

This can be set alongside statements made by many leading politicians of the British government of the 1980s. For example, the Chancellor of the Exchequer considered that 'we should now think about training young people for the jobs which are', as he put it, 'not so much low-tech as no-tech'. Recently an official at the Department of Education and Science said something similar. 'We are beginning to create aspirations which society cannot match . . . when young people . . . can't find work which meets their abilities and expectations, then we are only creating frustrations with . . . disturbing social consequences. We have to ration . . . educational opportunities so that society can cope with the output of education . . . People must be educated once more to know their place.' (Cohen, 1986)

This is not something new. It can be found in the arguments surrounding the very introduction of modern mass schooling in the 1870s. It can be found in the fears raised amongst the ruling classes from the earliest charitable initiatives in schooling the children of the working classes. The fear is that educated people might question their station in life, might look around them at the better off and begin to wonder why. Parents typically want the best for their children, and that often means the children doing better at school to have better jobs and life chances than they themselves. However, in an economy based upon inequalities of wealth and opportunities, such demands can be destabilising.

Apart from the economic sphere, education results in a radical shift of awareness. This in itself can be frightening. It can disturb the complacent acceptance of routines, habits and beliefs. All educational movements in history have unsettled the old ways of thinking. Socrates could not be tolerated by those who saw his teachings as corrupting the youth of the city. Thus he died. Think of the major revolutions in thought brought about by the work of Copernicus, Galileo, Darwin. In the twentieth century change has been rapid. Technological advance, riches and greater personal freedoms have been accompanied by war, great poverty and the rise of totalitarianism and fundamentalism. Education is not some luxury add-on, it is not just a warehousing of the young until they are old enough. Think of the controversies that in Britain have surrounded education, the charges of political indoctrination often levelled during the 1980s at some left-wing local councils. For example, the *Daily Express* (May 23, 1987) in the run-up to a general election, ran an article by Laurie Norcross, under the title *LEFT-WING MENACE DES-TROYING OUR SCHOOLS*:

> For education this is the most important election since the war, and perhaps the most crucial ever. The choice is clear. Do we want parents to be free to choose the best State schools, so forcing teachers to improve the quality in order to get their custom?
>
> Or do we want to see the onward march of left-wing socialism in education?

Together with this article was a catalogue of right-wing complaints against the alleged lunacies of the left-wingers. These included comments upon the left-wing causes such as anti-sexism, anti-racism and the publication of booklets with such titles as *Talking About Young Lesbians*, or the *Playbook for Kids about Sex*. An article by Frances Beckett in the *Times Educational Supplement* (June 5, 1987) exposed many headlines like these as being false, basing her article on a report by researchers at Goldsmiths' College. Whatever is the truth of these matters, it cannot be argued that education is not of political concern. It is deeply political. It cannot be otherwise, because it acts upon people. Schools are political devices, funded and fostered by governments to fulfil a range of social, economic and political goals. A school curriculum in a totalitarian state cannot be the same as that in a democratic state. The more tolerance a government shows for the diversity of opinion and action, the freer will be the curriculum of the school. Only truly free societies can tolerate a truly free education. Freedom and education are inextricably linked. If we as parents wish our children to grow freely, then we must watch carefully their progress through school and we must know what we mean by freedom. We cannot let politicians usurp our role and act upon our behalf.

It seems to me that any education worth the name should seek to:

1. create conditions in which children can freely, yet safely, explore the environment;
2. support the creative exploration of each child's creative energies, grasp of the world and inner experience;
3. provide access to cultural resources;
4. offer a means by which the expressions and actions of the child can find ever more creative and assured realisation in the world;
5. realise that education confers the dignity of having and expressing rights;
6. understand that education takes part within a community but is in itself and essentially an individual experience;
7. confirm that education serves the individual in the expression of individual experience and serves the community in facilitating the sharing of cultural forms.

These propositions were embedded in the educational experiences of my son's early days at school. Since that time I have been, as an educational researcher and a supervisor of student teachers, into many schools at every age level. In general, the younger the age range catered for, the more likely more of these propositions are realised in practice. Nevertheless, few schools are as committed to child-centred forms of education as the school my eldest son went to first.

I was reminded of that school and of another similar local school in which I frequently conduct research, when I saw, during a research period in Spain, schools desperate to move towards democratic forms of teaching. They were painfully conscious of their years of totalitarianism under Franco and were determined to eradicate from their forms of teaching those authoritarian styles which by engendering a passive response to authority supported totalitarian politics. I saw clearly the fragility of democracy, of freedom and of individual dignity, and I saw how essential was the role of education in supporting these.

In whatever modern mass society we look, school is the child's first model of the kinds of institutions mass society generates. In it can be found all the parallels with government, places of work, and the institutions of the welfare and social services. In it they meet all the personalities, learn all the social dramas, learn their place in society, and learn the degree to which they can challenge, change and manipulate. It is the first public stage upon which a child may hope to act educationally. Did we make the wrong decisions in still sending our children to school? At this point we are unsure. We hope the experience of meeting people, learning to deal with them on their own terms and yet still conserve an inner strength, still maintain a creative attitude to life, will later serve them well if they meet other difficult times. However we are sure that schools must change if they are to have a truly humanising and educational influence upon children and thus upon society. To that end the parents' last words must be to ensure the right of participation in the education for freedom of their children.

References

COHEN, G. A. (1986) 'No habitat for a shmoo', *The Listener*, 4 September.

HENRY, J. (1971) *Essays on Education*, 23, Harmondsworth, Penguin.

NISBET, R. (1976) *The Social Philosophers*, London, Paladin.

SCHOSTAK, J. F. (1986) *Schooling the Violent Imagination*, London, Routledge and Kegan Paul.

7
'They're too Young to Notice':
Young Children and Racism

Ian Menter

Introduction

Jane, a 19 year old White student teacher on her first teaching practice, will set the scene. She is working in a reception class at a medium sized primary school on a large council estate in a provincial city.

> The racism thing is very hard here because it's such a white area, so it doesn't come up naturally to celebrate Diwali or anything because you've got no children in your class that tell you about it at newstime . . .

> . . . I felt up to now I haven't trusted the class enough to . . . be able to take in a story book that say had African children in it. I'm not entirely sure what their reaction would be and I want to get more settled in and perhaps discuss it with the classteacher first . . . I think they'd all sort of shout out 'Oh they're Black!'

> We have a bookclub on a Tuesday . . . The parents and children are supposed to choose a book together, take it home, read it for a week and bring it back. That's quite interesting because the children either just pick the book up or the mums sort of push them into which to choose. There's one lovely story about an African boy called Jafta which no-one ever takes, nobody has borrowed it, which is quite interesting. So I think they're probably quite prejudiced already but I've not felt confident enough to start doing anything, because I don't want to start something which I can't carry on. If I was going to bring it in, just raise the issues one week and be gone again . . . It's got to be constant, not brainwashing, but constant ideas. You only become aware of things if you're constantly seeing examples.

> So it's the tricky situation of being aware but not being totally sure of how to overcome it, for me personally . . .

> I'm not sure what they'd come up with and I'd be very scared if I did start
> reading a story and they started shouting insults at the pictures and I said
> 'No, don't do that' and they said 'Why?', I'm not sure I'd know what to
> say . . . it's not worth doing something halfheartedly[1].

What Jane has expressed so well in these extracts is the power of racism among the
youngest infant children as well as the feeling, commonly expressed by those
teachers who do perceive racism, of powerlessness to counteract it.

In this chapter I want to explore the magnitude of the problem of racism for
those who work with young children. It is important to do this because the usual
portrayals of racism as disaffection are associated with older people[2] and because, as
will be demonstrated, the nature of the racism is so contained within the children's
own culture that it can be almost or completely invisible to adults, whether parents
or teachers. In addition, throughout the chapter, I will indicate how this racism is
not simply a matter of personal attitudes, whether of children or adults, rather, it is
part of a complex phenomenon which pervades the very structures of our society.

On one or two occasions I touch upon the way in which issues of racism and
sexism connect. Given the limitations of space, however, I am not able to give this
important question adequate consideration. Nevertheless, I hope that by reading
this chapter the reader will be able to identify some of the similarities and differences in the two areas. The separation is problematic for practitioners because both
issues occur simultaneously and so have to be acted upon or responded to simultaneously[3].

I start by discussing some of the problems in defining racism and in defining
disaffection. Both concepts are difficult to define and become even more difficult in
the context of understanding young children. Some of the problems in earlier
attempts to link these two concerns are considered. On the basis of my own understanding of the two terms I then discuss what I refer to as the social construction of
racism and how this may shape the experiences of young children, both Black and
White[4]. By then focusing on the question of whether young children can *be racist*, I
move towards a concluding discussion of the implications for those who work with
young children. Throughout the chapter I draw on the experiences of a number of
teachers and writers to illustrate the points I am making.

Defining the Problem

'Racism' and 'disaffection' share two features. They both carry negative conno-
tations and they are both difficult to define. The combination of these features
renders any attempt to discuss them inherently contentious and emotive. Nevertheless clear definitions are essential if progress is to be made. One of the first difficulties with 'racism' is that it is apparently based on an acceptance of the notion of
'race'. Certainly, 'race' has a strong common sense meaning in society, but biolo-
gists have shown that those differences commonly associated with 'race' — that is

external physical features — are of minute significance. That is, the range of differences **within** any 'race' is statistically more significant than the differences **between** 'races'. For most purposes therefore, there is, in the words of the slogan, but 'one race, the human race'. The notion of 'race' as a distinguishing feature of groups of humans must therefore be seen as an idea which has been socially constructed rather than as a scientific fact. From the strong belief in individuals having 'racial' origins, the creation of a strongly felt notion of 'us' and 'them' follows. 'Us' refers to members of 'our race and 'them' refers to members of 'other races'.

What then is racism? Though recognising the social basis of 'race' I am not denying the very real existence and significance of racism, to the contrary in fact. 'Racism' is the term which describes those inequalities in society which affect people according to their identification as members of one 'racial' group or another. It is also important to note that the term 'racism' has tended to replace 'racialism' in recent years. The latter term was usually synonymous with 'racial prejudice', a feature taken to relate to the psychology of individual or groups. 'Racism' as well as incorporating such notions is usually taken to emphasise societal and political aspects[5].

The formula 'Prejudice plus Power equals Racism' is often used to convey this contemporary understanding. I would argue that this can be misleading if it is still taken to mean that prejudice is the root cause of racism. Experience and history show that changing the attitudes of those in power by itself is not enough to remove racism. It is the power structure itself which must be changed as much as the individuals within it. This is the basis of the assertion in this society that racism is a White problem. That is, for historical and economic reasons, the 'racial group' which is in the position to benefit from racism in Britain is White people. Nevertheless, if the promotion of racism is based on the occupation of a position of power in society, an interesting question may arise in looking at young children. As members of a social group themselves, all children are relatively powerless, in this society at least[6]. The question must arise therefore, whether children can actually 'be racist'. This is a point to which I will return.

In common parlance the most frequent coupling of the term disaffection is with the word 'youth'. Thus 'disaffected youth' is often invoked in discussions of young adults and teenagers. It is less usual to see 'disaffection' applied with regard to younger children. However, when it is used in the context of schooling, it is normally associated in some way with the dispositions of pupils. It often equates with 'alienation' and certainly conjures up an image of children for whom school seems to be a problem and, simultaneously, children who seem to be a problem for the school. The effect of discussing disaffection in education is to focus discussion very much on the children, sometimes to the extent of ignoring the wider context which may well be what is giving rise to the problems.

When the two terms under consideration are brought together, this last point has particularly grave implications. In discussions on 'race' and education over the last thirty years there has been a recurrent tendency to 'blame the victim'. That is, discussions about race and disaffection in education have frequently been about 'disruptive Black children'. For example, if one looks at a well-known book on infant education by Alice Yardley, the underlying concerns in her discussion of 'immigrant children' are clear.

> In some schools the children have a good command of English and are not at all self-conscious about the colour of their skin, but still find great difficulty in fitting into an English way of life and our school system. Factors which give rise to cultural problems are:
>
> 1. Indefinite discipline in the home. In Indian families, for example, women have few rights and children have little regard for them . . . These children resist female discipline, yet need the love of a stable mother figure . . .
> 2. . . . Girls are as forceful as boys and go out for what they want with amazing drive and tenacity. The inferior status of girls in the home creates a deep-seated need to be noticed in school.
> 3. Many immigrant children are highly intelligent and often devise cunning ways of getting their own way in a society where they feel different and up against the odds[7].

Perhaps the crude stereotyping in such an extract has become much clearer with the passage of time since 1976 when this was written, but it is nevertheless startling. There is also a clear indication of how sexism and racism often intersect. Views such as these can be described as amounting to a pathological perception of Black children and their families. Such perceptions have been very influential in the thinking of educationalists during the 1960s and 1970s and, it has been argued, have been a major cause of the over-representation of Black children in special schools and special units, especially those for children who have been labelled 'maladjusted'[8].

In what follows now I seek to turn this approach upside down by showing why, if we are to focus on children, as we do when discussing disaffection, then it is the alienation represented by racism that should be given primary consideration. In other words it is the racist disaffection of White children that must be as much a part of our concern as the experience and behaviour of Black children. Furthermore, because of the way in which I have defined racism as structural as well as personal, the limitations of this discussion should be apparent. Working simply on the behaviour and experience of children, even if we do consider White as well as Black children, will not by itself solve the problem. Other steps must be taken, many of which may be deemed 'political', if we are to work seriously towards the elimination of racism.

The Construction of Racism

How then does racism in society impinge on the lives of young children, Black and White? Through answering this question we may start to see how children's understanding of 'race' and racism are created and to get some insight into how these understandings, in turn, are 'lived out'. Through taking five of the social institutions which shape everyone's experience — the state, the media, the community, the home, the school — we can appreciate the great pervasiveness and diversity of forms of racism to be considered.

Firstly then, the state itself can have a very direct impact on the lives of young children. The divisive effects on families of the Immigration Act and the general threat to all Black people raised by the Nationality Act must create insecurity for children in those families. With the help of one of her teachers at an infants' school in Hackney, Zeynep Hasbudak has told the story of the eventually successful attempts of immigration officials to deport her father. Similarly, the style of policing experienced by children who live in areas with large proportions of Black people, means that those children really do have experience of a police state, with all that that implies[9]. The popular media, such as TV and comics, have a profound influence on virtually all children. I was reminded of this on a recent visit to a nursery school.

A 4-year-old child was showing a painting, which she had just completed, to her teacher and some other children. She had painted a wide brown border all around the large piece of kitchen paper. Inside this frame was a large yellow sun, a human figure and some yellow 'ground'. She explained that this was a picture of Africa. The frame, she said, was because she had seen Africa on the television, in a programme about hungry people.

What was unusual about this incident was the apparent consciousness of the source of her image of Africa. I wondered how long it would be before the TV frame was forgotten and her image of sun, sand and starvation became real in her mind. The general absence on TV and in other media, of Black people, especially positive images of them, which has been well documented[10], provides a distorted picture for all children. Those children living in areas with large numbers of Black people don't recognise 'their society' in these images. Those children in predominantly White areas are left ignorant of the nature of the wider society in which they live.

Within the community also, children are exposed to manifestations of racism.

I remember as a probationary teacher the day a 6-year-old Black girl in my class came to school in an anxious state. Later in the day she told me that the letters 'NF' had been daubed on the front door of her house during the night. Her whole family had been very frightened by this.

Racist graffiti is all around in cities and in areas where Black people are in the minority they can experience outright verbal abuse. One young Black woman in Bristol has recounted how, as she walked her two young children home from school, a group of White youths called out 'There goes the nigger woman with her Black bastard children'. Recurrent experiences of this kind led her to seek rehousing in an area with more Black families. Her children were also able to go to school where there were other Black children[11].

The role of the home in constructing children's reality has long been seen as fundamental. The reproduction of racist myths is readily recognisable for teachers when children make such statements to them as 'My dad say Black people are taking all our jobs' or 'My mum says I mustn't take this book home again. It's for Black people'.

> A dinner assistant overheard this conversation between two white middle infant girls: 'Is Charlene [Afro-Caribbean] coming to your party?' 'No — whites only at my party'. When the little girl who was having the party was later questioned by her teacher about what she had meant, she said that that was what her mother had told her when she asked if Charlene could come.

This kind of assertion not only induces children into prejudiced ways of thinking, it creates the very categories themselves upon which racist ideologies are built, the notion of 'race' and the identification of an 'us' and a 'them'.

Finally, the school itself. How does the experience of school shape the 'racial' understandings of young children? One of the clearest messages for many children is that teachers are White. This can occur even in schools where the great majority of children are Black.

> November 1985 in an urban infants' school. It's lunchtime and seven 4-year-old children, four Black and three White, are being served by the (White) student teacher who is sharing their table with them. 'Could you serve out the potatoes, Amy, while I serve the meat, please?' Amy is White. Stephanie, the Black girl who is sitting next to Amy, says 'Miss, can I serve out the peas?' Before 'Miss' can answer, Robert, the Black boy on her other side, calls, 'No, Stephanie can't be the teacher. She's a little Black girl'.

Until recently the majority of resources in schools did little to reflect the reality of this society and still today it is common to find schools where representations of Black people are negligible or non-existent. Indeed it is still all too easy to identify biased or insensitive materials.[12] Several primary teachers from predominantly White schools, on a recent multicultural education in-service course, indicated that their biggest problem was convincing their colleagues that the books, pictures and play equipment in their school should reflect the cultural diversity of society. 'It's just not relevant here, they were told'.[13]

These five sources or sites of children's experience have been presented in this discussion as if they were all separate and distinct. In reality of course there is often a strong mutual reinforcement between them and an interlocking which may well have the effect of securing racist ideas in young children's minds.

Can Young Children be Racist?

Given the pervasiveness of racism which has been described in the foregoing section it should not be surprising that we can identify ways in which young children become involved in racism. White children can be drawn into the culture of racism and indeed become its active promoters. Alternatively, they may learn to identify and resist it. Black children on the other hand can personally experience the material and psychological effects of racial abuse and discrimination but they too may learn ways of resisting.

The views about young children held by many child-centred educationists, certainly until recent times, now seem very naive. For example, while the Plowden Committee devoted a whole chapter of their 1967 Report to *Children of Immigrants*, their view is essentially one of childhood innocence:

> Most experienced primary school teachers do not think that colour prejudice causes much difficulty. Children readily accept each other and set store by other qualities in their classmates than the colour of their skin. Some echoes of adult values and prejudices inevitably invade the classroom but they seldom survive for long among children. It is among the neighbours at home and when he [sic] begins to enquire about jobs that the coloured child [sic] faces the realities of the society into which his parents have brought him.[14]

This view contrasts strongly with some of the experiences already recounted but perhaps most strikingly with this story from an infants' school:

> A 5-year-old boy was sitting at a table looking at books in a corridor, where he thought he was unobserved and would not be overheard. He watched a Black YTS trainee walking towards him on her way to the staff room. As she drew level, he said: 'Ah, you Black bastard'. The young woman went over to him and quietly asked him how he would feel if she had called him a 'White bastard'. He was speechless. The Headteacher, whose office door was open, overheard all this and apologised to the YTS trainee. The trainee appeared quite unperturbed, saying that she was used to that sort of thing, 'Not to worry, it happens all the time'.

The notion that children do not notice skin colour nor make any valuative associations with it has been completely dispelled by research work carried out by social psychologists on both sides of the Atlantic. Ellen Goodman's classic work on race awareness in young children was first published in the USA as long ago as 1952. She studied 4-year-old children and showed that skin colour was a very significant aspect of the children's developing self-identity along with other aspects such as age and sex. Further she found:

> The fact is that mere intellectual awareness of the physical signs of race is not all of the story. There is another part which is not merely startling but quite shocking to liberal-humanitarian sensibilities. It is shocking to find that 4-year-olds, particularly white ones, show unmistakable signs of the onset of racial bigotry.[15]

Work of a similar nature was carried out in England during the late 1960s and early 1970s by David Milner. He carried out a number of experiments which suggested that many Black children were developing poor self-esteem and held negative self-concepts associated with their blackness, from a very early age. He advocated multiracial education approaches as a way of boosting Black children's self-esteem. Milner's work was strongly criticized by Maureen Stone who argued both that it promoted a 'deficit' view of black children and their culture and that multiracial education would do nothing to overcome the poor performance of Black children in schools. It was essentially a diversion from the main function of schools which was to equip children with the basic skills of literacy and numeracy.[16]

More recent empirical work by Alfred Davey and his associates indicates that Black children in Britain do not typically suffer from poor self-concept. Davey writes:

> In contrast to many earlier studies, which have stressed the importance of own-group rejection by minority group children, our findings demonstrate that both minority and majority group children have a strong sense of group identity. On the other hand, the pattern of ethnic group preferences showed that the majority children clearly perceived the advantages of being White. A well defined sense of personal worth, accompanied by a sharp perception of depressed relative status, is likely to prove a socially explosive mixture, unless we are more successful than we appear to have been in educating children for living in a multi-ethnic society.[17]

Most children had already developed these understandings by the age of 7 or 8.

The social psychological evidence then strongly supports the arguments advanced earlier in this chapter. Young children are growing up in a society in which racism is a pervasive feature and from a very early age they learn the significance of 'racial' identity. In other words, in this society, young children are strongly 'racialized'.[18] In spite of the research which has been carried out on the formation of racial awareness and identities, major problems remain however, arising from the lack of understanding of the process of attitude development and of the connections between attitudes and behaviour.

Firstly, it is often suggested that with young children there is a one-to-one correspondence between attitudes and behaviour, but some evidence from considerations of racism would suggest the contrary. Goodman, for example, found among her 4-year-olds a marked reticence about 'public' expression relating to race.[19] A story told by Robert Jeffcoate illustrates this phenomenon:

> The headteacher of an 'all-White' nursery school collected fourteen photographs which portrayed Black people in a variety of situations and in a respectful and unstereotyped way. The headteacher's intention was to present the photographs differently to two sets of children. With the morning children she would try to stimulate discussion by asking questions about salient features, other than those related to 'race', whereas with the afternoon children she would merely draw their attention to the pictures without asking questions and so presumably

encourage a freer response. Her hypothesis, that in neither group would there be reference to skin colour, nor indeed would any disparaging remarks be made, was fulfilled by the morning group, where the experience was 'mediated' by the headteacher. However, with the afternoon group, the response was very different. The children were observed and taped by a researcher who reported that after three or four minutes, the children began to make very negative and derisory comments about the people in the pictures. The discussion was punctuated with cries of 'Ugh, Blackies!' Eventually, hostility reached such a pitch that the headteacher felt obliged to intervene and close the session.[20]

Secondly, there is the question of whether attitudes shape behaviour or whether behaviour and experience lead to attitude development. Thirdly, there are great uncertainties about the longer term aspects of attitude development. For example, if a young White child apparently holds strongly racist views does that necessarily mean he or she is likely to be a racist as an adult? Might the reverse not be possible in fact? There is clearly a need for further research around these questions.

The problems raised for teachers are difficult indeed. If children are already learning to hide their racial attitudes from authority figures such as teachers, how can those teachers objectively assess the scope and nature of the problem, let alone respond to it? On the whole, teachers are better equipped to respond to children's behaviour than to their attitudes and have a repertoire of appropriate strategies. The theme of implications for teachers is one which will be developed in the last part of this chapter.

Before that however I wish to look at the closely linked question of young children's moral and political development. Those who have worked with young children or are parents will be all too aware of the strong sense of justice which children develop. While 'That's not fair'! often has an egocentric motivation, it is nevertheless based on a notion of morality. Furthermore, children often apply the same logic when supporting others, with what might be seen as altruistic motivation. Olive Stevens elicited the political understanding of 7- to 11-year-old children and demonstrated that the 7-year-olds were well on the way to developing abstract concepts such as equality, justice, authority and freedom. Many features of young children's social play provide the basis for the development of such concepts (turn-taking, sharing out). The children also demonstrated a high level of awareness of many current political concerns in society. This seems to come largely from television although also from discussions with adults, Stevens found.[21]

Nevertheless, in spite of the apparent sophistication of young children's awareness and understanding, racism persists. Indeed in many situations, the personal manifestations of it, such as name calling, are commonplace. A study carried out by Shahnaz Akhtar in first and middle schools in the provincial and 'quiet' city of Norwich led to the conclusion that 'non-White children face considerable and continuous racist abuse from white children'.

A four year old Asian boy reported: 'one boy in another class in my school hits me every day and he said, "I want to pull your skin off and I want to bring your White skin out".' Another first school boy said: 'I like my friends. They help me when gangs come to fight with me and my friend because we are not White, but we also hit them very hard. One girl and some boys call me and Haroun "chocolate". Then we fight with them. I tell my teacher. She tells them off but they forget and we tell the teacher again . . .'.[22]

In these schools it was apparently difficult to find any teachers who acknowledged the extent, or sometimes even the existence of the problem. Three kinds of rationalisation were proffered. Firstly, that 'there is not a problem'. Secondly, 'there is a problem, but it is not a racial one'. Thirdly, 'there is a racial problem, but it is not serious'.

Implications for Teachers

I have shown in these discussions something of the nature of the problem of racism with young children. It is pervasive, sometimes difficult to identify, but damaging to both black and white children. It is most clearly a devastating form of disaffection in the early years of schooling, but what sort of response can be made by those whose responsibility it is to work with young children? As has been indicated already, the first step is to recognise the existence of the problem. This is crucial, but having done this, there is a variety of levels at which responses may be made, although at each level the actual responses will of course depend on the nature of the particular problem identified.

Firstly, at the most immediate level, how can teachers respond to racial abuse or the articulation of racial stereotypes by children?[23] With incidents of racial abuse most teachers who have discussed this seem to be in agreement that discussion with the children concerned lies at the heart of an appropriate response.[24] It is as important to support a black child who has been abused as it is to explain to a racial abuser why his or her behaviour is wrong and unacceptable. At times it may also be important to raise the matter explicitly with the whole class. In instances of repeated racial abuse, especially if they are from the same children, the parents will have to be brought in. In any case it will be important, in order to create a secure and non-racist environment for all the children, that parents are not merely made aware of the concerns but are invited to support the stance of the school.

With the aim of creating such an environment, it is important to identify a second level of action for teachers. This is the matter of curriculum and resources. A school where incidents of overt racism are rare is likely to be a school where positive images of black people are promoted through books, displays, topics covered and so on. The under-representation of black people amongst the teaching profession will tend to undermine this, but that in itself is only likely to be solved if black school pupils experience school as a safe, stimulating and supportive environment. One of the ways in which many black children are disaffected from school is through the simple failure of the school to recognise the culture of its children. One black student teacher recalls her experience:

> As a non-English speaking 4-year-old I was thrust into the throes of the English education system in 1966. There I found myself in a sort of 'cultural limbo'. Having spent four very important developmental years of my life learning to talk, feel, think and even dream in Gujerati, I suddenly discovered that for a large percentage of my daily life this way of functioning was to be suspended. In fact I was strictly forbidden to speak Gujerati at school ... in the playground to speak Gujerati would bring forth hurtful taunts and jibes from non-Gujerati-speaking, monolingual peers. Mimicking was the most hurtful; the embarrassment and shame to ensue from the reflection of oneself in the gibbering, grimacing westerners was intense ... This sad state of affairs continued well into the fourth year of secondary school from which point I tentatively started to rebuild my tattered self-concept.

It is remarkable, but fortunate for the teaching profession, that the writer of this recovered sufficiently from such a severe experience of disaffection to enter teaching herself.

To recognise cultural diversity is in itself unlikely to be enough, for it does nothing to challenge the racism within society which the children are exposed to. One clear aim of anti-racist teaching will be the development of critical awareness in children, so that they are able to identify racial injustice when it occurs and themselves respond appropriately. This might range from questioning the portrayal of black children in a book,[25] through reporting of racist graffiti, to simply asking their teacher why there are no black teachers in the school. These are just examples of the kind of things which happen in a school which takes its opposition to racism seriously. Racism is a serious infringement of children's rights.

A third level of response is at the level of policy. A significant number of Local Education Authorities and schools have now adopted written policy statements on racism, racial equality or multicultural education. While the function of such statements will be different for schools and LEAs, what is certainly important in either case is the process of policy development. The discussions entered into between White and Black people, between professionals and parents and between professionals themselves will determine whether any written policy is worth more than the paper it is written on.[26]

To conclude, I return to Jane, the first year student on her first teaching practice who set the scene for this chapter. The school she went into is a school that is highly regarded for many aspects of its work, including the relationship between the school and its community. However, Jane's experience indicated very clearly how this is not a school which has yet developed its practice and policy in the way indicated above. While teachers and student teachers like Jane continue to identify the problem of racism there is hope that progress can be made towards limiting its damaging effects on Black and White children. As Jane poignantly demonstrated the task is a difficult one. However, the worst thing that could happen is that the issue is ignored. There remains an urgent need for teachers and other early years workers to unite around this concern. For, if racism is not countered during children's early years then what hope is there of successfully countering it later? While such work alone will not be enough to eliminate racism, without it there is little hope of a just and humane society emerging in the twenty-first century.

Acknowledgements

I would like to thank Gill Crozier, Penni Gregory, Kay McFarlane, Naseem Moolla, Iram Siraj-Blatchford and Mary West for their help in the preparation of this chapter.

Notes

1. 'Jane' is the fictional name of a student whom I interviewed while carrying out some research on the subject of teaching practice in initial teacher education during 1987. See I. Menter (1988) *A Study of Teaching Practice and Supervision at a Polytechnic Department of Education*, Research Report, The College of St. Paul and St. Mary, Cheltenham.
2. For an good example of this, see R. Cochrane and M. Billig (1984) 'I'm not National Front myself but . . .', *New Society*, 65, 255-258.
3. For further discussion of the connections between sexism and racism in education, see: L. Davies (1987) 'Racism and sexism' in S. Delamont (ed.) *The Primary School Teacher*, Falmer Press. Several chapters in G. Weiner (Ed., 1985) *Just a Bunch of Girls*, Open University Press are very pertinent.
4. Throughout this chapter I have used the word 'Black' as a political term to describe people who experience racism. I am therefore including members of a variety of 'minority ethnic groups'.
5. The definition of 'race' is discussed in S. Rose and K. Richardson (1978) *Race, Education, Intelligence*, National Union of Teachers. For further discussion of definitions of racism, see C. Jones (1986) 'Racism in Society and Schools' in J. Gundara *et al.* (Eds) *Racism, Diversity and Education*, Hodder and Stoughton. The development of racism is lucidly explained in a series of books published by The Institute of Race Relations. See especially Book 1, *The Roots of Racism* (1982) and Book 2, *Patterns of Racism* (1982).
6. The weak political position of children in British society is discussed by Bob Franklin in the first two chapters of B. Franklin (Ed.) (1986) *The Rights of Children*, Blackwell.
7. A. Yardley (1976) *The Organisation of the Infant School*, Evans. Elsewhere I have included a longer extract from this text, which regrettably reveals yet more sexist and racist stereotypes. See I. Menter (1987) 'The Primary Purpose of Swann', *Forum*, 29, 2, 50–54.
8. There is not the space in this chapter to give detailed consideration to the issue

of 'maladjustment' and Black children, nor to consider the processes by which negative teacher expectations are created and fulfilled. For further reading on these points see B. Coard (1971) *How the West Indian Child is Made Educationally Sub-Normal in the British School System*, New Beacon Books; C. Butler (1979) 'ESN Revisited?', *Issues in Race and Education*, 22; 'The Swann Report' (1985) *Education For All*, HMSO.

9. Zeynep's story is told and illustrated in Z. Hasbudak and B. Simons (1986) *Zeynep — That really happened to me . . . .* ALTARF (All London Teachers Against Racism and Fascism). See also *Issues in Race and Education* (1985), 45, 'Deportations, an issue for schools'. Further insights into issues raised concerning police and young people may be gained from *Issues in Race and Education* (1982), 36 ('Police Force the Issues').

10. On media racism see P. Cohen and C. Gardner (Eds) (1982) *It Ain't Half Racist, Mum*, Comedia/Campaign Against Racism in the Media.

11. *Black and White*, BBC1, 12 April 1988.

12. See S. Zimet (1980) *Print and Prejudice*, Hodder and Stoughton; G. Klein (1985) *Reading Into Racism*, Routledge and Kegan Paul. For a discussion of the promotion of positive images see N. Browne and P. France (1986) 'Unclouded minds saw unclouded visions': Visual images in the nursery' in N. Browne and P. France (Eds) *Untying the Apron Strings*, Open University Press.

13. The course referred to was a short course at the College of St. Paul and St. Mary, Cheltenham, called 'Multicultural Education — Strategies for Change in Primary Schools'. On the question of anti-racist education in 'all-White' schools, see C. Gaine (1987) *No Problem Here*, Hutchinson. There is an increasing amount of research evidence which demonstrates the way in which schools reinforce racial categories. See for example: C. Wright (1987) 'Black students — White teachers' in B. Troyna (Ed.) *Racial Inequality in Education*, Tavistock; G. Crozier (1989), 'Multicultural Education — Some unintended consequences' in L. Barton and S. Walker (Eds) Open University Press.

14. The Plowden Report (1967) *Children and their Primary Schools*, Vol. 1, HMSO, paragraph 179. For a recent critique see D. Winkley (1987) 'From Condescension to Complexity: Post-Plowden schooling in the inner city', *Oxford Review of Education*, 13, 1, 45–55.

15. M. E. Goodman (1964 edn.) *Race Awareness in Young Children*, Collier-Macmillan, p. 245.

16. Milner reviewed his original research, partly in the light of Stone's criticisms. The debate has been discussed by Madan Sarup. See: D. Milner (1983) *Children and Race Ten Years On*. Ward Lock; M. Stone (1981) *The Education of the Black Child in Britain*, Fontana; M. Sarup (1986) *The Politics of Multiracial Education*, Routledge and Kegan Paul, Chapters 3 and 4.

17. A. Davey (1983) *Learning to be Prejudiced*, Arnold, p. 173.

18. The notion of racialization has been used to describe developments in education policy by Bob Carter, Barry Troyna and Jenny Williams. See, for example, B. Troyna and J Williams (1986) *Racism, Education and the State*,

Croom Helm or B. Carter and J. Williams (1987) 'Attacking racism in education' in B. Troyna (ed.) *Racial Inequality in Education*, Tavistock. However, the way in which I am using it here to describe an aspect of identity formation has affinities with studies of gender differentiation. See, for example, E. Belotti (1975) *Little Girls, Writers and Readers*, Schocken, for an 'early' classic study, or S. Askew and C. Ross (1988) *Boys Don't Cry*, Open University Press, for a more recent analysis.

19. Goodman, *op.cit.*, p. 266.
20. Adapted from: R. Jeffcoate (1979) *Positive Image, Writers and Readers*, see pp. 13–14.
21. O. Stevens (1982) *Children Talking Politics*, Martin Robertson.
22. S. Akhtar and I. Stronach (1986) 'They call me blacky', *Times Educational Supplement*, 19 September, 23. See also the report: Commission for Racial Equality (1988) *Learning in Terror*, CRE.
23. In an interesting report on a survey of infant teachers in 1986, a team from Leicester University found that 22 per cent of their sample had experienced discussions between children in which racial stereotypes were used. The authors suggested a variety of strategies which teachers might use to deal with these or other difficult incidents. See: A. Anning *et al.* (1986) 'Attitudes and the infant teacher', *Child Education*, June, 15–22.
24. A very clear and concise approach to tackling racial abuse in schools is set out in G. McDougall (1986) 'Racist Incidents in the Primary School', *Primary Teaching Studies* 1, 2, 12–15.
25. An interesting example of this is provided in the film 'Racism — the Fourth R', when some young children write letters to a publisher about the use of grey colouring to denote Black children. This film is available from ALTARF, Room 216, Panther House, 38 Mount Pleasant, London WC1X 0AP.
26. For assisting in the development of policy and practice within schools the following may be useful: chapters by Tibbetts, Walsh, Mulvaney, Milman and Francis in M. Straker-Welds (Ed.) (1984) *Education for a Multicultural Society*, Bell and Hyman; ALTARF (1984) *Challenging Racism*, ALTARF: D. Houlton (1985) *All Our Languages*, Arnold; D. Houlton (1986) *Cultural Diversity in the Primary School*, Batsford; J. Durrant and J. Kidner (1988) 'Racism and the under-fives' in A. Cohen and L. Cohen (Eds) *Early Education: The Pre-school Years*, Paul Chapman; ILEA (1984) *Education in a Multi-ethnic Society: The Primary School*, ILEA, or write to 'Building Blocks', Castlemead Estate, The Rampway, Camberwell Road, London SE5, for a copy of 'An early years curriculum for a multi-cultural society'.

8
School Ethos and the Individual within a Community

Val Wood

Introduction

As a new head of a primary school, I started to keep a diary. Five years on, I wrote:

> The school has changed over a period of five years. It has become more
> open to change. My feelings have changed — I no longer want to drive
> past the school each morning rather than meet the challenges each day
> brings. The people in the school are working together towards common
> purposes. There is a sense of unity though not uniformity. Visitors say the
> children are friendly, open and confident, and that they are engaged in
> purposeful activity. The adults, in the main, listen to the children with
> interest and with respect and treat them with friendliness. The people in
> the school and in the neighbourhood care about the school. There is
> virtually no vandalism directed at the school and it has not been broken
> into for three years. Parents still tell their children to hit back when
> someone hits them — we're still working at that as well as many other
> things. Things like helping a mum to see that although she thinks 'Come
> here you 'orrible dirty little . . . ', 'get out and shut up' are terms of
> endearment, there is a possibility that little Jimmy will not only grow up
> thinking he's horrible and dirty but also that he may shut up altogether.
>
> Situated on the edge of a large estate of Local Authority Housing on
> the fringe of a northern city, we need to work very hard at belonging to
> the community of which we are part. Traditionally, schools have been
> seen almost exclusively as the places where children go to learn. Parents
> have in general stayed out — they may even have been kept out. As a
> result of changes in attitude on a national level, parents' role in children's
> learning is gradually becoming acknowledged and given recognition.
> Parents who achieved well in the school system themselves may easily be
> persuaded that their support and help is wanted and is valuable. They
> may feel comfortable relating to teachers and openly discussing such
> things as children's books and learning to read. Parents who were less

successful in the school system are not only reluctant to discuss reading because their own literacy skills are inadequate, but frequently find the school environment and teachers in particular very threatening. This school welcomes its parents and makes provision for them. It tries to accept the differences in their experience and to convince them that they have something to offer.)

We don't think 'we've cracked it' but we do believe that through adopting sharing attitudes which have implications for every part of the institution — organisation, responsibility, care and control of children, curriculum, parents and community — we are creating an 'atmosphere', an 'ethos' in which children can learn and want to learn. The organisational structure of the school and the attitudes it portrays are designed to give out messages of welcome, respect and involvement in an attempt to counteract the feelings of fear and alienation that may be experienced.

Individuals in the Institution — Some Implications

An average-sized 5 to 9 years first school like this attempts to cater for two to three hundred children. Each child is a unique individual, and although it may be possible to describe an average 5-year-old or an average 8-year-old in terms of height and weight, or a reading or maths score based on national statistics, it is virtually impossible to estimate the level of skills acquisition both practical and cognitive, or the amount of knowledge stored or attitudes developed with any degree of meaningful accuracy.

Within the school institution, working alongside the children are a number of adults: teachers, parents, cleaners and ancillary workers, each one an individual. Any attempt to achieve good working relationships in the institution must take account of that individuality and make provision within its daily life for expressing personal opinions and for meeting individual needs. By providing opportunities for individuals to take an active part in the running of the institution each person is helped to feel that he or she belongs to the whole institution.

The knowledge, skills and attitudes held by adults are the result of large numbers of experiences and situations through which the individuals throughout their lives have been enabled to make better sense of the world in their terms. A framework of understanding is built to which reference can be made as each different and new experience is encountered. The flexibility of the individual framework is of paramount importance, but as individual experiences are different, likewise the degree of flexibility will vary. The notion of flexibility and openness of mind is an apparently desirable state and as such will be identified and owned by many adult individuals, yet, because of differing perceptions, it will mean different things to different people.

The range of experiences, attitudes and knowledge which children bring with them on entering school is also vast. It may be hard to envisage a point of contact or establish common goals for a child who regularly goes rabbiting with his grandad and another who spends his/her holidays in Tenerife. The gaps in understanding between them provide pitfalls for curriculum planning. Barret[1] highlights the implications of differences in children's experience and consequent understanding. School does not always take account of these differences in its expectations of children and raised levels of anxiety can often result. Anxious children are not free to learn from what is offered. Pringle[2] identifies four basic emotional needs which must be met from birth and that enable a child to grow to mature adulthood. These are: the need for love and security; for new experiences; for praise and recognition; and for responsibility. Parental responsibilities are paramount in these areas for the infant and toddler. The fact that the necessity of meeting these needs may extend into adult life reinforces the desirability of a growing and continuing understanding and cooperation between home and school. In a school like ours this is doubly important.

Home and School

In the early 1900s Margaret McMillan's pioneering work in her nursery in Deptford set out to decrease the gap which she felt existed between home and school.[3] She deliberately tried to convince parents that their attitudes to education played an important part in shaping their children's educational attainment. The Hadow Report on the Primary School[4] gave importance to Parents' Associations, open days and sports as 'opportunities for contacts between teachers and parents', but was a pale reflection of McMillan's vision. Isaacs[5] and Mellor[6] both made important contributions to the developing debate. The Milwaukee Project and the Head Start programme in America concentrated on family intervention and compensatory education in support of children who were socially and culturally deprived. An alternative concept, and one that would attribute due regard to the worth of individuals and their right to accept responsibility and to make choices, would be complementary rather than compensatory education. The school needs to come to terms with the values and aspirations of the community it serves rather than implicitly opposing them, thus establishing a smoother and more understanding relationship between the home and the school. This is what we hope we are working towards.

School then, in an area of so-called 'deprivation', has a daunting task to perform over a long period to make itself a welcoming place and to help parents realise that teachers are people (as well as to help teachers realise that parents are people).

Sharing 'baby talk' and informal discussion about homes and families can help. The first ten to fifteen minutes of each day is 'children and parents time'. Parents come in to talk with teachers and to change their children's books. A relaxed beginning to the day at which information can be exchanged between parents and teachers helps to build confidence and again assists in bridging any gap that might exist.

Any one of our parents is likely to be a so-called 'school failure' who did not understand or enjoy school and maybe even encountered rejection. Feelings of failure may have engendered hostility and a considerable amount of blame. Parents who themselves had a poor experience of school are especially fearful of failure for their children but may not know how to prevent it. Do teachers understand this, I wonder? Teachers themselves have experienced success in the education system. Few of their parents are manual workers, skilled or unskilled. Burgess (1973)[7] suggests that those who have such parents quickly adopt attitudes and aspirations which make them indistinguishable from the rest. All this means that the background, education and life style of teachers in a school like ours is vastly different from that of most of the children they teach and most of the parents with whom they come into contact. Middle class or aspiring middle class parents identify with teachers' attitudes and assumptions. People who live in poorer areas, so-called socially and culturally deprived, tend to have different values and assumptions and find it difficult to fit naturally in school, they may find school remote and be put off by attempts to attract and interest them.

> 'We don't like meetings'. 'There's too much reading in letters you send home'. 'Why don't you do writing like you do for the kids?', have all been given as reasons for not reading invitations to come to school. Twenty-one parents attended our annual parents' meeting this year — an increase of eight on last year. A free crèche was offered to enable them to come. Not many of those who attended had read the governors' report to parents that had gone out to each family in school two weeks earlier. 'There was too much reading' was given as the main reason.

Lack of understanding and a minimum of close contact by teachers with children from poor backgrounds may have profound and far reaching implications. Teacher expectation affects children's school performance[8][9] but teachers' expectations are rooted in their own background and upbringing. Is it possible that teachers spot ability in middle class children more easily than they do in children from less advantaged backgrounds? Personal experience has shown that this happens with frequency and consistency.

> Ability in children from advantaged homes often manifests itself in facility in spoken language, book skills and personal confidence. Children whose homes are devoid of books and in which reading is not valued will not show the ability that is expected by teachers. An assessment such as 'lacking in ability', 'low ability' or 'has no language' may then be made.

If this discrepancy is seen by parents, and I suggest that there is every reason to suppose that this is so, it is hardly surprising that parents from less advantaged homes find school remote, difficult to approach and to identify with. It seems likely then that the parental involvement movement may widen the gap rather than close it unless of course we adopt positive strategies in our schools to ensure that parental involvement is effective regardless of background.

In the current pursuit of excellence and what conversely is seen by some as a levelling down to equality we are in danger of losing the real concerns between the apparently opposing viewpoints. We have seen how the school may be perceived as an alien environment and how much better equipped and closer to 'the system' some children are on entering school because of the match between middle class children and teachers' thinking. It cannot be argued then that all children are equal but to be offered equal opportunity is the right of every child. What may not be equal is individual capacity to make use of opportunity, so we need to cater for, accept and value individual difference, making full use of the range of knowledge and experience that individual children bring to school with them. Excellence should not be viewed narrowly in terms of achievement within a single subject area but across a broad spectrum of human skills and endeavour. Do we build on what children know, think, and are, or do we as Holt[10] suggests 'foster bad strategies, raise children's fears, produce learning which is usually fragmentary, distorted and short-lived, and generally fail to meet the real needs of children'? How do we start to meet these needs?

Changing Schools, Changing Teachers

'A good school, in short, is not a place of compulsory instruction, but a community of old and young, engaged in learning by cooperative experiment' (Hadow 1931). To what degree does this contain an accurate description of today's teacher let alone a teacher in the 1930s? Regardless of developments in thinking and trends in teacher education, many young teachers, unless appointed to a school in which they are encouraged to think and question and enabled to grow and develop, appear to regress to a comfortable, clearly defined framework of teaching based on either their most recent memory of teaching (usually their own secondary school) or a contemporary model (sometimes a bad one). This is not intended to be a criticism of teacher education, although sometimes that is appropriate, but rather a comment on the inadequacies of early post training experience and to emphasize the immense responsibilities that are carried by school staff in the ongoing training of teachers. That probationary teachers are still faced with 'you can't sit there, that's my chair' or 'we don't want any of your new-fangled ideas here', is a sad reflection on parts of the teaching professions and could be viewed as an expression of fear. Fear of change, fear of altering the status quo or rocking the boat. What people know and understand, what is predictable feels comfortable; change, the unknown can be full of fear and anxiety and threat.

If a school is to meet the wide variety and ever changing needs of the people who serve it and whom it serves it must itself be conversant with change and grow and develop according to the needs of those people. Its curriculum must be a living entity, growing and developing as new thoughts and ideas emerge.

There is little to be gained from talking about 'learning through drawing' and 'the value of work based on first hand experience'. What makes it a reality is seeing the children's skill developing through observational drawing and recognising that by digging a bucketful of potatoes they are learning a whole range of skills, concepts and knowledge. Knowledge — that potatoes grow under the ground. Skills — peeling, cutting, cooking. Concepts — cutting, sharing. Does a kilo of potatoes produce a kilo of chips plus peelings? How many people will be fed? The potential for learning from digging one's own bucketful of potatoes is vast and wide ranging but has to be seen to be believed.

The school's organisation should develop and change as the people working in it make new demands on themselves and on the children. Change at its most effective does not come from above but from among and is a response to a perceived need, but change may lead to stress and maybe conflict. The reactions will be as many and varied as the individuals involved and will range through denial and avoidance to confrontation. To say that the key to effective change is communication seems almost to trivialize the complexities but in a climate where discussion is encouraged, where consultation is the norm and where to say what one thinks is acceptable and what one says is accepted, there is likely to be a greater confidence in the system as well as an increased view of individual self worth. It is obviously important that the words actually used in the communication convey the same meaning as the actual messages behind the words.

Opportunity for dissension must always be given. The courage needed to voice dissension when there is consensus all around is hard to achieve.[11]

As well as communication a significant key to change is the notion of acceptance. The value of the individual, his/her uniqueness and worth as a person, child and adult, is central to a view of school that I wish to portray. That each individual child and adult has thoughts and opinions, needs approval, has values, aspirations, fears and anxieties, experiences stress, is sensitive and has immense potential for learning are fundamental and pervasive principles. The practicalities of reflecting all-pervading beliefs in the life and work of a school are monumental. There are implications in terms of leadership and management, organisational structure,[12] decision making, curriculum, teaching and learning, care and control, the school environment, equipment and materials, communication,[13] interpersonal relationships, attitudes to parents and the community, responsibility, equal opportunities — in fact every aspect of the life and work of the school needs to be an expression of the beliefs it holds. Acceptance, respect and recognition, regardless of attitude, race, gender or background are the rights of all people. Parents need to know that we respect them as their children's teachers as well as people. To show them that this is our belief demands change in the attitude of some teachers. 'Parent support' and 'parent cooperation' are terms reminiscent of fund raising and parents' associations — very good of course in their own way. 'Parent involvement' is suggestive of a much more fundamental, all-pervasive role for parents in which the natural course of events is followed from birth, parents being almost exclusively the child's teachers until he/she enters the education system. Then the child's education becomes a partnership in which each participant recognises and values the role of the others[14] and in which parents actively support the work of the school by becoming involved in children's learning.

Children's needs for love and security, for new experiences, for praise and recognition and for responsibility, identified by Pringle and mentioned earlier in this chapter, certainly appear to be needs which, if met, promote growth and learning throughout human life. That people need new challenges, need to be recognized, praised and encouraged and to learn to accept responsibility with increasing competence not only applies to children and parents but to all the school's people, adults and children. It is the supportive framework however, the building of open and trusting relationships, by *being* increasingly open and trusting that enables this development to take place.

Changing Leadership

'It's OK not to know all the answers' is one of the first things that the leader needs to learn.

> Gradually I am learning I don't have to be in total control. 'Ted will be able to help you with that' or 'I don't know, Sharon might', contributes to the idea of building a team of people who are valued as individuals and for the skills they offer. Individuals then develop in leadership roles themselves.

Gradually after that realization dawns and is declared, the leader's position moves from the top or the front to somewhere in the middle. He/she moves from a leading leader to an enabling leader. There can be other changes too. Not everyone needs to look to the leader for all decisions. Individuals recognise that their contributions are capable of influencing the development of the institution. There can be dialogue between all the members. Other individuals can feel confident 'not knowing' and take steps to 'find out'. The enabling leader needs to recognise potential in another person, assist in its realization and then have the ability to stand back and watch that person take initiative and assume a leadership role. In this way, not only are individual needs met, but there is benefit to the whole institution.

A school built on traditional lines with individual classrooms is not necessarily conducive to the promotion of cooperation and continuity. An Open Plan school lends itself not only to cooperative planning but also to sharing ideas, mutual support, continuity of approach and of learning. The climate of the school in which the leader leads from among, in which it's all right 'not to know', in which opinions are sought and valued, where individuals are respected and where responsibility is accepted as a means of growing, promotes corporate planning, meaningful dialogue, free flow of ideas and sharing of space and resources. This kind of climate is also indicative of a view of children as intellectual beings who deserve a high level of educational provision.

Older children in the school research the story preferences of younger children, write stories to match the research and then both read the stories to them and present the books for their bookshelf. Young children are thus presented with a good model for learning — quality handwriting (so that it can easily be read by young children) clear story line and high quality illustration as well as book making skills.

Teaching and Learning for Everyone

'I hear and I forget. I see and I remember. I do and I understand', has been a guiding principle of many effective teachers through the ages. A curriculum that focuses on first hand experience as the most meaningful way to learn underlines once more the view of children and their intellectual development. Experiences range from artefacts to examine, through simulated situations in drama, to visits near and far.

Children need to learn about the potential for learning in the immediate environment of their homes but also to have the opportunity of a wider view of the world. To go to market and bid for ducklings, buy their food, build their shelter, measure their weight gain as well as their food intake, to rear them for several weeks before returning them to market to sell is an experience packed with real and relevant learning. A real-life situation of conflict transferred into a problem-solving experience in drama makes high demands on children's intellect and its resolution has tremendous implications for learning what it feels like to stand in someone else's shoes.

Identification of purpose and careful detailed planning reinforce the centrality of the value of the individual. That work is presented with care, is well matched to individual need, is interesting and stimulating and makes use of high quality materials also reflects the principle of individual worth. Communication between learners, both adults and children, reinforces the importance of the learning process as more greatly to be valued than the end product. Discussion between teacher and child helps towards the realization that the result need not always be either right or wrong. Children can find out that making mistakes is an acceptable and comfortable way of learning and not to be feared. Teachers learn much about the thinking and reasoning processes of children.

Children's art has been a contentious issue in many a staffroom I have known. Opinion has ranged from 'I want it to look like what it's meant to be' to a genuine recognition that children's drawing is related to their understanding of the world and how they perceive it and needs to be valued as such. Children's own original work is what is important to achieve, not second-rate adult work filled in by children. Much discussion has taken place about the need for teacher intervention, the use of ready mixed paint and the over-use of felt tipped pens. Children can and do learn to mix their own colours, choose appropriate paper for their work, select their media. They learn in the process about size, colour, texture, shade and relationships and the product is individual and unique. Within the process the individual child has been enabled to develop further understanding, thinking and his/her perception of the world.

Organisation of and choice of equipment and materials, the way in which work is marked and presented, the standard of cleanliness and tidiness, are all a reflection of how an institution views itself and its people and how it wishes to present itself to the outside world. Materials and equipment that are carefully labelled and stored enable children to accept responsibility and assist them towards working independently. Equipment and materials that are selected for their high quality are not only more durable but they are also more pleasant to use and often encourage higher standards of work.

The way children's work is marked directly relates to how people are viewed and valued and the way they learn. Pages of ticks are hardly indicative of active learning or of learning through a process. They may be telling us that this child has had enough practice. To receive a piece of work looking like a battlefield must be soul-destroying, especially if 'I thought it was my best ever story'. Marking work when the person who produced it is not present is a denial of the whole purpose of learning. The learner's perception of both the process and the product is an essential part of learning. Dialogue between the teacher and the learner is what consolidates the learning and poses questions for future learning.

The books we choose, if they are to reflect our view of individuals and their worth, must not only be of the highest quality in every way but must also depict males and females in a range of roles as well as give value to a diversity of cultures. Equal opportunities must be an integral part of our whole school approach and all the members of the institution need to be aware of the subtle ways in which stereotyping occurs and actively work to prevent it in all its forms.

School must be pleasant, relaxed and as comfortable and clean as possible, always enhanced by interesting and stimulating displays and a variety of children's work. Children know the extent to which we value their work by what we say about it and by the way we present it for public view. It is also another way of showing value for the individual. Carefully mounted work with unobtrusive use of colour enhances the environment, shows the work is valued and also assists in increasing expectation. Examples of all children's work need to be displayed — never 'the best' — who can judge that anyway? Criteria for selection need to be various, 'I like your use of colour', 'This time you've managed to use several different greens in your leaves', 'I got really scared when I read your story', 'Your poem really made me hear the sea'. HMI believe that the headteacher is the key person in the establishment of the ethos of the school. Ethos is concerned with attitudes and values, but appearance is also important. If the school caretaker/superintendent and the cleaning team feels valued as part of the whole school team and support the values and beliefs of the other members of the team then its aims are more likely to be achieved.

Recognition, praise and encouragement, new experiences and responsibility have been suggested as needs not only of children but also of adult people and are important throughout life. To have corporate or collective responsibility for the work, life and attitudes of a school as a member of the teaching team can be daunting but it can also be stimulating. It certainly ensures participation and gives individuals recognition. Consultative decision making, at times corporate decision making, is also demanding but it makes the theory of individual worth a reality.

> By presenting, for example, several alternatives for discussion with regard to the organisation of the open plan area for the new school year; through discussion to reject one, then another and finally to adopt an adapted third is more likely to achieve commitment to the plan than if it had been imposed.

It means too that all opinion is listened to, accounted for and utilised in making decisions that affect the whole institution. It can mean greater job satisfaction but it can also mean greater commitment. Individual development is dependent on openness to new learning and on a view of education as a life long learning process which is fed by new experiences and greater responsibility and nurtured by recognition, praise and encouragement. Teachers need to be offered opportunities to learn new skills and to practise forgotten ones just as children and parents do. Similarly they should have a framework of support — knowledge that it's all right 'not to know' and 'it's OK to make mistakes'. Praise and encouragement could lack enough precision to be meaningful so it is important for people to know how they are performing. Reports and references must be discussed openly between the individual and the leader and used as a basis for further learning.

Policy and Action

Careful planning of the communication system in a large institution is vital if it is to be successful. Topics ranging from, who bumped his head at dinnertime, who is visiting today, how much capitation money is left, to the development focus for this term, need to be communicated. Strategies that ensure that the appropriate messages are communicated to the people who deal with them must be implemented.

How do children know we like them? Is it obvious to them that the underpinning value of our institution, its very life blood, is the worth of individuals? Are children's experiences those of fairness or favouritism? Criticism or encouragement? Do they experience love, care and respect or are they ridiculed, despised and rejected? Are they enabled to learn in a stress-free supportive environment or are unrealistic expectations made? The reality is that children carry with them any anxieties and stresses that are their experience in other parts of their lives. Part of function of the school is to understand this and to be supportive while at the same time creating the kind of environment that is conducive to learning, that will not tolerate destructive criticism, ridicule, favouritism and stereotyping, and which practises fairness, love, care and respect regardless of race, gender, age or handicap.

It is one thing to have a clear philosophy and clear principles. Where implementation makes demands on resources — in-service training for teachers, visits for children, curriculum planning — principles are not enough. The provision of a rich learning environment, raising teachers' expectations, the establishment and maintenance of home school and community links, and a broadly based relevant curriculum are all principles clearly set out in Local Education Authority initiative of which this school has been a part.[15] Resources, personnel as well as financial, have been made available to enable development to take place. Change and development of this order could not have happened so quickly without the level of support that has been available. It has been a city-wide initiative, a response to need whose stated aims happen to reinforce the beliefs held in our school. No one is suggesting that this model is definitive. A lively developing school is constantly growing and changing, not changing for change's sake but responding to the demands, ideas and challenges of its people as well as looking further afield to influences which it believes will be beneficial to its development. When we think 'we've cracked it' it's time to pack up and go home!

Notes

1. Barrett, G. (1986) *Starting School: An Evaluation of the Experience*, Final report of an evaluation of responses of reception children to school. Commissioned by the Assistant Masters' and Mistresses' Association.
2. Pringle, K. (1975) *The Needs of Children*, London, Hutchinson.
3. Margaret McMillan's work is described in Bradburn, E. (1976) *Margaret McMillan: Framework and Expansion of Nursery Education*, Denholme House Publishing.
4. Haddow, (1931) *The Primary School — Report of the Consultative Committee*, London, HMSO.
   It is interesting to compare the ideals set out in this report with the practice in primary schools today, e.g., Introduction p. xix 'Subjects are not independent entities, but divisions within the general field of knowledge, whose boundaries move and should move, backwards and forwards'. 'The pursuit of primary school studies in the form of distinct and separate subjects was not the method best calculated to meet the needs of young children'. 'What is necessary is that the curriculum of the school should make every use of the environment of the pupils'.
5. Isaacs, S. (1930) *Intellectual Growth in Young Children*, London, Routledge and Kegan Paul.
6. Mellor, E. (1950) *Education Through Experience in The Infant School*, Oxford, Oxford University Press.
7. Burgess, T. (1973) *Home and School*, Harmondsworth, Penguin.
8. Barker Lunn, J. C. (1970) *Streaming in the Primary School*, Windsor, NFER.
9. Jackson, B. (1962) *Streaming: An Education System in Miniature*, London, Routledge and Kegan Paul.

10 Holt, J. (1965) *How Children Fail*, New York, Delta.
    Other work by John Holt includes *How Children Learn* and *The Under-achieving School*. All his work underlines the importance of the individual.
11. Easen, P. (1985) *Making School-centred INSET Work*, Beckenham, Croom Helm/Open University. See Chapter 11 particularly. This book is part of a set of Open University materials called P536: Making School-centred INSET Work. It is a pack, not a course.
12. *Organisational Structure*. It is important to the smooth running of the institution that there is a clear and easily understood structure. In this instance children are arranged strictly in classes chronologically. Because we work in an area of profound need, we have enhanced staffing levels. This enables us to have three teachers to each two classes. The structure can be represented in this way:—

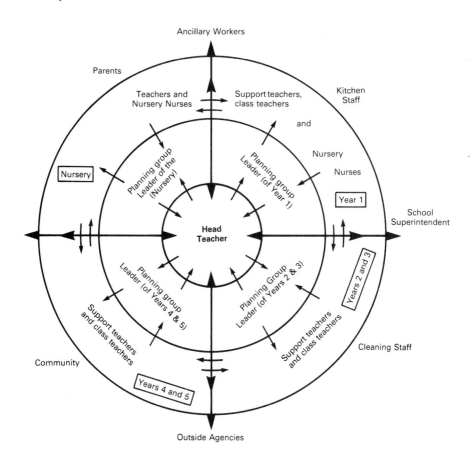

13. *Communication*. It is important that all possible means of communication are used and everything possible is communicated.

Meetings of the four planning groups take place every week.

The four planning group leaders meet with the Head every two weeks.

Planning groups discuss curriculum, organisation, topics of whole school concern as well as individual children.

14. Griffiths, A. and Hamilton, D. (1984) *Parent, Teacher, Child: Working Together in Children's Learning*, London, Methuen.
15. Leeds Local Education Authority set up a Primary Needs Project in 1985 supported and funded by the City Council. Schools are gradually being drawn into the additional resourcing and support that inclusion provides in relation to the needs of communities and teachers. The work of the school is therefore fully supported by advisers, additional staffing etc., because of the commitment, policies and practices of the LEA and Council.

Part IV
Learning and Knowing: Policy and Practice

9
'School starts at five . . . or four years old?' The Rationale for Changing Admission Policies in England and Wales

Martin Woodhead

Introduction

Exploration of disaffection in the early years of school inevitably leads to consideration of the policies that stipulate the period of compulsory schooling. This chapter examines the creation of the laws and policies concerned with children starting school.

The 1944 Education Act requires that children commence full-time education in the term following their fifth birthday, but many local authorities now admit children at the beginning of the school year following their fourth birthday. This trend breaks with long established conventions about the kind of educational environment that is appropriate for children above and below the statutory starting age. The origin of these conventions is explored, first in the debate surrounding the 1870 Act and secondly in reports in the first decade of this century which led to exclusion of under-fives from school and establishment of a separate nursery education sector.

The recent break with convention has come about because of the opportunity created by falling school rolls to meet parental demand for early educational provision. The specific policy of annual admission has been justified educationally as helping to compensate for the disadvantages experienced by summer born children under termly entry arrangements. While annual entry may be the most equitable way of arranging school admissions, questions are raised about whether setting this a year younger will necessarily be to the advantage of summer born children, especially if resources, teaching and curriculum are not modified to suit the very youngest entrants.

This is a shortened version of a paper which first appeared in the *Journal of Education Policy*, Vol. 4 No. 1 1989.

A Small Revolution

Over the past few years a small revolution has been taking place in arrangements for children to start school. Five is the age for beginning full-time schooling in Britain, or so the textbooks say. More precisely parents are required to ensure their children receive full-time education from the start of the term following their fifth birthday. In practice increasing numbers of children are now being admitted to primary school well before their fifth birthday. The purpose of this article is to examine the rationale that appears to underlie these trends towards earlier school admission. The focus will be on England and Wales; developments in Scotland have followed a somewhat different path.

The age of five was first introduced into English educational legislation as part of the 1870 Education Act. However, at that time it was not set as a national requirement. Instead, W. E. Forster proposed five as a minimum age for making education compulsory, with thirteen as the maximum age, and gave local School Boards discretion on the precise policy within these limits. The move towards compulsion from five was strengthened by Lord Sandon's Act of 1876, with the clause that it be: 'the duty of the parent of every child to cause the child to receive elementary instruction in reading, writing and arithmetic', and defined the child as 'between the ages of five and fouteen years'. The relevant clause of the legislation within which current practices are framed strongly echoes that statute of nearly seventy years earlier: 'It shall be the duty of the parent of every child of compulsory school age to cause him to receive efficient full-time education ... etc. (Education Act (England and Wales) 1944, Section 36).

The upper limit of compulsory education has shifted several times since Forster introduced thirteen and Sandon increased it to fourteen. For example, the 1936 Education Act set fifteen as the normal leaving age, and this became universal in 1947. The age of sixteen was anticipated in the 1944 Act and finally implemented in 1972/73.

Meanwhile at the other end of the spectrum, there has been no change at all to the statutory age for starting school, since the 1880 Education Act finally endorsed five as a national requirement. Of course, there has always been some room for manoeuvre over the precise interpretation of starting ages. For example, since the 1960s children have commonly been admitted as 'rising fives', in the term in which they become five (i.e. one term earlier than the law requires). However, in recent years a much more fundamental shift in policy has been taking place. Although this still does not entail a change in the legal requirement for starting school it has important repercussions both for children and for their families. There are two aspects to this shift in policy: increasing numbers of local authorities are opting for single-point annual rather than three-point termly entry, and they are setting this single point as the start of the school year following children's fourth birthday. In a survey carried out in 1986, 37 out of 81 LEAs in England and Wales had a predominant policy of single-point annual admission in their schools; a further 13 had a predominant policy of biannual admission; leaving the remaining 31 with traditional termly entry, although many of these were also admitting children below the age of eight. Indeed the survey only identified 8 LEAs with official policy conforming to the statutory age of entry. (Sharp, 1987, 1988; see also Cleave *et al.* 1985). If present trends continue, it will not be many years before virtually all children will enter primary school before they are five. The age of starting school will have become four, in practice if not in statute.

Probably few parents bringing up young children towards the end of the 1980s are aware of how different their children's experience of starting school will be depending on which local authority is responsible for the schools in their neighbourhood. The two extremes will illustrate the point. In an LEA following the policy of annual entry, a child born on 31st August 1985 would be admitted to primary class at the beginning of the school year beginning in September 1989, (i.e. immediately after his or her fourth birthday). In an LEA following the statutory requirements, a child who is up to four months older than the first child, (i.e. born after Easter 1985, would not be admitted until 12 months later, i.e., September 1990), a discrepancy of 16 months. Such discrepancies are not related in any way to the developmental maturity of the children, or their readiness to receive instruction. They are entirely a consequence of different LEA and school policies on admission.

Such changes in policy may not on the face of it seem to justify the term 'revolution', but there are three important respects in which annual admission is more than a matter of administrative convenience. First, in so far as education can be measured as a commodity in terms of years, it means that children in some LEAs are now receiving up to a year more primary schooling that their contemporaries in others. This policy might seem more dramatic if the year were at the other end of schooling, for example if some LEA's set the school-leaving age a year later than others. Second, at the age of five years old, a year is a very long time in terms of maturation and learning. The new policy means that some children are being introduced to the reception class who have had 20 per cent less developmental life-experiences than children admitted under statutory admission arrangements. Again, to emphasize its significance, the equivalent might be if some universities proposed to admit young people from the age of fourteen and a half, rather than eighteen. Thirdly, unless major modifications are made to the planning of reception-class work, it means that classroom organization, curriculum objectives and teaching styles designed with one age group in mind are being applied to children up to a year younger.

In all these respects recent trends are deserving of much closer scrutiny than they have generally received to date. Accordingly, the first part of this chapter examines these trends in more detail in the context of what little public discussion there has been at a national policy level. This is followed by an historical analysis of the formative influences on traditional patterns of educational provision at school and pre-school level. Against this background, the significance of recent changes in admission policy and practice become much more clear. The next section examines the rationale for such changes in some detail. Finally the chapter explores the specifically educational questions raised by the general trend towards early entry.

Towards a National Policy on Early Entry

Recent trends towards early school admission have come about mainly as a result of local responses to local conditions and pressures, (as a later section will elaborate). Accordingly, national discussion of these trends has largely been responsive too (Farley, 1985; Woodhead, 1986). The nearest thing to a central government policy is to be found in the Parliamentary Select Committee report *Achievement in Primary Schools* which recommended that:

> 'there should be no change in the statutory age of entry into school. However, we consider that local authorities should, if they do not already do so, and under suitable conditions, move towards allowing entry into the maintained education system at the beginning of the school year in which the child becomes five'.
>
> (House of Commons, 1986, para. 5.44)

Only the issue of compulsion seems to stand in the way of this recommendation displacing the statutory definition of the 'school age' child.

Nursery or Primary Classes for 4-Year-Olds?

There is nothing new about a policy of admitting under-fives into the maintained education system. State nursery education was first established under the Fisher Act of 1918, and has had an important if patchy role in local authority provision ever since, especially in helping combat disadvantage and deprivation, (Central Advisory Council for Education 1967). The idea of near universal availability to four year olds, is not new either. The Department of Education and Science White Paper *Education: A Framework for Expansion* (Department of Education and Science 1972) and subsequent Circular 2/73 (Department of Education and Science 1973) took recommendations of the Plowden report (Central Advisory Council for Education 1967) in proposing that sufficient provision should be made available for 50 per cent of 3-year-olds and 90 per cent of 4-year-olds. However, the Select Committee recommendation is not about developing nursery education in the form of the nursery classes envisaged by the proposals of the early 1970s. It is about early admission to the reception classes of primary education, whether in infant, first or primary schools, and while there has been a significant growth in nursery education provision since the early seventies, early admission to primary classes has also seen marked increases.

Statistics for England report that in January 1986 there were 235,867, or 20 per cent of 3 and 4-year-old children in infant classes. The equivalent figure for nursery schools and classes was very similar at 246,893, or 21 per cent of the age group, (Department of Education and Science 1987a). In fact these statistics seriously underestimate the number of children who attend infant classes before they are five. They refer only to children who were under five at the beginning of the second term of the school year. They thereby exclude the 192,376 children admitted as

4-year-olds at the beginning of the school year (in September 1985) who had already become five when the statistics were collected in January 1986 (Department of Education and Science, personal communication). Altogether, over 400,000 children under five attended infant class during the school year 1985/86.

Furthermore, breaking down the figures by age indicates that infant classes are now the dominant form of school environment for 4-year-olds. Only 57,557 of the children in nursery schools and classes in January 1986 were 4-year-olds. The vast majority, (almost 70 per cent) were 3-year-olds, along with a significant number of 2-year-olds. These statistics are for England. In Wales there is a much longer established convention of admitting young children into primary classes, so in January 1986, there were 56,325 children under five in these classes, compared with only 3,927 in nursery schools. (Welsh Office 1986, Table 2.04).

There are marked differences between nursery and infant settings in terms of organisation, staffing, philosophy and curriculum. Most children attend nursery education on a part-time basis, whereas full-day attendance is normal in infant classes, at least after the initial settling-in period. Staffing is more generous in nursery education because of the employment of professional nursery assistants, (NNEB trained); in England in 1986, the ratio of children to adult staff was on average 10.7 to 1 in nurseries (Department of Education and Science 1987a), by contrast with 22.1 to 1 in primary classes. (Department of Education and Science 1987b). Nursery classrooms are dominated by a wide range of play activities and the daily programme flexibly organised around children's preferences. While there is still a place for play-activities in many infant classrooms, systematic introduction of literacy and numeracy skills is a major goal and children's learning is much more strongly structured.

The appropriateness of drawing such a strong organisational dividing line between nursery and primary sectors is of course open to debate; whether primary school teaching might be improved by more generous staffing ratios and greater emphasis on play and imagination, and equally whether nursery teaching might benefit from a more explicit curriculum or even some structured teaching. Indeed, what makes recent trends so significant is the sense in which they challenge long established traditions about the kinds of school environment that are appropriate for children above and below the age of compulsory education. For example, the White Paper *Better Schools* observed:

> 'It is unrealistic to expect a teacher simultaneously to provide an appropriate education for younger four year olds and for children of compulsory school age. Very young children can be introduced too early to the more formal language and number skills and they miss the essential exploratory and practical work through which a good nursery programme forms a sound basis for later learning. Some four year olds are now moved up too early from nursery class or school and suffer similar disadvantage'.
> (Department of Education and Science 1985, paras 125 and 126).

In a joint statement from the two major groups representing those working with pre-school children, the point was put even more strongly:

'We regret that in deciding on a once a year entry policy, the local authorities have turned away from any consideration of children's needs to an arrangement which is mainly concerned with administrative tidiness and convenience.... Most four year olds are not ready to be confined to crowded classrooms without scope for physical and imaginative play. They are still mastering physical skills for which they need opportunities not generally found in the primary classroom...'.
(Pre-school Playgroups Association/British Association for Early Childhood Education, undated).

In fairness, the House of Commons Select Committee also recognised some of the problems created by the early admission policy they advocated:

'The teachers are seldom experienced or trained for children of these younger ages; they commonly have no ancillary help of the kind that a nursery gives; they may have up to 34 or even more children in a class and with an age span from three or four to six or even older; they must give a considerable amount of their time and attention to the development of literacy and mathematical skills in the older children; they rarely have sufficient equipment or the space needed by the younger children'.
(House of Commons 1986, para 5.41)

The Select Committee's response to these problems was distinctly ambiguous. First, they seemed to accept the general demand attributed to parents for early attendance provision with educational objectives, but, while they argued that a nursery school or class may be the appropriate provision for these children, they did not propose their exclusion from school until such time as a nursery school or class could be established. Instead, they argued that where no nursery is available young children should continue to be admitted to infant classes, but at the same time that local authorities should work towards providing conditions in these infant classes (in terms of staffing and equipment) 'which can compare in all appropriate respects with the requirement for nursery classes'. (House of Commons 1986, para 5.45). This goal of improving quality was also hinted at in the White Paper *Better Schools* (Department of Education and Science 1985, para 130).

It is not clear what rate of progress constitutes 'working towards'. But it seems unlikely that local authorities will be quick to enhance the resources available to reception classes to this standard. One of the main reasons for early admission policies is that they go some way to meeting unsatisfied parental demand for pre-school provision, while sparing the cost of capital and recurrent expenditures on building, or converting, staffing and equipping classrooms to nursery specifications. If provision for 4-year-olds were brought into line with nursery classes 'in all appropriate respects', it is debatable whether this would represent a marked saving over establishing nursery classes for all 4-year-olds in the first place. Even if the Select Committee's recommendations on equipment and staffing were implemented within the foreseeable future, important questions would remain about the curricular objectives and style of teaching that is appropriate for 4-year-olds:

whether they are the beneficiaries of spending less time in play-based activities and being introduced earlier to instruction in reading and number work.

These emerging policies represent a break away from long accepted principles about the educational 'needs' of this age group. So as a first step in this exploration of the rationale for policy change, it may be instructive to rehearse what the major influences were on the traditions of schooling from which the new policies deviate, without, of course, implying that these traditions are in any way sacrosanct. Two questions in particular are pertinent. First, what was the rationale for setting five as the age of starting school? And, second, how did nursery education emerge as a separate and in many ways distinctive form of education for children under five?

The Rationale for Setting Five as the Age of Starting

The age of five was introduced into the 1870 Education Act as part of the much wider parliamentary debate about establishing a national system of elementary education. In fact there was remarkably little discussion about the choice of age, no more than fifteen brief exchanges in Committee on July 11th 1870. (Hansard 1870 Vol. 203, Cols 56–59). What little debate there was on this question, was very much subordinated to the issue of compulsion, which aroused strong passions, and took up a good deal of parliamentary time. On the one hand there were those who objected in principle to the denial of parental liberties to decide what was best for their children, and others who argued that for some children school attendance might not be a necessary nor appropriate form of education. On the other hand it was argued that compulsion was only to be seen as a last resort, as a way of ensuring that schooling was available to all children, even those from the most inadequate and neglectful homes. For these children schooling was a form of protection against the evils of life 'in the gutter'.

A rather different kind of argument centred on the role of children in the work force, and it was from this issue that some of the strongest arguments about age of attendance originate. By compelling children to go to school, the State was thereby preventing them from earning a living, which in many cases, it was argued, may have caused real hardship to them and to their families. Add to this the problem of disruption of traditional arrangements for school-age brothers and especially sisters to look after younger ones, and the impact on family economics and organisation would in some cases have been felt severely, but the strongest concern was expressed about the impact of compulsion on the older school-age child. As an example here is a short extract from the Hansard report of Mr. Welby's contribution to the debate.

> He took his stand on the ground that it was necessary that after 10 years old there should be absolutely no restrictions on the labour of boys, such as would be involved by compulsory attendance at school.
> (. . .)

he should show how from them — first, the immense inconvenience to farmers; secondly, the grievous hardship to labourers which would be caused by keeping their boys at school after 10 years old: and, thirdly, that such inconvenience and hardship were wholly unnecessary.
(...)

(Hansard 1870, Vol. 203, Col. 53–54)

Appealing to the problems of 'agriculture' and 'struggling poverty' he then went on to propose an amendment to the Bill to limit compulsion to the early years of childhood:

Send the children to school at five by all means; keep the girls there till 12 if you liked; encourage the boys by every possible inducement to stay as long as they could; but do not prevent them by force, after they were 10 years old, from earning all they could towards the support of themselves and their little brothers and sisters. He would beg to move in page 24, line 22, to leave out 'children', and insert 'boys above the age of five years and under the age of ten years, and of girls'.

(Hansard 1870, Vol. 203, Col. 56)

It was this perceived necessity of an early school completion date and hence an early start date that dictated the course of the brief debate in Committee on this issue. Forster took Welby's proposed recommendation as a cue to clarify the government's position. He proposed that instead of setting fixed ages for compulsion, a minimum of 5 and maximum of 13 be provided as guidelines within which School Boards would have discretion to set their own limits; thereby diffusing the appearance of this being an unprecedented level of State intervention.

The next stage of the debate was dominated by those who considered five years old too early. Two members argued that five was 'too tender an age for compulsion' while another drew attention to the inappropriateness of demanding attendance of young children suffering ill health. At this point Forster showed that his views were not fixed on this issue, saying that 'he was willing, if the Committee wished it, to make six years the minimum' (Hansard, 1870, Vol. 203, Col. 51).

In some respects, six years of age would have been an obvious choice for marking off the age of compulsory schooling. As Szreter (1964) has argued:

Until a few years before the passing of the Forster Act, there had been little in the educational thought and practice of 19th century Britain to suggest that the age of 5 would constitute the dividing line between voluntary and universal education. Thus in Robert Owen's infant school, which he established in 1816, half-time attendance was reserved for the 2–6 age group; Roebuck, as early as 1833, i.e. a few years before it became at all practicable with the passing of the Registration of Births and Deaths Act, advocated in Parliament compulsory education from 6 to 12. Again, Wilderspin, Stow, and infants schools organized in accordance with their ideas, grouped 2–6 year old children together. Froebel whose views became influential in this country in the 1850s, also set his borderline at the age of 6. Generally, only the 'close, crowded, and dirty' dame schools took in children aged 2–6, while charity, parochial, and monitorial schools admitted their pupils at 6, or more commonly at 7.

In most other countries of the world, six *has* been chosen as the age of starting, possibly reflecting underlying developmental changes at this time, for example, in terms of Piagetian theory, children begin to make the transition to concrete operational thinking from around six (Inhelder and Piaget, 1955).

While willing to consider six, Forster's original proposal and preference was for five, and it was five that entered the statute book. The reasons for this being the eventual outcome are clear from the rest of the brief debate. Educational considerations only make up a part of the story. The next major contributor, Mr. Dixon, advocated five by reference to the Factory Act under which 'children were worked as early as they could earn wages. It was right, then that they should go to school early' (Hansard 1870, Vol. 203, Col. 57). He drew attention to cases of children of three years old and even younger attending school. There is certainly something in this argument, albeit a somewhat dubious one. The context of the 1870 Act was an economic system in which as one commentator noted 'Children begin to have a money value as soon as they can shout loud enough to scare a crow, or can endure exposure to the weather in watching cows in the lane'. (Newcastle Commission 1861). It may have seemed to contemporaries inconsistent to argue at the same time that children could not endure the more benign environment of the school from an early age. Besides there was another reason for taking children into school from an early age which had equally little to do with an educational rationale in any direct sense. The next two contributors to the debate weighted up the pro's and cons of recognizing the custodial function of elementary schools in a situation where many homes were of poor standard and both parents were out at work. As Mr. Melly put it: '. . . it would be well that children should be sent to school without the intervention of the gutter, and without the risk of the fire at home'. (Hansard 1870, Vol. 203, Col. 58).

At this point in the debate W. E. Forster reinforced his preference for five as the appropriate age, but the dissenters did not readily acquiesce to this view, and Mr. Candlish now 'moved to amend the Amendment, by substituting six for five'. (Hansard 1870, Vol. 203, Col. 58). Mr. Stephen Cave intervened making clear that he would vote against Candlish's amendment, because he believed that children were better off in school than in the gutter:

> they could not be taught much book learning, and certainly dogmatic theology would run off them like water off a duck's back, yet it was not too early to inculcate good habits

He went on:

> 'The difficulty was to obtain time for education without trenching on the time for gaining a living. He believed that a *system of beginning early and ending early* would present a solution of that difficulty, and that the

infant school and night school would well supplement the ordinary school.'

(Hansard 1870, Vol. 203, Col. 58, emphasis added).

There was only one other contribution to the debate, which had nothing whatsoever to do with the issues at stake, but which had a decisive influence on the acceptance of Forster's original proposal, without further debate, and without a division on Candlish's amendment that would have set six as the starting age. Benjamin Disraeli, then Leader of the Opposition, had been listening to the debate, and he was evidently frustrated about the slow progress that was being made on what to him must have seemed a trivial point. For he now chose to speak, as Hansard reports:

'Mr. Disraeli said, he hoped the Committee would not divide. He was prepared to support the proposition of the Government whether it was 'five' or 'six', as that was the only mode by which they could make real progress with the Bill.

(Hansard 1870, Vol. 203, Cols. 58–59)

The authority of the elder statesman was sufficient to silence the dissenters, Candlish's amendment was withdrawn and the age of five went forward to the statute book.

It is instructive to reflect on this debate of over a century ago in two respects. Firstly, it makes clear that the decision of five was in many ways an arbitrary one, which the Members of Parliament sitting in Committee that day in 1870 could hardly have imagined would have such an enduring impact of the experiences of starting school for successive generations of young children. It is, then, entirely appropriate that the rationale for this tradition be reviewed over a hundred years later. Secondly, this debate demonstrates quite clearly that any specifically educational considerations about when children could most profitably benefit from school learning were overshadowed by a complex of other issues to do with the social conditions affecting families and children at the time and the continuing place of children in the work force. Both these sets of issues pointed towards providing school for children as soon as they were sufficiently mature to cope with the setting and the demands of instruction.

Clearly, in the latter part of the twentieth century, neither of these issues apply in the same way, or even at all. The living conditions of the vast majority of children have improved markedly and certainly the original economic reasons for concentrating their formal education on the early years no longer apply. On the contrary, the prospects for employment are in many cases receding into the distant horizon, and as noted earlier, the age of completing education is becoming extended. Set against this background, the present trend to admit even younger children to school might seem a curious one, but before going on to look in more detail at the rationale for recent trends, we need briefly to consider the second question posed at the end of the last section, about the development of a separate nursery education sector.

The Development of Nursery Education

In the introduction to this paper, reference was made to the Fisher Act of 1918 as having first made possible the provision of state nursery schools for children below compulsory school age. But this was not the first occasion that under fives had been in school. On the contrary. The establishment of nursery education was actually associated with a sharp decline in the number of young children in school! Official statistics show a peak in 1899–1900 when 622,498 three and four year olds attended public elementary schools in England and Wales, or 43.36 per cent of the age group. (Board of Education, 1909, Table 3). Only in recent years has this percentage been matched. For example in 1986 there were 508,623 under-fives in nursery or primary classes in England, or 43 per cent of the age group. (DES 1987a).

What is the explanation for this apparent paradox? The Acts of 1870 and 1876 set five as the age from which attendance at school was to be compulsory, but they set no lower limits on attendance on a voluntary basis; indeed parents had the right to seek admission for their younger children. In practice, children under five had been attending in considerable numbers throughout the middle years of the century, 269,031 in 1869–70, and their numbers rapidly increased towards the end of the century, e.g. 384,046 in 1879–80, and 464,756 in 1889–90 (Board of Education 1909, Table 3, England and Wales). The willingness to admit young children to school stemmed firstly from concern about their care and welfare, especially those vulnerable to the hazards of cramped slums and urban street life. Secondly, and probably more significantly, there was a good deal of pressure from working parents for schools to accept the younger brothers and sisters of older pupils who, prior to compulsion, would have played a major part in their daily care. Even in the 1850s, Matthew Arnold observed from his inspection of young children in elementary schools that 'parents will not send the older children without sending these also'. (quoted by Whitbread 1972).

The authorities' acquiescence to this arrangement is demonstrated by the inclusion of children under five in the calculation of grant, but there was a third factor which also reinforced the trend. The system of *payment by results* introduced by the Revised Code of 1862 extended down to children six years and over. Part of the rationale for early admission at that time was that children were more likely to reach the required Standard I, if they had been introduced to the classroom from an early age (Szreter 1964).

However, the widespread extension of formal elementary schooling among children in their early years during the last century was not without its critics, especially amongst those who had become familiar with the educational principles embodied within the European kindergarten movement, which were inspired by the philosophies of Rousseau and Froebel amongst others. Two official reports in particular can be singled out as most influential both in arresting the trend for young children to be taken into elementary school before the age of five, and establishing the principle of a separate nursery education sector.

The first was the product of an enquiry into the age of admission carried out by five women inspectors, reporting in 1905. The strongest condemnation of contemporary arrangements came from Katherine Bathurst, and caused some official embarrassment (see Introductory Memorandum by the Chief Inspector of Elementary Schools', Board of Education 1905, p. 1). Here is a brief extract from an inspector's on elementary school life in Manchester at the turn of the century, taken from a paper written in 1905, advocating the establishment of a national nursery system:

> Let us now follow the baby of three years through part of one day of school life. He is placed on a hard wooden seat (sometimes it is only the step of a gallery), with a desk in front of him and a window behind him, which is too high up to be instrumental in providing such amusement as watching passers-by. He often cannot reach the floor with his feet, and in many cases he has no back to lean against. He is told to fold his arms and sit quiet. He is surrounded by a large number of other babies all under similar alarming and incomprehensible conditions, and the effort to fold his arms is by no means conducive to comfort or well-being.
> (. . .)
> What possible good is there in forcing a little child to master the names of letters and numbers at this age? The strain on the teacher is terrific. Even when modern methods are in vogue and each child is provided with coloured counters, shells, beads or a ball game, the intellectual effort of combining three plus one to make four, or two plus two for the same total, has no value at such an age. The nervous strain must reduce the child's physical capacity, and this, again, reacts unfortunately on the condition of the teeth, eyes and digestion.
> (Katherine Bathurst 1905, reproduced in Van der Eyken 1973).

These views were echoed in the Chief Inspector's introduction to the 1905 report:

> 'No formal instruction' is the burden of all the recommendations, 'but more play, more sleep, more free conversation, story-telling and obser-vation'. The aim of big town Infant School is too often to produce children who at the age of six and a half have mastered the mechanical difficulties of Standard 1 work. It should be to produce children well developed physically, full of interest and alertness mentally, and ready to grapple with difficulties intelligently'.
> (Board of Education 1905)

The impact of these and other expressions of concern was immediate. In the Code for 1905 the Board of Education introduced the following addition to Clause 53:

> where the Local Education Authority have so determined in the case of any school maintained by them, children who are under five years of age may be refused admission to that school (quoted in Board of Education 1908).

Subsequently the numbers of under fives in school dropped dramatically. For example in England and Wales the figure of 622,498 in 1899–1900 fell to 382,069 in 1909–10 and 186,843 in 1919–20 (Board of Education, 1914, Table 3b; Board of Education 1927, Table 32).

The second influential report at this time was produced by the Consultative Committee of the Board of Education (1908). Thoroughly reviewing the issue of school attendance before five, including extensive reports on practice in other European countries, the Committee came down strongly against school attendance for the majority. However, they recognised that conditions of living and availability of parental care made some form of public provision desirable, and outlined in some detail the kind of provision that would be appropriate:

1. The proper place for a child between three and five is, of course, at home with its mother, provided that the home conditions are satisfactory [...]
2. Under existing economic conditions, however, the home surroundings of large numbers of children who attend elementary schools are not satisfactory [...], and children from these homes should be sent during the daytime to places specially intended for their training.
3. The Committee consider that the best place for this purpose is a Nursery School [...].
5. Formal lessons in reading, writing, and arithmetic should be rigidly excluded from the curriculum of younger infants, and also everything that requires prolonged complex operations of the nervous or muscular systems. Freedom of movement, constant change of occupation, frequent visits to the playgound, and opportunities for sleep, are essential [...] (Board of Education, 1908)

The immediate impact of these positive proposals for young children's education was much less dramatic than had been the impact of the concern expressed about their experience in elementary schools.

It was only after the experience of establishing wartime nurseries that the potential benefits of a nursery education system to serve all children became officially recognized, as, for example, in this extract from the 1943 White Paper:

> ... even when children come from good homes they can derive much benefit, both educational and physical, from attendance at nursery school.
>
> (quoted by Blackstone 1971).

Over the intervening years, some local authorities, especially the large urban conurbations in the north of England, have achieved high levels of nursery education provision, for example in 1986 serving 55 per cent of 3 and 4-year-olds in Manchester, 51 per cent in North Tyneside, South Tyneside and Liverpool, 40 per cent in Sheffield, and 31 per cent in Leeds, (Department of Education and Science 1987a), but provision is patchy and there are vast areas of the country that offer only a very low level of provision, where nursery education is a Cinderella service, whose development consistently takes second place to the more demanding pressures of the statutory sector.

In summary then, '5 years old' has emerged not merely as the somewhat arbitrarily disgnated age for starting school, it has come to mark off two quite distinct sectors of education. On the one hand it marks off a system of universal elementary or primary education which virtually all children attend from the age of five and which has its origins in the need to provide a grounding in the basic numeracy and literacy skills demanded by an industrial economy. On the other hand, it marks off a much less well developed system of nursery education which was established in part in reaction to the conditions of schooling and style of teaching in elementary education at the turn of the century, and is characterized by a distinctive child-centred approach to working with young children. Although the influence of the 'progressive' movement in the 1960's, (especially through the Plowden Report, Central Advisory Council for Education 1967), brought many infant classrooms more into harmony with the informal methods of nursery education, differences in staffing and equipment, curriculum priorities and teaching methods remain to this day.

Viewed against this background of established traditions of education for children above and below the statutory admission age it is much easier to understand why what on the face of it seems a relatively insignificant change in policy on starting ages justifies the term 'revolution'. The next section returns to the contemporary debate, and the rationale that has been offered for breaking away from traditional arrangements.

Breaking with Tradition: Pragmatic Response or Positive Policy

No single clear-cut rationale can be offered for changes in admission arrangements. Since they are not a direct response to national initiatives or trends, but rather to local priorities and circumstances, the reasons for changing policy will vary from one part of the country to another. Indeed, in some cases it may not even be appropriate to apply the idea of 'a changing policy' to what is essentially a piecemeal response to local conditions affecting individual schools. Nonetheless, it is possible to identify certain general features held in common in many situations.

The Context of Early Admission

Firstly, the context of recent developments has been the substantial demand for pre-school provision which, as we have already seen, is only patchily met by a system of nursery schools and classes. We may speculate that a largely unarticulated demand has existed at some level ever since young children were excluded from elementary schools at the turn of the century, but it was not until the early 1960s that the hiatus in publicly-funded nursery education led to the establishment of voluntary, parent-run playgroups. These have grown so rapidly that in terms of children served they now outnumber all other forms of pre-school provision put together. Although they originally emerged as a substitute for state nursery education, playgroups have now adopted a parent-centred philosophy as a distinctive alternative to nursery education and received a good deal of public attention (Plowden 1982; Finch 1984). Experience suggests that, even so, parents frequently seek out explicit educationally-oriented provision where it is available, especially as their children approach compulsory school age. This is presumably in the not unreasonable belief that children will thereby stand a better chance of making good educational progress.

Another attraction of early entry to primary school concerns its convenience to the circumstances of families. Whereas nursery schools, classes and playgroups offer mainly part-time places, the full-time attendance patterns normal in primary classes are frequently more convenient to the increasing number of parents who by choice or necessity are employed in full or part-time work outside the home. Finally, of course, unlike many private and voluntary pre-school facilities, school comes free of charge.

The consequence is that instead of serving as pre-school alternatives, a linear pattern of attendance is often established, with the youngest children attending playgroup and then being transferred to a nursery school or class for a few terms prior to admission to reception class at four or older, according to local practices. This is not to say that all parents necessarily wish their children to be in primary school at the earliest opportunity, but they are likely to feel under strong pressure to comply with early admission policies, for several reasons. Delaying entry might prejudice their chances of gaining a place in the school of their choice, (under the 1980 Education Act), which may already have filled its quota of places at the beginning of each year. There is also the fear that their children might have difficulty catching-up with the educational progress of early-entrants to school.

In passing we may note that introduction of a foundation curriculum from the age of 5 linked to systematic attainment testing as early as 7 years old, (Department of Education and Science 1987b), may well have the effect of reinforcing this pressure for early admission to an educational environment in which emphasis is given to instruction in the competencies covered by the tests. There is a compelling parallel between these trends and the practice of testing to Standard 1 at 6 years old which encouraged early admission in the latter part of the nineteenth century (as discussed above). In this respect it is salutory to note the comments of Edmond Holmes, Chief Inspector at the Board of Education during the first decade of this century, reflecting on the effect of the Revised Code on teachers and children:

> For a third of a century 'My Lords' required their inspectors to examine every child in every elementary school in England on a syllabus which was binding on all schools alike. In doing this, they put a bit into the mouth of the teacher and drove him, at their pleasure, in this direction and that. And what they did to him they compelled him to do to the child.
> (...)
> They must have believed that the mental progress of the child — the only aspect of progress which concerned educationalists in those days — would best be tested by a formal examination on a prescribed syllabus, and would best be secured by preparation for such a test; and they must have

accepted, perhaps without the consent of their consciousness, whatever theory of education may be implicit in that belief.

(Holmes 1911, reproduced in Van der Eyken, 1973)

In short, a combination of educational aspirations and custodial requirements encourage strong parental demand for early entry. These coincide with local authority considerations of efficiency and economy, which, as we noted at the outset, make acceptance of young children into primary classes seem, on the face of it, a more attractive option than nursery education, because of the 'savings' in both capital and recurrent expenditure.

The Opportunity for Early Admission

These considerations of demand and costing provide the context for recent developments, but they have only recently become salient to local authorities and schools because of the opportunity presented by falling school rolls. The birth rate in England and Wales fell from 783,000 in 1971 to 584,000 in 1976. By 1985 it had increased again somewhat, to 656,000 (Office of Population, Censuses and Surveys 1987, Table 2.19). Translated into a supply and demand equation, the effect has been that in 1985 primary school capacity was calculated as 4.6 million places, but only 3.7 million children were in attendance. (Department of Education and Science 1987d). For many schools confronted with the prospect of undersized classes and redundant staff (on conventional assumptions about class sizes and teaching ratios) extending the age range of the school to embrace younger children has been seen as one way of maintaining its established size. For village schools in particular, which have often been threatened by the prospect of closure, early admission has been seen as a way not only of keeping the numbers up, but also of ensuring an early commitment to the school from parents, who might not be able to secure such an early entry from other schools in the area.

From the discussion so far it may appear that changing admission policies are merely a pragmatic response to parental demand and changing school circumstances, but the practice of taking 4-year-olds into school has in many cases been presented as the expression of a much more positive policy. This is especially so where it has been tied to a decision to adopt a single-point entry system, i.e. all new children starting at the beginning of the school year after their fourth birthday. The argument is that single-point entry helps compensate for the long-recognised disadvantages that can be suffered by the summer-born children under a termly entry system (Rogers 1984). In one local authority, for instance (the London Borough of Ealing), a lengthy discussion paper was prepared by the Campaign for the Advancement of State Education (CASE) which successfully argued the case for single point entry at 4+ almost entirely on the basis of this issue. Respects in which summer-born children are at a disadvantage under termly-entry arrangements also informed the Select Committee's recommendation that local authorities move towards allowing entry at the beginning of the school year in which children become five (House of Commons 1986, para 5.42). Accordingly this educational rationale for single point-entry deserves detailed scrutiny.

The Case for Single-point Entry

The law requires that children commence formal education at the start of the term following their fifth birthday. The resulting pattern of three intakes during the year has been traditional throughout the century, and has also been justified as ensuring that all children start school at approximately the same level of maturity or school-readiness (allowing, of course, for the considerable individual variation within any group of same-age children). For over twenty years now, however, questions have been raised about the wisdom of this policy. These questions centre on the experience of summer-born children. Evidence began to accumulate that children born during the summer were over represented amongst lower achieving groups in the school population. In the days when ability-streaming was commonplace in primary schools, a disproportionate number of summer-born children were found in the lower streams, and conversely a disproportionate number of autumn-born children in the upper streams. (Jackson 1964). Another researcher examined a sample of children described by teachers as 'backward readers', and found that nearly half (46.7 per cent) were born during the summer months (Freyman 1965). The same pattern was found in schools for the educationally sub-normal (Williams 1964). Other research showed a similar effect on children passing the 11-plus examination. In one County Borough in the early 1960s, 59.4 per cent of successful candidates were born in the first six months of the school year; of children born in the second half of the year (i.e. including summer-born children) only 40.6 per cent were successful (Jinks 1964).

The explanations for these findings are, it can be argued, all linked to conventions of school organization. Certainly, they do not reflect any differences in the native ability of children born at different times of the year. Indeed, if anything research on intelligence during the very earliest years, before school has made any impact, suggests that summer-born children perform, on average, very slightly better than autumn or spring-born children (Barker-Lunn, 1972).

The first disadvantage suffered by summer-born children is due to the convention of organising children into year groups, based on a school year beginning in September. Through this convention, summer-born children are always the youngest in the group. At every stage in their educational career, for every assessment, however informal, and in every selection procedure, either internally within the school or as public examination, they are the youngest in the group. If their relative immaturity were always taken fully into account, (as in standardized tests for example) this might not matter. In so far as they are judged by simple comparison with other members of the group, then their relative immaturity may place them at a disadvantage. Also, there is evidence that despite their claim to treat children as individuals, primary school teachers do tend to judge the older pupils in the class to be the more 'able' pupils (Bouri and Barker-Lunn 1969). Needless to say, since this disadvantage is the result of a convention about setting the start of the academic year in September, any change to it would enhance the position of the summer-born child relative to other birthdates. While schools are organized into year groups based around the month of September, children with summer born birthdays will always be the youngest in the class. It is important to note at the outset that this disadvantage is not remedied by a move to annual entry.

The second disadvantage faced by summer-born children is based on another convention, and is modified by a move to annual entry. The traditional interpretation of the statutory requirements for commencing school produces a pattern of admissions three times a year, at the beginning of each term, as children become five, but every other school transition is normally organized on an annual basis, so while children join the reception class on a termly basis, they are moved into the second and third classes as a year group each September. Since the summer-born children will not have attained the required age until late on in the reception class year they will have experienced less schooling than older members of the group, in fact two terms less than autumn-born children. For example, within an infant/junior school system the older autumn-born children would receive eight or nine terms schooling compared to the youngest summer born children who would only have had six or seven terms. In short, under conventional admission policies summer-born children are doubly disadvantaged: the younger they are the less schooling they receive.

To these disadvantages can be added two more which may also be modified to some degree by a change in entry arrangements. When summer-born children come into the reception class, they are joining an already established group as the youngest members. As a result they may have difficulty establishing their position in the group, competing for the attention of the teacher, keeping up with the level of the work which may be pitched more towards the more mature, experienced, older children. This has been termed the 'age-group position effect', (Williams 1964). Fourthly, a consequence of the age group-position effect may be that teachers who believe the youngest children in the group to be less able carry a lower expectation for their progress and make fewer demands on them, so their perceived lower ability could become self-fulfilling. (Rosenthal and Jacobson 1968).

Empirical demonstration of the disadvantages suffered by summer-born children in a termly entry system has added to the weight of argument favouring a change in policy, but proposals for a single-point entry system are not particularly new. Annual entry was advocated in the Plowden Report (Central Advisory Council for Education 1967) although their proposal was that the statutory age for children starting school be redefined as 'the September term following their fifth birthday'. The rationale for proposing this later uniform legal start date included the desirability of (i) organizing infant schools to provide a full three year course; (ii) eliminating the inequalities in length of education related to date of birth; and (iii) releasing resources for provision of part-time nursery education for all who want it'. Plowden also proposed that in order the ease the transition to school especially for the youngest children, full-time school should not be obligatory until the child's sixth birthday.

The Plowden proposals were themselves informed by earlier proposals to modify school-starting arrangements drawn-up by the then London County Council and submitted as evidence. Work on the so-called London plan was continued by the Chief Primary Education Inspector and eventually published as a detailed analysis of the merits of various policy options which attempt simultaneously to ease the experience of transition and equalize the opportunities available to children irrespective of birthdate (Palmer 1971). However, each of these proposals presumed development of comprehensive nursery education provision. While this became government policy in the early 1970s (Department of Education and Science 1972), it was only partially implemented, as noted earlier. Consequently, the recent trends to apply the idea of single point entry are taking place against a background of very varied and sometimes limited opportunities for preschool experience. The policy of annual admission is also being applied to children a full year younger than envisaged in the proposals of the late 1960s and early 1970s, and in many cases without major modifications being made to the organization and goals of infant school teaching. Finally it is frequently being applied with rather less opportunity or encouragement of part-time attendance in the early terms, not least because of family circumstances which frequently lead parents to seek a full school day at the outset, (as discussed above). These present day realities need to be taken into account in evaluating the merits of the policy.

While there are certainly respects in which single-entry admission policies can be viewed as progress towards offering more equitable access to education, there are other respects in which the position of summer-born children has changed little, and may even have become worse. First, as noted above, it is mainly the second disadvantage that is alleviated by the new policy; namely that they have achieved a superficial equality in terms of 'quantity' of schooling, but in other respects they remain in a disadvantaged position. They are still the youngest in the class. What significance this has, if any, will depend on the character of the school environment and the expectations placed on them by teachers. For example, there is evidence from the American system, where single-point entry is widely practised, that the youngest children in the class perform less well, at least in the early stages (Kinard and Reinherz 1986). This brings the discussion back to the concerns raised at the beginning of this paper about whether the buildings, staffing, and equipment of primary classes are appropriate to the developmental level of children who are barely 4 years old. Insofar as they are not, then it is the youngest that are most likely to suffer, and the youngest are the summer-born children. At worst the early school experiences of summer-born children might be more prejudicial to their adjustment and progress under the new arrangements than they were under traditional supposedly non-egalitarian arrangements.

This is an empirical question, which must await the test of time. Meanwhile, it is also worth reflecting on whether these new arrangements have really solved the problem of inequality of school experience, or merely pushed it back a stage. Admission policies to nursery education, as well as other pre-school groups, commonly confer exactly the same advantages on autumn-born children. For example, in cases where children are normally admitted at the start of the term after they become three, the autumn-born children could remain within the nursery for up to two years, until they are nearly 5, while summer-born children would only gain the benefit of a pre-school group for one year, until they are just 4. On the principle of equality of school experience the only logical solution, short of using totalitarian birth control techniques to ensure that each year's stock of young humanity celebrates its fifth birthday on the first day of the autumn term, would be to apply the single-point entry system to nursery. This could be achieved either by refusing admission to autumn-born children until they are nearly 4, or by encouraging summer-born children to enter when they are barely 2 years old! Pushed to this level, the absurdity of treating education as a commodity whose value is to be measured in years is shown in stark relief.

In conclusion, there may be a good case for adopting the single annual entry policy followed in many other European countries, although the case for doing so is not nearly so strong as advocates have sometimes suggested. In particular, if primary schools simply lower the entry age without any other adjustments to staffing, equipment, curriculum and teaching then it is doubtful whether this change in policy will be in the best interests of the youngest and least mature members of the class, the summer-born children. In short, an increase in the *quantity* of schooling is unlikely to bear fruit unless it coincides with considerable attention to enhancing the *quality* of educational experience for young children.

In drawing this conclusion, it is important to note that England and Wales are not alone in facing questions about the appropriateness of school experiences for young children. For example, in Sweden a government enquiry has been carried out into the advantages and disadvantages of reducing the age of starting compulsory school. The context of this enquiry was very different since the beginning of compulsory school (and with it the introduction of reading, number etc.) is normally set at 7 years of age in Sweden. No statutory changes have resulted but the National Board of Education has proposed that efforts should be made 'to develop a basic pedagogical consensus between pre-school education and compulsory school' (Swedish National Board of Education, 1987). In the USA, where children start school at 6, extensive discussion of the issue in State legislatures has in many cases resulted in an extension of kindergarten opportunities in elementary schools for 4 and 5-year-olds. In one case, New York, kindergarten has been made mandatory, but not without concern being expressed about the inappropriateness of formal teaching for young children (Elkind 1986, Zigler 1987).

An Education Fit for 4-year-olds

In this final section, it seems appropriate to set aside the many complex considerations that bear on admission policies in the past and present, and briefly address the issue of what 'quality' of education might entail in the early years, what kinds of learning and teaching are appropriate for 4-year-old children as they make the transition into school.

The first thing to acknowledge is that starting school can be a daunting experience for any child, even a child with nursery or playgroup experience, and for very young children the potential for stress is presumably that much greater. A recent study identified three respects in which starting school can be a stressful experience (Cleave, Jowett and Bate 1982). First, there is the new environment, both the scale and the size of the territory that children must find their way around, and also the greater constraint on where and when they may and must move between areas. Second, there is the curriculum, including the range and type of activities, the organization of the daily programme and the more restricted choice of activity for the primary school child. Finally, there are the people, both the numbers of strange children and adults as well as the limited availability of individual adult attention, and the much greater degree of impersonal group control by teachers.

Other research has identified the way problems of adjustment to school are manifested and the numbers of children affected. Diverse studies have found that teachers judge between thirteen and fifteeen per cent of children to have difficulties adjusting to school (Chazan and Jackson 1971, 1974; Davie *et al*. 1972; Hughes *et al*. 1979). This percentage remains virtually constant during the first eighteen months to two years, although it is not necessarily the same children who are judged to have difficulties at each stage. Indeed a detailed analysis of teachers' ratings after one term and again after five terms has shown the changing pattern of adjustment problems. Some are common to both ages, for example, approximately similar numbers of children are perceived as having difficulties verbalizing in school work and following instructions. Others are characteristic problems of initial entry, for example, difficulties in coping with personal needs, and lack of fine motor control, reflecting the relative immaturity of young children. Later in the infant school other problems emerge more strongly, such as problems of cooperation and concentration (Hughes *et al*. 1979). Acknowledging that admission to school can present problems for a significant number of primary age children, is there any clear educational virtue in reducing the admission age by as much as 12 months in some cases? In particular is there any research evidence that in terms of later educational attainment, the principle of 'the earlier the better' applies? There are two potential sources of evidence, neither entirely conclusive, but both suggesting that great caution is needed in applying that particular principle in this case.

The first source comes from recognition that in terms of admission policies, Britain is set apart from countries in the rest of Europe, and indeed the world, which have in almost every case adopted six or seven years old as the age of compulsory education. Simple comparisons are somewhat misleading because in some countries there is a very well-established pre-school care and education system such that a much higher proportion of young children are in educational establishments than in Britain, despite our early starting policies. For example, in the mid 1970s over 90 per cent of 3 to 5-year-olds were attending pre-school in Belgium; 79 per cent of 3-year-olds and virtually all 4 and 5-year-olds were in pre-school in France; and over 90 per cent of 4 and 5 year olds were in pre-school in the Netherlands (Woodhead, 1979). Even so, formal teaching of the 3 Rs does not usually commence until primary schooling, so there is some sense in enquiring whether there is any evidence that British traditions of early starting are associated with higher educational attainment in these respects than in other countries where a later pattern of starting formal instruction is normal.

Some years ago, the International Association of Evaluation of Educational Achievement, (IEA) conducted an analysis of mathematics scores obtained on a representative sample of 13-year-olds in twelve countries, according to whether 5, 6 or 7 was the age of starting. Their results were somewhat puzzling, in that 6 appeared to be the optimum age, producing higher scores than amongst children from school systems starting at 5 or 7. (Husen, 1967). The early start in countries like England and Scotland does not appear to be of great benefit, although at the same time it must be acknowledged that other variables such as style of teaching and emphasis on formal curriculum objectives may account for the differences in results.

If this evidence is to be believed, there does not appear to be a strong case for taking the opportunity of early admission to introduce children to 3 Rs teaching, but at the same time, the second source of evidence appears to point to the potential value that carefully planned early education can have for this age group. In particular recent studies have for the first time demonstrated that participation in a pre-school programme can yield long term benefits in terms of positive educational attitudes and progress in school, which can be sustained through to school completion and beyond. Almost all of the studies have been conducted in the USA, focused on pre-school intervention programmes for socially disadvantaged children, of which the major publicly-funded Head Start Project is the best known example (Zigler and Valentine 1979).

A whole series of experimental projects has reported positive results individually (Gray *et al.* 1982; Schweinhart and Weikart 1980; Clement *et al.* 1984) and collectively as the Consortium for Longitudinal Studies (Lazar *et al.* 1982). These projects show no long term effect on ability, and in most cases little effect on actual attainment, but they do show quite clear effects on children's ability to meet the requirements of schooling and (within the American system) avoid retention in grade and referral to special education, and go on to complete High School. A small number of studies also report favourable effects on levels of employment and juvenile delinquency. There are severe constraints on the generalisation of these results to other cultural and school systems and to a wider population of young children (Woodhead 1985; 1988). However, although these American findings cannot be directly translated into British early years policy, there is one respect in which they may be able to inform the issue under debate here. All the pre-school projects which demonstrated strong positive effects shared certain features in common. They were well resourced, carefully planned with the age-group in mind, generously staffed (1:6 on average) and supported, with extensive parent contact and involvement. They were, in short, high quality pre-school programmes, very different indeed from the quality of some reception class experiences for four year olds described in the White Paper and Select Committee reports referred to at the outset (Department of Education and Science 1985; House of Commons 1986).

Taken together, these two very different kinds of study suggest that improved educational attainment does not necessarily follow from early school admission,

but that given the right conditions, resources and planning, early education programmes can reap benefits in the long term. They reinforce the argument against
passively absorbing these children into the regime and learning requirements set by
the primary school curriculum at a much earlier age. Instead some active
development of primary education is required to ensure that it is appropriate to
their maturity and interests. As mentioned at the outset, this is unlikely in the long
run to entail making financial savings over provision that would meet the standards
of nursery education. Indeed it might be more appropriate to recognise these
developments as representing a consolidation of the pre-school sector, as much as
an extension of primary education. Whether it is appropriate to do so depends on
more than just resourcing issues. It also depends crucially on resolving rarely
acknowledged issues about the educational rationale for early admission policies.
Many of these issues are reminiscent of those that confronted education inspectors
and policy makers in a more extreme form several generations ago (Board of
Education 1905; 1908). These can be expressed as a series of questions: about the
kinds of learning and teaching that are appropriate for 4-year-old children; about
the quality of the relationships they should be developing with their teachers; and
about the curriculum priorities for the age group. For example, to what extent are
the early childhood years most profitably spent anticipating demands of later
schooling for literacy and numeracy based skills? Is it inevitable or desirable for
children to learn the discipline of constraint on personal expression and acceptance
of directed activity that is required if specific teaching objectives are to be attained
in a large group setting? How far should they, rather, be encouraged to develop and
explore a broad range of creative possibilities for learning in their environment
under the guidance of adults trained to work with this age group? In other words, to
what extent should the design of early learning take its cue from understanding of
the developmental features of the age group: their pre-occupation with playful
activity, their powers of creativity and imagination; their physical energy and
enthusiasm for mastering a wide range of practical skills and competencies? These
are not straightforward questions that can be answered simply by reference to the
literature of child development and educational research. They also depend on
attitudes to childhood and beliefs about the purposes of education. But this does
not mean that they should not be addressed. These are crucial policy related
concerns which have a direct relationship with disaffection and the effectiveness of
schooling experiences offered. The suspicion is that because the lowering of
admission ages has come about partly as a pragmatic response to changing
circumstances, and partly as an egalitarian measure intended to help summer-born
children, the precise educational rationale for the school environment being
offered to 4-year-old children has been given inadequate attention, or overlooked
altogether.

References

BARKER-LUNN, J. (1972) 'Length of infant school and academic performance', *Educational Research*, 14, pp. 120–7.

BLACKSTONE, T. (1971) *A Fair Start: The Provision of Pre-School Education*, London, Allen Lane.

BLATCHFORD, P., BURKE, J., FARQUHAR, C., PLEWIS, I. and TIZARD, B. (1987) 'A systematic observation study of children's behaviour at infant school', *Research Papers in Education*, 2(1), pp. 47–62.

BOARD OF EDUCATION (1905) *Reports on children under five years of age in Public Elementary Schools by Women Inspectors of the Board of Education*, Cmnd. 2726, London, HMSO.

BOARD OF EDUCATION (1908) *Report upon the School Attendance of Children below the Age of Five*, Cmnd. 4259, London, Board of Education Consultative Committee.

BOARD OF EDUCATION (1909) *Statistics of Public Education in England and Wales, Part I. Educational Statistics, 1907–08* London, HMSO.

BOARD OF EDUCATION (1914) *Statistics of Public Education in England and Wales, Part I. Educational Statistics, 1912–13* London, HMSO.

BOARD OF EDUCATION (1927) *Statistics of Public Education for the year 1925–26, England and Wales*, London, HMSO.

BOOKBINDER, G. E. (1967) 'The preponderance of summer-born children in ESN classes: which is responsible: age or length of infant schooling?' *Educational Research*, 9, pp. 213–217.

BOURI, J. and BARKER-LUNN, J. (1969) *Too Small to Stream*, Slough, NFER.

CAMPAIGN FOR ADVANCEMENT OF STATE EDUCATION (undated) *First School Admissions: the case for September entry for all*. London, CASE.

CENTRAL ADVISORY COUNCIL FOR EDUCATION (1967) *Children and their Primary Schools, Vol. I, The Plowden Report*, London, HMSO.

CHAZAN, M. and JACKSON, S. (1971) 'Behaviour problems in the infant school' *Journal of Child Psychology and Psychiatry*, 12, pp. 191–210.

CHAZAN, M. and JACKSON, S. (1974) 'Behaviour problems in the infant school: changes over two years', *Journal of Child Psychology and Psychiatry*, 15, pp. 33–46.

CLEAVE, S., JOWETT, S. and BATE, M. (1982) *And So to School*, Windsor, NFER-Nelson.

CLEAVE, S., BARKER-LUNN, J. and SHARP, C. (1985) 'Local education authority policy on admission to infant/first school' *Educational Research*, 27 (1) pp. 40–43

CLEMENT, J. R. B., SCHWEINHART, L. J., BARNETT, W. S., EPSTEIN, A. S. and WEIKART, D. P. (1984) 'Changed lives: the effects of the Perry Pre-school Program on youths through age 19' *Monograph 8* Ypsilanti, Michigan, High/Scope.

DAVIE, R., BUTLER, N. and GOLDSTEIN, H. (1972) *From Birth to Seven*, London, Longman.

DEPARTMENT OF EDUCATION AND SCIENCE (1972) 'Education: A Framework for Expansion', *Education White Paper*, Cmnd. 5174, London, HMSO.

DEPARTMENT OF EDUCATION AND SCIENCE (1973) 'Nursery Education', *Circular 2/73*, London, DES.

DEPARTMENT OF EDUCATION AND SCIENCE (1985) 'Better Schools', *Education White Paper*, Cmnd. 9469, London, HMSO.

DEPARTMENT OF EDUCATION AND SCIENCE (1987a) 'Pupils under five years in each local education authority in England — January 1986', *Statistical Bulletin 9/87* London, DES.

DEPARTMENT OF EDUCATION AND SCIENCE (1987b) 'Pupil-teacher ratios for each Local Education Authority in England — January 1986', *Statistical Bulletin 8/87* London, DES.

DEPARTMENT OF EDUCATION AND SCIENCE (1987c) *The National Curriculum 5–16: a Consultation Document*. London, DES.

DEPARTMENT OF EDUCATION AND SCIENCE (1987d)'Providing for quality: the pattern of organisation to age 19' *Circular 3/87*, London, DES.

ELKIND, D. (1986) 'Formal education and early childhood education: An essential difference', *Phi Delta Kappan*, May.

FARLEY, S. (1985) 'Sooner the Better?' *Times Educational Supplement*, 28.11.85, p. 21.

FINCH, J. (1984) 'A first class environment? Working class playgroups as pre-school experience', *British Educational Research Journal*, 10(1), pp. 3–17.

FREYMAN, R. (1965) 'Further evidence on the effect of date of birth on subsequent school performance', *Educational Research*, 8(1) pp. 58–64.

GRAY, S. W., RAMSEY, B. K. and KLAUS, R. A. (1982) *From 3 to 20: The Early Training Project*, Baltimore, University Park Press.

HOUSE OF COMMONS (1986) 'Achievement in Primary Schools', *Report of the Select Committee on Education, Science and the Arts*, London, HMSO.

HUGHES, M., PINKERTON, G., and PLEWIS, I. (1979) 'Children's difficulties on starting infant school' *Journal of Child Psychology and Psychiatry*, 20(3), pp. 187–196.

HUSEN, T. (Ed.) (1967) *Internal Study of Achievement in Mathematics: A Comparison of Twelve Countries, Vol. II* London, John Wiley and Sons.

INHELDER, B. and PIAGET, J. (1955) *The Growth of Logical Thinking from Childhood to Adolescence*, translation published 1958, London, Routledge and Kegan Paul.

JACKSON, B. (1964) *Streaming: An Education System in Miniature*, London, Routledge and Kegan Paul.

JINKS, P. C. (1964) 'An investigation into the effect of date of birth on subsequent school performance', *Educational Research*, 8(3), pp. 220–225.

KINARD, E. M. and REINHERZ, H. (1986) 'Birthdate effects on school performance and adjustment: a longitudinal study', *Journal of Educational Research*, 79(6), pp. 366–372.

LAZAR, I., DARLINGTON, R. B., MURRAY, H. W. and SNIPPER, A. S. (1982) 'Lasting effects of early education: a report from the Consortium for Longitudinal Studies' *Monograph of Society for Research in Child Development*, 47(2-3).

NEWCASTLE COMMISSION (1861) *Report of the Commissioners on the State of Popular Education in England*, p. 180, British Parliamentary Papers, Education General 3, 1969 edition (Dublin, Irish University Press).

OFFICE OF POPULATION, CENSUSES AND SURVEYS (1987) *Social Trends* London, HMSO.

PALMER, R. (1971) *Starting School: a study of policies*, London, University of London.

PLOWDEN, Lady B. (1982) *Speech to annual conference of Pre-school Playgroups Association*, April 1982.

ROGERS, R. (1984) 'Born at the wrong time of year', *Where*, June 1984, pp. 6–10.

ROSENTHAL, R. and JACOBSON, L. (1968) *Pygmalion in the Classroom: Teacher Expectation and Pupils' Intellectual Development*, London, Holt, Rinehart and Winston.

SHARP, C. (1987) 'The first year at school' in NFER/SCDC. *Four year olds in School: Policy and Practice*, Slough, NFER.

SHARP, C. (1988) 'Starting School at four', *Research Papers in Education*, 3,(i), pp. 64–90.

SCHWEINHART, L.J. and WEIKART, D.P. (1980) 'Young children grow up', *Monograph 7* Ypsilanti, Michigan, High/Scope.

SZRETER, R. (1964) 'The origins of full-time compulsory education at five', *British Journal of Educational Studies*, 12, pp. 16–28.

SWEDISH NATIONAL BOARD OF EDUCATION (1987) 'Starting School in Sweden' personal communication.

VAN DER EYKEN, W. (Ed.) (1973) *Education, the Child and Society*, pp. 120–122, Harmondsworth, Penguin.

WELSH OFFICE (1986) *Statistics of Education in Wales, No. 11*, Cardiff, Welsh Office.

WHITBREAD, N. (1972) *The Evolution of the Nursery — Infant School* (London, Routledge and Kegan Paul).

WILLIAMS, P. (1964) 'Date of birth, backwardness, and educational organization? *British Journal of Educational Psychology*, 34(3), pp. 247–255.

WOODHEAD, M. (1979) 'Pre-school provision in Western Europe' in Council of Europe *From Birth to Eight: Young children in European Society in the 1980's* Windsor, NFER-Nelson.

WOODHEAD, M. (1985) 'Pre-school education has long-term effects, but can they be generalised?' *Oxford Review of Education*, 11(2), pp. 133–155.

WOODHEAD, M. (1986) 'When should children go to school?' *Primary Education Review*, No.25, Spring.

WOODHEAD, M. (1988) 'When psychology informs public policy: the case of early childhood intervention'. *American Psychologist*, 43, 6, pp. 443–454.

ZIGLER, E.F. (1987) 'Formal schooling for four-year-olds? No.' *American Psychologist*, 42(3), pp. 254–260.

ZIGLER, E.F. and VALENTINE, J. (Eds) (1979) *Project Head Start: A Legacy of the War on Poverty*, New York, Free Press.

10
Needs of Teacher Education for Early Years Teaching

Peter Heaslip

Introduction

It is now common practice for children to enter infant school in the year in which they turn five. This has meant that in many parts of the country children are beginning their primary schooling just after their fourth birthday. This makes experience based learning situations, commonly called 'play', essential for these children at least. There is general concern for the children, but too little concern for the teachers who have to face the task of providing them with nursery education while others expect them to be treated as infant children. This chapter broadens the teaching range for our consideration to 3 to 8 years, to include nursery teachers, who together with the teachers of 4-year-olds feel particular disaffection about their training for their roles.

Six months after completing their Post Graduate Certificate of Education Course, five probationary teachers met together to compare notes. They had been part of a group of twenty students who had undertaken a year's initial training at a College of Education where their course had been geared to the early years known as the '3 to 8 Track in the Primary Course'. PGCE Courses which are completed in one year have been able to make a more immediate response to the demands for early years teachers than the four-year B.Ed. courses and the five probationers are typical, both in terms of pre-service experience and in the range of teaching situations, which early years probationers may expect on their first appointment.

Ranjit was 24, with a BA (Hons) in Social Science. She came to her teacher training with general work experience not directly related to teaching. Although in recent years she had helped in her father's business she had spent most of her time since university working in service industries. Now in her probationary year she was working in a large nursery school in London. With too few representatives from ethnic minority groups in teaching, she was readily appointed to an area where she would be seen as a positive black authority figure. The staffing ratio in the nursery was generous and Ranjit led a team of two NNEB trained staff, one who was nearing retirement and the other newly appointed from a B Tech. course. Unlike the other four probationers she was given regular weekly assistance and had frequent meetings with other probationary teachers where issues and concerns were discussed. It was the teaching role to which she had aspired when she decided to enter the profession.

David was 31, married with two children and a third on the way. He had studied for a B.Sc. in physical sciences, having previously worked in a bank. The joy of his own children had sparked off his interest in early childhood education and his intention had been to work in a nursery. His background in science and particularly his strength in maths had attracted the interest of a local infant school, and although his intention remained to be a nursery teacher, the lack of nursery teaching positions in the area, combined with the prospect of moving house just before the arrival of another baby had prompted him to accept the infant position. The school was the one in which he had undertaken his final teaching practice and many of the children in his vertically grouped infant class were children he had already taught.

Penny, 24, had read theology and then worked for two years with mentally handicapped children. During this time she also studied English as a Foreign Language, an area in which she then had little experience. Her intention had been to train on a course specialising in children with severe learning difficulties, and ultimately she hoped this would be where she worked. Now however, she was in the North, in charge of a large nursery unit attached to an infant school. All the children were part-time pupils; a total of nearly fifty 3-year-olds. The nursery nurse had been at the school since the unit opened ten years earlier, but Penny was the first teacher to be appointed who had trained for early years. Previously there had been a redeployed secondary teacher and a mother returning to teaching after having had her family. The nursery nurse, having felt that she had trained the two previous teachers about the needs of nursery children, considered that Penny also needed this same direction. There seemed to be very little support for probationary staff from either the Local Education Authority or from the head teacher who left her to 'get on with the little ones'.

Karen, 23, had married at the completion of the course and had followed her husband to one of the Shire Counties. Her initial degree was in fine arts where she majored in graphics. Although still dabbling professionally in that area, she had worked as a care assistant in an old people's home before jointly running a refuge for battered wives. Like David, she wished to work in a nursery and it was for this reason that she had applied for the particular PGCE course, for there were few that catered for those who wished to specialise in the nursery sector. When she had applied through the pool system for a nursery position in the Shire county, she was disappointed to be placed in an infant school. Although she protested to the LEA she was informed that her knowledge of young children could be best used with a reception class in a large city infant school where the children were admitted just after their fourth birthday. By the end of the first term she found herself with thirty-two 4-year-olds and no staff assistance.

Jackie at 39 had been the oldest member on the course. She had first trained as a nursery nurse and worked in a day nursery. Then while she was at home raising a family, she completed her A levels and studied at the Open University for a degree in Education. Her last challenge had been to obtain 'O' level maths. As well as bringing up her three children, Jackie had been involved in the playgroup movement as a mother, leader and sometime tutor. Now, Jackie was teaching in the school her children attended, in the infant department of a large primary school where parents checked daily to see that reading books were brought home, and where Parent-Teacher Association meetings were well attended especially when maths or reading evenings were held. The head teacher believed in old fashioned values and a proper emphasis on the three Rs. He believed that standards had slipped, 'but with the correct approach to hard work in the infants you can put us back on the rails. It's what the parents want, and I believe they are right', he told her. The local adviser, while sympathetic to current thinking, had not yet been seen by Jackie, and to date the probationary meetings had been about child-abuse and implementing an anti-racist policy in the classroom. There had been nothing about the curriculum or classroom management.

These five probationary teachers were not surprised to find that their professional situations differed so greatly. Differences occur no matter what the age range for which a student trains, but there are features of the training for early years which are particular and problems which arise from the specific situations in which they are working.

Brief consideration of the PGCE course on which these five, together with twelve others, undertook their initial teacher training indicates that it was typical of many courses of initial teacher education. All students had been given the choice of completing one of their teaching practices in a nursery or infant class — this was more than some other courses offered. The assessed practice had been in an infant class. There had been ample opportunity to discuss experiences, and to debate what were deemed to be key issues, but although the particular track was designated 'early years', not one of the tutors had ever taught in a nursery and only one had previously worked in an infant school. The tutors, while knowing their subject area well, seemed unable to relate to the practical demands which faced students, especially when they were working in the nursery. The tutors had 'supervised' teaching practice rather than used the school experience as a basis for considering issues. Some student disaffection with their training was only to be expected. How much of the disaffection was based on common need, and how much was particular? Common concerns may give ground for changed course content or emphasis while specific worries may be individual and situation specific. Let us draw from each of these probationary teachers an expressed concern.

First we take Ranjit in her nursery school in London. She is fortunate that the Inner London Education Authority has a policy which supports teachers in their probationary year. Many of the issues which relate to the development of professional competence are common to all probationers irrespective of the age range they are teaching. The regular meetings with other probationers and the support given by the local authority is gratefully received by Ranjit.

There are opportunities too to discuss the more particular concerns of a nursery teacher, which although included in her initial training course can only be worked out 'on the job'. The major concern for Ranjit is that of leading a team, especially with a very young nursery nurse whose B. Tech course, while encompassing the wider areas of welfare, has been less than specific on the demands and needs of nursery children, and of motivating the nursery nurse nearing retirement and disillusioned by earlier promises of career prospects which never eventuated.

David, whose intention remains to work with nursery age children, finds that the school sees him as the maths expert and he feels in danger of his child-centred approach being squeezed out by an increasing demand of subject specialism, especially with the emphasis from the core curriculum. He has difficulty putting into practice his 'Plowden ideas'. The Ginn 360 reading and the Scottish maths seem more important to the school than active learning, and parents are discouraged from making contacts with the teachers unless by appointment. Somehow he seems to be slipping into a pattern which just a year before he had been the first to criticise.

Penny has a far greater problem than Ranjit. She has little support from the head teacher and there is no early years adviser in the authority. She maintains a clear belief in involving parents, but with fifty sets of parents this is some task! Her greatest challenge however comes from trying to implement a purposeful curriculum with no cooperation and considerable opposition from the nursery nurse who believes in 'letting children play', and who has in effect directed the previous teachers, a redeployed secondary teacher and a junior teacher, along these lines.

Karen faces the challenge that has been a nightmare experience for many probationers employed to teach 4-year-olds. Although believing soundly in play being the basis of learning and of children being 'active agents in their own learning', she finds the demands of thirty-two children aged between 4 and $4\frac{1}{2}$ years, without staff assistance, a task with which she can scarcely cope. She lives one day at a time, and each Friday is grateful that she has got through another week. Is there any way that an initial training course could have prepared her better for the position in which she finds herself?

Jackie faces a similar conflict. Her firm belief in an appropriate curriculum and of child-centred methods is being undermined by the 'return to basics' mood from both parents and head teacher. Jackie knows from talking to her friends that they are sympathetic to this viewpoint even if their children are sometimes reluctant to go to school, but she is unable to justify to them with sufficient conviction exactly how children learn through play. She finds herself reluctantly going along with the school policy, even though she believes it is inappropriate.

Could their initial training have assisted these students, and to what extent is their disaffection with their course valid? The changes which have taken place in teacher training over the last two decades highlight the difficulties of the early childhood educator. With the introduction of B.Ed. degrees in 1965 students have been expected to undertake a main subject at an advanced academic level as well as their professional studies and school experience. Curtis (1986) suggests that

> The approach towards professional studies varied from college to college,
> but in general those institutions specialising in early childhood education

adopted a child centred approach and attempted to integrate the various areas of the primary curriculum rather than presenting students with discrete subject areas. In many colleges the main subject specialists (who usually had secondary school teaching experience) taught the methodology of the various curriculum topics leaving the education tutors the task of attempting to relate theory learned to the practice in the classroom. Generally it was the education tutors who were experienced classroom teachers with expertise in the early childhood field.

However, in practice, this has not always been the case as the following analysis demonstrates.

Following the James Report in 1972, there was a dramatic cutback in student numbers in initial teacher training and many colleges which trained nursery/infant teachers were closed or became part of new institutions. Many early childhood tutors who were 'Crombied out' in the 1970s did not have the paper qualifications now demanded, but their first–hand experience of nursery education gave their teaching a depth and an appropriateness that was missed when subject specialist tutors were deployed onto early years courses. When new courses emerged few members of staff had had any experience of working with young children. An HMI report highlighted this problem (*Training in Schools: The Context of Initial Training*, 1983).

The British Association for Early Childhood Education conducted from 1979–81 a survey of staffing for teachers preparing to work with 3 to 5-year-old pupils and found that there was not only a shortage of trainers, but those who were taking early retirement were not being replaced. Other staff without early years experience were taking over their courses. Many training institutions were recruiting students for the 3 to 9-years phase. As a result there was in the 1980s not only a decrease in the number of teachers trained to work in the nursery age range at a time when the provision was expanding, but many of those with a nursery/infant qualification were 'very inadequately prepared to work in nursery schools and classes' (Curtis, 1986).

In a written reply to the Tutors of Advanced Courses for Teachers of Young Children in 1983, Her Majesty's Chief Inspector Perry stated that 'tutors who are required to teach students preparing for early years should have a most carefully structured and substantial in-service training, including a careful programme of observation work with young children in order to prepare themselves for this field' and further added that at that time, of the eighty-five total training institutions, 'only a few are capable of offering initial training for the early years'. In 1984 less than 3 per cent of tutors in teacher training institutions had ever taught children under the age of 8 years, and yet 40 per cent of students were training for that age range.

In the DES (1983) document it is stated that 'The professional element in the student's preparation should be taught by people who are successful and experienced members of the teaching profession'. This means that there are serious implications for staffng early years courses. The current shortage of early years teachers has resulted in training institutions expanding course provision to cover early years without ensuring that the younger age range is being tutored by staff with appropriate experience. There is widespread concern that the content of the courses may not be matched to the role demands of the early years teachers. However, uncertainty about the government's commitment to under fives has placed training institutions in a dilemma. Should early years staff be appointed when there is no historical reason to suggest that commitment is likely to be anything other than intermittent? I believe that we are now entering a more stable situation. Nationally the nursery provision programme is relatively static and the provision of schooling for 4-year-olds is increasing, nor are we faced with a falling birthrate. Training institutions have responded positively to DES requests that consideration be given to increased early years initial training courses. Now they must face the challenge of either appointing suitably experienced and qualified staff, and ensuring that courses are appropriate to the needs of those working in nursery and infant schools, or not accepting the invitation to expand or develop early years courses.

The variety of roles that these trained teachers will face is indicated by the five probationary teachers considered earlier. The quality of their training and its relevance to their immediate professional challenges is made more important by another national trend. Many local authorities are replacing early years advisers and inspectors by appointments with an overall primary responsibility. The Early Years Adviser is becoming an increasingly rare officer. Many probationary teachers find that their contact with advisory staff is limited but also that those without appropriate early years experience seem unaware of the particular nature of their role, especially in the nursery school. If a student has been trained by tutors, works in a school with a head teacher and is under the guidance of an adviser/inspector, *none* of whom has early childhood experience, disaffection is almost certain to occur, in both new teachers and their pupils.

All early years courses which cover the range of 3 to 8 years should require a student to have school experience in a nursery. This in itself presents problems, for some training institutions, especially in the South, may have limited nursery provision and even in areas where provision is richer, the competition for nursery placements from a host of other agencies training for multi-disciplinary workers with the 'under 5s', often results in a scarcity of places on offer. There is now increasing acceptance that the role of the teacher in the nursery and in the early years of schooling, is specialised but there is seldom an emphasis in training that would validate this, and almost never an analysis of either why this is so or what these roles are. The following seeks to reflect the needs expressed through the five teachers introduced earlier.

Leadership Skills

Both Ranjit and Penny found that from their first day as probationers they were required to lead a nursery team of other professionals and paraprofessionals. Each faced particular challenges. Penny was responsible for a nursery nurse who 'had trained the last two teachers' because they had not previously worked with young children. Like many nursery nurses who are part of a nursery team this nurse had many years of experience in working with young children and was reluctant to take a supportive role. In a survey undertaken in Avon over half the nursery nurses interviewed in a study of nursery schools and classes believed they were either equal to or better qualified to work with young children than teachers or that teachers were unnecessary in nursery education (Heaslip, 1985).

There are minimal opportunities for promotion in education for nursery nurses and this lack of career structure is reflected in an absence of attendance at inservice courses. Halloran (1982) found that 40 per cent of currently working nursery nurses over the age of 30, and 61 per cent under the age of 30 in social services and education had not undertaken *any* in-service training. Very often courses available to teachers are not made available to nursery nurses. The resentment felt by many nursery nurses (see below) will need to be understood by the nursery teacher who, as a newly qualified probationer may well have to lead a team and promote the professional development of staff who harbour latent and sometimes overt feelings of antagonism to the teaching profession. Management of staff and sensitive leadership of a nursery team should be a major component in any early years course. The Avon Study (Heaslip, *op cit*.) showed that most nursery teachers were reluctant to be seen taking a direct leadership role, preferring not to lead positively on educational issues because of latent discontent which could sour working relationships. While no initial training course could be expected to resolve this, students should consider the particular staff management issues which are likely to confront them from their first days of teaching. One important factor in leadership is understanding and using the strengths of other adults available in the classroom. These need to be explained further.

Nursery Nurses

There is no other sector in education where two separate professionals each with different training and career structures work side by side as they do in the nursery or reception class. In general, there is very little knowledge by either nursery nurses or by teachers of either the extent or content of each others' courses. The Avon Study suggested that a widely held view by nursery nurses was that a teaching course was theoretical and did not deal with practical work with young children. Although teachers tended to know more about an NNEB qualification, the changes being introduced by the Board and the CPQS (Certificate of Post Qualifying Service) are less well known. If the two professions are to work together, there is a need for both sectors to have a clearer understanding of each other's roles and training. Teachers of four year olds in infant schools may often have some timetabled support from a general assistant who very often has an NNEB qualification. To gain greatest benefit for the children from this support, the teacher needs to know how to deploy the trained nursery nurse so that her training is utilised to the full.

Nursery nurses can harbour a cluster of grievances, both real and imagined, imposed and self inflicted. The teacher must not only work in cooperation with nursery nurse, but she must also develop the skills to ease these grievances and accept responsibility for the professional development of her staff. To enable her do this, training must focus on issues which are strongly felt by NNEB staff.

Other professionals

With open recruitment, staff employed as nursery assistants may not be NNEB trained but may come from any care service. Their contributions will differ according to their training and experience, and the teacher must be aware of this. Social workers, health visitors, child minders, play group leaders and many others all have direct professional contact with the nursery and reception teacher, many of them spending time observing in the classroom. The teacher needs to liaise with and utilise the services of these persons so that the children and families with whom she is working are best served. Few other newly qualified teachers could expect this responsibility in their probationary year.

Visitors

Nurseries play host to an increasing variety of visitors, students and observers from other professions. Although in her probationary year the teacher may be relieved of some of these, it is likely that she will be expected to have attachments from FE courses and secondary school pupils on work experience or child care courses. These attachments will often be made with minimal guidance from the host institution and often with limited communication with those responsible for the attachments. The teacher is often left to *tutor* and supervise these students while they are in the nursery. The demand is often considerable. One ex-student had fourteen such attachments in her first two terms as a probationary teacher.

Some GCSE courses require students to spend time with young children, and this has created a responsibility on secondary teachers whom may have little knowledge or experience of young children. Too often much of this responsibility seems to be transferred to the nursery or infant teacher. With this demand increasing and with the probationer faced with the task of accommodating and informing these students, this aspect of their role needs to be considered in their initial training course.

Parents

Quite often the school shields a probationary teacher from parents until she has come to terms with the demands of the classroom. For the early years teacher the reverse is true. From her very first teaching day the probationer is expected to interact fully with the parents and these very early contacts are likely to be extremely important for both parties. The nursery and/or infant teacher is often the first contact that the parents will have had with the education sector since they left school. The quality of the interaction and the relationship established from it are of vital importance, for on these first contacts are likely to be laid the foundations on which the complementary role of parents and teachers will be built.

Although there is general acceptance of the need for parental involvement, the Avon Study indicated what I believe to be a widespread pattern. With some notable exceptions, 'parents as partners' is given low weighting in practice, and seldom were issues of parental involvement said to have been an integral part of an initial training course. The motivation to involve parents should not be a response to government legislation, or to suggestions of accountability to parents. For continuity of experience for the child, parents' and professionals' cooperation needs to be basic to our teaching. Often this relationship which a parent and early years teacher have built results in the parents using the teacher as an adviser and consultant on later infant and primary education, and this creates new demands of knowledge and counselling.

Essential in any primary course, but particularly in those training for the early years should be a substantial element on the exploration of the manner in which staff and parents can complement each other in the education and care of the child and in which the child is seen within the broader framework of his family and community. In an early years course it should be a permeating theme and a constant focus of attention. It should also be noted and stressed in the courses of student teachers that, despite the adult team that may be involved, there are also strong possibilities that the teacher of young children may be isolated, physically at least, from other colleagues in the school. Strategies for (a) coping with this and (b) overcoming it should be developed.

Curriculum Issues

Curriculum considerations also become a major concern, for until recently there has been little direction on what constitutes an early years curriculum. Traditional subject-based considerations are inappropriate. In a climate where the demands of a national curriculum are at the forefront of teachers' minds, the teacher of 4 to 8-year-olds must ask herself whether a 70 per cent time allocation to English, maths and science is appropriate for young children. If not, in the absence of clearly defined national or local guidelines, she must be able to set out the principles which will determine her curriculum design.

At the present the early childhood teacher can concentrate on developing the whole child. Division of the curriculum into subjects or even categories of social, emotional, physical and moral development is awkward. The child needs to be considered as a whole, and it is the teacher's responsibility to create a learning environment that is appropriate for her or his development, one that is print rich and language heavy, where curiosity can be cultivated, thinking challenged, and competences enhanced. This can not be done in discrete compartments, learned in subjects, assessed, recorded and transferred onto paper.

To state that a traditional subject-orientated approach to an early years curriculum is inappropriate without providing a more suitable alternative is unhelpful. Students on initial training courses must be given the basis for developing a curriculum appropriate to the needs of the children and the constraints of the teaching situation. Dowling (1988) suggests that effective curriculum planning involves:

1. a knowledge of how young children develop and learn most effectively
2. familiarity with the materials, activities and methods that promote different types of development and learning
3. the resources available in terms of time, staff numbers and expertise, accommodation and equipment.

To do this the teacher must have a deep understanding of the contribution of play and a development of the art of appropriate adult intervention both physically and through resources. This is the essence of effective early years practice.

The role of play in children's learning and developing should be a major pre-occupation of students on an early years course, both during school experience and through their course-based work in reading and discussion. One of the dilemmas the probationer faces is convincing parents, colleagues and politicians of the value of play. To do this effectively, not only has the teacher to understand and believe in play as a medium through which much learning takes place, s/he must be able to articulate this and then translate this theory into effective classroom practice.

Two other factors also contribute to the arguments for play as the basis for planning in the classroom and they are mutually supportive.

1. A thorough grasp of child development
2. A trained skill in observing children.

Each will complement the other; a knowledge of child development will inform the observations and these will support an understanding of the stages and levels of a child's development. These with play are fundamental to a teacher's curriculum provision and should be central in the training of the early years teacher.

Asserting the Case for Early Years Curriculum

Ranjit, David, Penny and Karen are all dependent on the above foundation in order to be effective in their teaching, but Jackie, with the demands for a 'return to basics', needs this foundation most strongly. As a newly qualified teacher, faced with conflict between demand for tangible results and the real needs of the children, she must be clear in her philosophy of what early years teaching is about and what she should be doing. Further she needs to be articulate so that she can inform and influence others. Too often the teacher of young children is seen in Joyce Grenfell terms of a caring, slightly eccentric soul dispensing sweetness, tissues and the occasional admonition with motherly charm and a professionally modulated voice. The actual role demands, together with the warmth and genuine care, an intellectual rigour, a professional concern, a self assurance and belief in what one is doing and a competence that can only develop from this.

The curriculum in early years is not delivered to children, it results from the interaction the child has with the environment which the teacher provides and of which the teacher is an integral part. Disaffection in the children and in the teacher may well arise when the teacher is aware that inadequacies in her training have left her unprepared for the role she is undertaking, and for the challenges she faces, or when she is unable to articulate the appropriateness of what she feels and knows is right for the children but lacks the training in reflection, analysis or study to substantiate it. The provision of in-service education which is drawn from the expressed needs and actual role of the early years teacher would seem to be a priority, especially for those whose initial training was at the best less than appropriate and at the worst irrelevant.

Katz (1984) states 'All of us who teach, at whatever level, have to face the fact that we cannot offer our learners all the possible advice, suggestions, commentary or information that might be helpful or instructive to them'. Teacher trainers, however, have a responsibility to ensure that courses are relevant and provide a basis for sound practice, so that the quality of the teacher, which is the key to effective schooling, will overcome any disaffection in school which the young children in their care could begin to harbour.

References

CURTIS, A. (1986) 'Educating Early Childhood Educators', in: Heaslip. P. (Ed) *The Challenge of the Future*, Bristol Polytechnic.
DEPARTMENT OF EDUCATION AND SCIENCE (1983) *Training in Schools: The Content of Initial Training*, HMI discussion paper, London, DES.
DOWLING, M. (1988) Education 3 to 5: A Teachers' Handbook, London, Chapman.
HALLORAN, H. (1982) *The Diverse Role of the Nursery Nurse and its Implications for Future Education and Training*, M.Ed. thesis, University of Manchester.
HEASLIP, P. (1985) *The Training and Roles of Nursery Staff*, TACTYC, Vol. 5 No. 2, pp 1–105.
KATZ, L. (1984) *More Talks with Teachers*, ERIC, EECE:, University of Illinois.

11
Conditions for Disaffection?

Gill Barrett

Disaffection is a policy issue and is not simply a problem for pupils, parents and teachers. However, underpinning my interest in disaffection are implicit concerns about individuals and their ability to function effectively, with choices, in society. Associated with this is an awareness that schooling fails to make confident learners out of the majority of pupils and is therefore ineffective. Other chapters in this book have shown how the early years at school may initiate this process. This chapter examines some broader concerns. It looks in more detail at some of the anomalies inherent in the current context of schools that appear to create conditions for disaffection.

Three propositions are explored within the chapter

1. that personal and socially constructed ways of thinking affect what we see, know, and do in all spheres of living;
2. that curriculum and its presentation are the outcome of experience and ways of thinking and are necessarily open to criticism;
3. that effective learning is not the result of external imperatives, or curriculum content per se, nor necessarily to be recognised in conformity of result.

Central to this discussion is an argument which many might regard as at least surprising because of the limitations we impose on our thinking and beliefs about learning and knowledge within society. This argument has direct relevance to our understanding of disaffection in the early years because it concerns the value we place on the thinking, knowledge and understanding of young children. The chapter argues that there is an important relationship between the thinking and subsequent speech and action of children, and the thinking of subject areas and/or commonsense ways of solving problems with people or things. If we fail to recognise and value children's thinking as learners, disaffection will continue to be a problem and schools will not enable pupils to be effective either as individuals or within a societal role.

The rest of this chapter examines the ways of thinking that affect the behaviour of teachers, and school policy and curriculum makers. This involves examining concepts of society and the individual and the relationship between them that exists in education and schooling. Specifically, it includes looking at concepts of knowledge and learning and their relationship to curriculum in schools. It also entails looking at the perceived needs of children if they are not to become disaffected from learning; and of society, if we are to continue to develop on all levels. Finally I will explore the relationship between needs of the individual and the society in which they live and demonstrate the dangers of creating conditions for disaffection of the individual from learning.

What is Society? And how does it think?

Society is a much contested term and can be defined in many different ways depending on theoretical perspective. For this chapter we will consider society to be those socially constructed expectations, policies and behaviour which impinge upon the child in school. The predominant ways of thinking within that context would stem from those with the most power to disseminate and enforce their ideas. In the late 1980s it might be said that the most publicised way of thinking in the media and through government policy is 'Thatcherism'. This is based on a theory which promotes market forces as the major way of deciding what shall exist, or not, and who will succeed, or not. Initiative and competition are key concepts and promoted ways of operating. The 1988 Education Reform Act applied this way of thinking to schooling. It is now possible for schools to opt out of Local Education Authority control which is significant in terms of local long term planning and policy making. Schools and LEAs no longer have the right to fix yearly limits to admission numbers in order to equalise numbers in schools or to keep places for local admissions during the year. Market forces, or parental choice, will decide which schools are supported, and ultimately which are to close. It would seem that the testing of individuals at age seven, eleven and fourteen, also provided for in the Act, is designed to ensure that children will know whether they are succeeding, or not, in relation to the National Curriculum. The accountability of the schools to the market is being emphasised in ensuring that aggregate results of schools must be published. This will ensure that others too know whether schools are achieving high or low scores, and low scoring schools can be forced to either close or improve. Competition and individual initiative, rather than cooperation are the key ways of thinking being promoted and there are few state funded options left open to those who see education or society in other ways.

However another view of what 'society' is, and what its ways of thinking are, can be obtained by looking at what it has created, what it does, and what the relationships are between its history and present and between its peoples. This is to see society in terms of evolution, growth, and a sum of its different people, history and contemporary thought and action. In some people's eyes this would be referring to culture but I want to stress that this view of society takes into account people's actions, as well as ideas in symbolic forms in words, pictures and three dimensions. In these terms our society can be conceptualised in terms of polarities. Opposing ways of thinking and acting face us in all social environments. For example:

1. collaboration and cooperation is taking place in work places, in communities, between institutions and individuals, but competition is promoted, and operates in relation to established norms on many levels (e.g. academic achievement; success in work through promotion; winning; financial gain; etc.);

2. hard work and recognition of existing societal rules is juxtaposed by many who are out-of-work and increasingly question these socially constructed expections;

3. change and growth in the environment in which we live and the communication systems we use (consumer demands, industry, technological and scientific understanding for example) is juxtaposed by groups, institutions and individuals who resist learning, growth and change or seek a return to simpler ways of living;

4. concepts of equal opportunities, and growing understanding of our society as multi-cultural and a society of the world is juxtaposed by male conceptions of success, nationalism and intolerance of differences from the predominant culture;

5. growth of understanding about learning in classrooms through reflective practice and research at all practioner levels of education, is juxtaposed with increasing control of schools, teachers and curriculum by many who have no extended experience of education;

6. calls for appropriate workers for society able to think, learn, apply what they know and initiate action is juxtaposed by demands for a return to a curriculum founded on academic discipline based subjects.

I could go on but I think this illustrates a society poised on the divide between history and its future with elements of both uneasily operating together in all spheres of existence and society. This also illustrates that society is made up of people who can and do think in many different ways. They use their thinking to many purposes but largely to enable themselves to feel more effective within it. Interpretations of that effectiveness will vary but together these forms of effectiveness, and thinking that underpins them create different industries, ways of organising and categorising people, ways of bringing up children, ways of interacting with people, ways of displaying authority or power, and ways of educating children and creating the curriculum. These are but a few of the areas in which individuals illustrate effectiveness and hence create differences. But how does this view of society link with that of society promoted by its policy makers?

One of the most important ways of creating a relationship between society as defined through dominant policy, and the society created by people within it, is through the structure and function of schooling and the form and content of school curricula. But do schools simply have a controlling and regulating function in that the curriculum and values of school only allow 'success' to limited numbers; or do they serve an educative empowering function of the individual in order to give them choice and control over their own lives? Given these alternative accounts the question that remains is whether schooling and education are, or can be,

What is the relationship between the needs of society as defined the dominant ways of thinking in society o

synonomous. Can schooling empower, and thus enable individuals to become critically aware of their own lives in order to take action, make choices, and become confident learners? Is this possible despite home conditions and parents' perception of themselves in society, and despite the apparent needs of society for particular forms of labour? What is the relationship between the needs of society as defined by the dominant ways of thinking in society and individual needs within the curriculum of schools?

Knowlege: Ways of Thinking and Knowing for Effective Learning

Before I address the question of societal and individual needs it is essential to look at ways of thinking about knowledge and learning that are subsumed within the assumptions and actions that people make.

First, let us take a commonly received view of knowledge. Learning, knowledge and success in schools, in the minds of many people, is related to the measured success resulting from a test set by someone else. Knowledge, i.e. facts, is learned in order to pass exams in order to show one is successful. On this understanding knowledge is conceived as an aggregate of subject related facts which are easily reduced to writing or other currently testable forms, having been produced by 'experts'. This view of knowledge has been traditionally associated with secondary schooling and higher education. In the last ten years changes have been initiated in secondary education, TVEI and CPVE for example and even the General Certificate of Secondary Education examinations which completed their first cycle in 1988. All these examples are more concerned with processes of knowledge and the thinking and skills required to create history, engage in vocational skills or to be a chemist. However attempts to build on this by promoting an alternative style of exam for entry to universities, and even a report suggesting a broader base for the existing Advanced Level Certificate of Education was soundly crushed by the Conservative Government in 1988. (Just to reinforce the point I was making earlier, this happened alongside initiatives by the University Grants Committee to open up University entrance to non-standard qualifications of mature people.) Knowledge as written, subject based and largely factual remains the predominant gatekeeper to university and other Higher Education. These criteria are supported by a government which appears to resist changes although some universities and the examination boards are now prepared to re-examine them. Most teachers therefore would have experienced a predominantly information subject based curriculum prior to starting work in schools, and would have been valued because of their ability to succeed in it.

Knowledge in these subject based factual terms does not readily equate with the knowledge that children in the early years of schooling appear to have, or to learn within their curricula. So how does society appear to think about their learning and knowledge? Primary and particularly first school children would not in these terms be engaged with learning knowledge. They are learning 'skills' required prior to learning knowledge. Skills are those activities that children 'do'

Primary years schooling recieves less funding and sense of value worth than Secondary.

and are not always perceived as requiring intellectual processes or to involve thinking, understanding and knowledge. Intentionality of action may be ascribed to adults but rarely to children unless their 'bad' behaviour is being discussed. The early years skills, or in our terms the knowledge of early years children, are apparently thought of as less important by those policy makers providing finance or manning committees: primary children receive less capitation, have higher pupil-teacher ratios than secondary children, their teachers are less likely to be on an additional allowance and representatives with primary experience are less likely to serve on, for example, National Curriculum and Examination Councils. Thus the thinking of policy makers about the value of early years schooling and knowledge is reflected in the financial support it receives and the value attributed to its teachers.

There is however, an alternative understanding of knowledge which applies to all forms of knowledge and age of learner. This is essentially related to learning and experience and recognises the role the individual has in making meaning of their experience through thinking processes. This concept of knowledge shows how the individual continually creates knowledge through experience and social opportunities to test out, re-formulate and use the knowledge they create. Increasing experience (thinking, doing, discussing, reading, writing etc.) can lead to new understanding and thus new knowledge. Knowledge is usable and may involve knowing how (action), or knowing that (information etc., to inform decision making and action). What is important is that in making meaning and ultimately knowledge from experience the learner knows the context from which it arose and knows therefore the way it might be used and hence communicated.

The two concepts of knowledge need not be considered as dichotomous, however. There is an essential relationship between them. We all have preferred ways of thinking and thus of perceiving the world and this applies equally to young children as it does to adults. Let me give you an example in relation to the latter. I told a friend from the School of Biology at the University of East Anglia that I had just heard a talk about 'Trees in the Political Landscape' which had totally altered my perception of what I saw as I drove to work. Prior to that I tended to notice the form, structure and juxtaposition of trees as spatial and artistic forms but had started to see their significance as boundary markers and expressions of ownership. He thought for a minute and said, 'That's interesting. When I look at a Norfolk landscape I think about the transpiration rate that day depending on what the weather is like.' How do you 'see' a landscape?

Children too have preferred ways of thinking, and very soon after starting school teachers will observe preferred activities, or children will say which activity they like in school even if they apparently engage in them all. For instance, after a year of researching children learning I had learned that if a child continued to engage with an activity voluntarily, their thinking and understanding of that activity was changing. It changed because it was becoming broader and accommodating more information, and, or because it was developing conceptually and being applied in an increasing number of contexts. In most instances this involved out of school learning but in the infant class in question pupils were given scope to develop their own interests. Some children expressed their growth of

Policy makers: have a single way of thinking.

thinking in words, particularly when they were accommodating increasing amounts of information. However others with ways of thinking which were multi dimensional, or less easily reduced to words, for example those who expressed their thinking in making three dimensional models, in social situations, or in expressing feeling and aesthetic forms were more likely to be silent about their thinking. Access to their thinking came through their talk about what actions they were doing in order to express the complex thinking and understanding they had growing in their heads.

They are using preferred thinking and the activities that make use of that thinking to make sense of the words. However they are usually doing so in ways that we could recognise if only we listen carefully enough for the thinking that underlies the apparently unsophisticated language or actions. In five years of research I have only encountered one child whose apparent thinking as demonstrated by his patterns of speech and action, was not consistently similar to principles and ways of thinking underlying subject knowledge or other common sense based problem solving with people or practical problems of survival. It must be said however that some of these ways of thinking would not simply fit into the school curriculum even since the addition of technology and science to early years curriculum through the National Curriculum. The sophisticated social psychological knowledge of some children would simply be dismissed as girls playing in the house corner, or boys playing fighting games. Is this thinking ever given a language and valued as knowledge? It is possible that disaffection from schooling could be grounded on an alternative and complex framework of knowledge and understanding which goes unrecognised because of the limits we set ourselves.

However, all children it would seem have the basis of thinking and knowledge learned through preferred modes of thinking and experience, long before anyone starts formal teaching. Given an appropriate approach to learning children's thinking and ways of experiencing the world can be used to construct their own knowledge and understanding of existing discipline based knowledge. The two forms of knowledge do not need to be seen as dichotomous. What links them are forms of pedagogy and ways of thinking about learning, children and curriculum. This leads me to explore the understanding of children in school and their needs as members of society.

Children's Needs in Society

One of the problems that exists for children is that they are in an essentially powerless position in relation to knowledge. Adults can always claim to know more. There are a number of factors that affect the relationship between adult and child knowledge: the dependency relationship between the child and adult; the division of labour to protect the child from early exploitation; the adult notion of 'childish' and the ego-centrism of adults in relation to what counts as knowledge. All of these mean that much of what children learn and know is not labelled as knowledge by adults. It is always seen as important that children move on to learn something new and even the thinking processes they have learned are not recognised as knowledge. Thus the thinking and experience they are using to make sense of the world are not necessarily valued. In terms of self esteem and continued learning, this is a problem. If we want children to be confident learners, a *first need* for them is that adults recognise and use their experience, thinking, and knowledge.

But we have to understand that children have to operate in a society. They need to know how to function as people among other people, and they need to know how their thinking relates to existing knowledge, and other ways of thinking that they will encounter. They need to understand too, that there are different questions that can be asked, and there are different ways of thinking about and interpreting experience. They also need to share ideas and discuss with others to understand these different ways of thinking and experiences that relate to them. In doing this they can become unafraid of differences, or similarities, and can learn to test out, articulate and adjust their own understanding. They will learn that some forms of thinking, algorithms for instance, produce the same answer whoever applies them, whereas others do not. They need to be able to communicate freely and assert their perspective if the need arises. They need to keep a critical perspective on their own thinking, and actions, and on that of representatives of society. For instance in recent years it has been necessary to enable children to think and act critically in relation to the behaviour of adults in order to encourage them to say 'No' to abuse from potential molesters.

Thus the *second major need* that children have is for opportunities to intellectualise their thinking, actions and knowledge in order to lead them to new ways of thinking about experience, and to understand the disciplines which underpin the thinking of our society.

Thirdly there is a need for children to have opportunities to reflect on, know, and value themselves as people (i.e. their feelings, thinking, behaviour and learning processes) in social contexts and be able to think and act as 'critical citizens' within society.

The Needs of Society

What about schools and the curriculum? How will these 'people', these individuals who are able to think and reflect, meet the needs of society and fit into alternative ways of thinking in which they may have to work? This is of course an important and difficult question. What, indeed, are the needs of society? Whose society? Within all the different responses that could be given, two principles might be in common: needs which relate to life and society as it is now, and needs in relation to how we would like it to be in ten, twenty, or more years time. Thus needs of and for society, to which schooling is expected to respond, include elements of both maintenance of the existing structures (e.g. particular service industries; local government; curriculum) and ways of thinking, while providing for processes which weed out the outmoded ways of thinking, acting and working. This creative process will allow for change and development towards a society which functions cohesively while valuing differences. What might the needs of society look like?

1. Effective learners and workers (in paid or unpaid work) able to initiate and develop practices and to co-operate and communicate their ideas and thinking.
2. Personally responsible, and socially responsive people able to learn and change as need is perceived.
3. People who have a sense of community/society and citizenship which makes them conscious of their role in enabling and developing society and of their wider responsibilities in social structures.
4. Policy makers who have a wider vision than a single way of thinking and who are willing to learn from the expertise of others while maintaining their wider pragmatic concerns for the community of people they serve.

Visions of life, whether centred round the success of the individual or equality of value to individual differences, would affect the reading and interpretations of these needs. These differences would affect the action taken in society and the actual curriculum promoted for children despite any National Curriculum there might be. But is this necessarily a bad thing? Do we really need to be the same? Aren't all these qualities part of what makes up our society of people and what makes living so potentially exciting? In these terms are there such differences between the needs as identified for the individual and those for society? I think not when both are translated into educational terms and into schooling.

Schooling and Curriculum

The sort of schooling which would respond to the needs of the individual and society would necessarily value the early years of schooling. This would not be thought of as simply opportunities for learning 'basic skills' in the context of an integrated (or not) approach to science, English studies, maths and aesthetic and physical aspects of the curriculum. It would be thought of as a means of enabling the child to know and develop their way of thinking and knowing about the world through giving it appropriate forms of expression and opportunities to intellectualise it. For example if a child has skill in and understanding of social interaction, or in the power structures and relationships embodied in many childhood games, or in the workings of cars, this should be recognised and utilised in order to aid their learning in other areas. I am not saying anything new here. This has been said in many ways for centuries but many educationalists who are involved with older pupils, or policy makers still do not seem to understand the effective learning process. If we want pupils to learn to read and write they need to have opportunities to use what they know in symbolic forms (e.g. 'play' situations), to be given language to talk about it, and appropriate genre of reading material and writing tasks in order to aid the move to intellectualising and communicating their thinking an understanding. This may mean a number of different approaches to reading and writing because a scientific way of thinking does not use the same form of language as that of an engineer, or someone with social understanding. We cannot easily 'read' that which is created by an alien way of thinking.

Pupils can also be helped to articulate new questions they can ask of real experiences so they can further develop their understanding and effective knowledge through new ways of thinking. These strategies are important because the child is learning a model of abstracting meaning — of disembedding concepts from the experiential, and imposing cognitive frameworks (e.g. questions) on the experiential giving them access to critical ways of thinking about their own thinking, knowledge and actions.

Fundamentally, however, they are learning that their thinking is valued and valid, and they can lead themselves to increasing knowledge and understanding. Within this process they will be exposed to experiences within the classroom where other children are doing things and thinking in other ways. They can be encouraged to watch, ask questions, learn new ways of thinking and language that goes with it. The mechanical, spatial thinker, can find relationships with problem solving in other spheres; or can be helped to see the aesthetic or historical way of thinking and talking about the machinery, cars etc. s/he usually sees in terms of function. This in turn may lead to other ways of thinking.

The period of education covered in this book can be seen as a time of developing and valuing the ways of thinking that children have if they have not been disaffected from learning and making meaning by adults and parents who cannot see the wisdom and thinking of children nor the knowledge of relationships burgeoning in childhood games.

Effective Learning or Disaffection

Adults frequently fail to understand children's knowledge and thinking, because of the assumption that knowledge lies in language and that it has inherent meaning outside the context in which it is produced or learned. Thus 'abstract' thinking is presumed to lie in abstract language developed in the context of subject areas. The analytical thinking and experience embedded in the question and the response of this conversation for example would not necessarily be recognised:

Mark (5-year-old) Is your brother a baby, Michelle?

Michelle (also 5) Oh no! When you're two you're a baby but not when you're three.

But this sort of abstract thinking is patently not the case in the vast majority of school learning because the language does not belong to the learner's experience. During three years of research into 'Learning in the Schooling Process from 4 to 16' the only consistent abstract thinking that I saw children engaging in (i.e. that which was related to the taught curriculum) was in the playgroup and the vertically grouped infant class.

The secondary children were using 'abstract' language which they learned in their lessons but those words were firmly tied to the context in which they were learned and in most cases were not used outside that situation because their thinking had not become abstracted from the experience in which they were learned. Playgroup children, and those in the vertically-grouped infant class, frequently abstracted ideas and concepts from the context in which they were learned and manipulated them — created or applied theory if you like — in relation to other contexts. Thus a seven year old abstracted a concept of story genre from the numerous stories she had heard and started to write, and together with other abstracted concepts concerning the place, characters and romantic plot of her story she created a story. Many of her friends had been writing stories for nearly a year but she was a very logical thinker, was good at maths and doing things, but had been slow to come round to reading and writing. Did the genre offered match her thinking?

Unless we take as central to schools and curriculum the understanding of pupils — and find ways to offer them models of the thinking and practice of subjects, skills and practices that we wish them to engage with, we are in danger of increasing disaffection. At a personal level individuals are aware of their feelings, their rights, the emotional abuse they feel when they are devalued as young children or learners. Children's feelings may be related to the way that dominant ways of thinking in society affect women, working class people, black people, or overworked and over stressed middle management or teachers. We all have a responsibility to society and the future — should we allow disaffection from society and learning to become rife? With pluralism, and a will to work towards equal value for all forms of intelligent (i.e. reflective) activity and not simply that believed to be 'academic' or language based, individuals may feel free enough and confident enough to become learners and knowers in their own terms.

Unless we are very careful the ways of thinking being promoted through the policies of government and embodied in the curriculum, testing and powers of the 1988 Education Reform Act will create a framework for disaffection of the thinking of the individual rather than a framework of learning. Initiative and the ability to take effective action in the work place, are not found in either school failures who become disaffected with academic curricula, or from those who simply fail to use their creative ways of thinking while learning the procedures and facts laid down by prescriptive curricula. If, as I suggest, young children are thinking, knowing persons then those whose lack of experience is not taken into account, or those whose thinking and knowledge is never recognised, will inevitably feel disaffected if they are never enabled to feel effective in the potentially alien environment of the school. The received view of young children is that they are egocentric and unwilling or unable to see the world from the point of view of others. This is patently untrue in circumstances where they are enabled to learn within a social context. So we may ask, 'Are these childish attributes?' Or are they adult attributes that children learn from adults around them who are themselves disaffected learners?

the language does not belong to the learner's experience.

167

Contributors

Clem Adelman is Reader in Education Research at Bulmershe College of Higher Education. He has taught and researched in all areas of the formal education system in England and has a particular interest in the early years of schooling. A comparative perspective on education has been provided by his recent research and evaluation in America.

Gill Barrett is Principal Lecturer in Education Policy Studies at Bristol Polytechnic. She taught all phases and abilities in her seventeen years of teaching which she followed by doctoral research into *Learning in the Schooling Process* and funded research into starting school. She is particularly interested in innovation and change and has researched the Education Reform Programme in Spain in this light. Her current concerns are effective approaches to Initial Teacher Education and development of teachers' thinking and practice through In-Service Programmes and Action Research.

Annabel Dixon is Deputy Head of an urban primary school in Hertfordshire. She has taught both infant and junior children for twenty-five years in a variety of schools. She qualified as a psychologist after five years of teaching. She has published widely in relation to curriculum and has written books on scientific and information topics for children. Currently she is investigating aspects of young children's writing on an S.C.D.C. grant.

Peter Heaslip is a Senior Lecturer in Nursery and Early Years Education at Bristol Polytechnic. He has been concerned with nursery and infant education for many years as a teacher, researcher, writer and teacher educator. Currently he is Chair of TACTYC and as such is concerned at national level with promoting curriculum and policies for the under-fives in schools.

Ian Menter is a Lecturer in Nursery and Infant Education at Bristol Polytechnic. He taught for ten years in central Bristol and is a founder member of the Campaign Against Racism in Education (Avon).

Anne Saunders until recently was working as a research officer for the National Children's Bureau where she was evaluating under-fives provision within a voluntary organisation in the North East of England. The main concern of her teaching and doctoral research has been to develop a grounded theory of nursery and infant curriculum. She is currently a Research Fellow on a project researching curriculum and learning issues funded by the Scottish Education Department at the Northern College of Education, Aberdeen.

John Schostak is a parent of two sons. He has researched, lectured and written extensively on the theme of disaffection and the alienating structures of schooling. He is currently lecturer in Special Educational Needs in the School of Education at the University of East Anglia

Val Wood is head teacher of a large first school in Leeds. She had been concerned with Special Educational Needs in relation to the culture of schooling for some years and has been developing these ideas as practices in schools, as teacher, deputy and head. Currently she is interested in management issues that emerge when school ethos ceases to be normative and relationships require collaboration and negotiation. She is now seconded to the LEA Teacher Appraisal Team.

Martin Woodhead is a Lecturer at the Open University. He has researched and published extensively on psychological and policy related aspects of pre-school and early years education.

Index